"Gripping, brutal, riveting—Rother delivers a thrilling account of murder and mayhem."

—M. William Phelps

"A true-crime triumph . . . Rother solidifies her star status."

—*The San Diego Union-Tribune*

"This gruesome story is fast-paced and will grip any lover of the true crime genre."

—*North County Times*

POISONED LOVE

"A true-crime thriller that will keep you on the edge of your seat."

—Aphrodite Jones

"Absorbing and impeccably researched . . . a classic California noir story of passion and betrayal and death, with a beautiful, scheming adulteress at the center of the web."

—John Taylor

"With integrity, class and skill, Rother weaves this complex story seamlessly in the page-turning fashion of a suspenseful novel."

—M. William Phelps

"A lively and immaculately researched book."

—Carol Ann Davis

"A devastating portrait . . . an unwavering look at how one young woman fantasized herself into murder."

—*The San Diego Union-Tribune*

"A page-turner."

—*San Diego Metropolitan*

"A gripping account."

—*San Diego Magazine*

Praise for Caitlin Rother

BODY PARTS

"A must read . . . well-written, extremely intense; a book that I could not put down."

—Kim Cantrell, *True Crime Book Reviews*

"Excellent, well researched, well written."

—Don Bauder, *San Diego Reader*

"Page-turning excitement and blood-curdling terror . . . riveting, fast-paced, and sure to keep you up at night."

—M. William Phelps

"Rother paints every page with all the violent colors of a malignant sociopath's fever. This kind of frightening and fascinating glimpse into a killer's mind is rare."

—Ron Franscell

"A superior study of the formation of a serial killer and his lost and lonely victims."

—Carol Anne Davis

"Shocking, chilling, fast-paced . . . a book crime aficionados will be loath to put down."

—Simon Read

LOST GIRLS

"A close look at a killer . . . deeply reported, dispassionately written . . . done superbly by a writer who knows how to burrow into a complex case."

—Los Angeles Times

"Disturbing . . . This book will be popular with fans of Ann Rule and other popular true crime writers."

—Library Journal

"Thoroughly reported, well-written, terrifying . . . I doubt that there will be a better book on this tragedy."

—San Diego Reader

"Well-written, thought-provoking . . . if ever a 'true crime' deserved a book-length study, this is certainly that crime."

—San Diego Union Tribune

"A nuanced look at Gardner, from rapist-killer to charmer with girlfriends aplenty."

"A gripping account of the chilling disappearances of two San Diego area schoolgirls, a compelling picture of the victims' families' heartbreak, a nuanced inside look at the two police investigations. A must-read."

"Rother is at her best when she boldly dissects how a boy with psychological problems formed into a man indifferent to his monstrous acts toward two young girls."

"A frank and riveting look at the life and mind of San Diego rapist and killer John Gardner."

DEAD RECKONING

"Well researched and a quick, engrossing read, this should be popular with true crime readers, especially the Ann Rule crowd."

"This gave me chills, and that's not easy to do."

"Gripping . . . Rother gives readers compelling insight to an unthinkable American nightmare. The book is frank and frightening, and it sizzles."

"Impressively reported in a forthright narrative . . . a pitch-perfect study of avarice, compulsion and pure California illusion."

"We've finally found the next Ann Rule! Caitlin Rother writes with heart and suspense. *Dead Reckoning* is a chilling read by a writer at the top of her game."

BODY PARTS

CAITLIN ROTHER

PINNACLE BOOKS
Kensington Publishing Corp.

http://www.kensingtonbooks.com

Some names have been changed to protect the privacy of individuals connected to this story.

PINNACLE BOOKS are published by

Kensington Publishing Corp.
850 Third Avenue
New York, NY 10022

All Kensington Titles, Imprints, and Distributed Lines are available at special quantity discounts for bulk purchases for sales promotions, premiums, fund-raising, and educational or institutional use. Special book excerpts or customized printings can also be created to fit specific needs. For details, write or phone the office of the Kensington special sales manager: Kensington Publishing Corp., 850 Third Avenue, New York, NY 10022, attn: Special Sales Department, Phone: 1-800-221-2647.

Pinnacle and the P logo Reg. U.S. Pat. & TM Off.

ISBN-13: 978-0-7860-3511-3
ISBN-10: 0-7860-3511-0

First Printing: March 2009

10 9 8 7 6 5 4 3

Printed in the United States of America

PROLOGUE

Rodney Ford had just gotten home after quitting his job on Monday, November 2, 1998, when his brother, Wayne, called.

"I'm in some real bad trouble and I think the police are looking for me. I need your help," thirty-six-year-old Wayne said, crying. "I need you to come get me."

Rodney was nearly two years older than Wayne and had always been stronger emotionally than his little brother. They'd been close since childhood, when they weathered their parents' divorce and had only each other for company in faraway places, like Okinawa, Japan.

When they were boys, their personalities were as stark contrasts as their hair color. Rodney, who had brown hair, had always been easygoing and outgoing; Wayne, a blond, kept mostly to himself and seemed to have a harder time dealing with life. *Much harder.*

It was already 7:00 P.M. when Wayne called, and Rodney was tired after a long, frustrating, and final day as a general superintendent for a big construction company, especially after commuting two and a half hours each way to South San Francisco.

He didn't relish getting back on the road, but he could hear in Wayne's voice that something was wrong—more wrong than the half-dozen times Wayne had asked for help in the past. Wayne needed him. And Rodney wanted to be there for his brother.

They were family, and family was important to him.

So Rodney quickly threw some things in a bag and hit the highway, heading north to the Ocean Grove Lodge in the seaside town of Trinidad, California. His destination was a five-hour drive from his house in Vallejo, and about a half hour north of Eureka, the coastal city in Humboldt County where he and Wayne grew up.

It was after 1:00 A.M. when Rodney pulled off the coastal Highway 101, headed east, and turned into the driveway of the motel, which was surrounded by a commanding stand of redwood trees, some three hundred feet tall.

Immediately to the right was the main motel building, which housed the office, a restaurant, and a bar, where Wayne had spent most of the day, drinking and playing pool with the bartender. A giant neon sign on the roof that read COCKTAILS lit up the night.

To the left of the driveway was the rustic cabin where Wayne was staying, and the phone booth he'd used to call Rodney.

There were eight of these cabins, most of which were split into two units with queen-size beds. Wayne had asked for the cheapest one, which cost only $38.50 and was also the smallest of the lot. They called it room zero.

Years earlier, room zero had been a barbershop in the same unit known as room one. When the barbershop closed, the motel owner turned it into another sleeping unit, thus the strange name. Room zero had two twin beds, a color TV, and a shower, but no kitchenette like the bigger rooms. The décor was simple: white walls and gray carpet.

Rodney parked in front of the cabin and walked up the stairs leading to a wooden deck, where Wayne was standing in the open doorway, waiting for him, with the television on.

Wayne looked bad. Unkempt and emotionally ragged. His hair, now brown and straight, was an unruly mess. He was crying as Rodney came up and gave him a hug

"What's going on?" Rodney asked, genuinely concerned.

"I'm glad you're here," Wayne said through his tears. "I really needed you to be here. I really wanted your help."

They went into the cabin and closed the door behind them. As they talked for nearly two hours, facing each other on the twin beds, Rodney often couldn't follow what Wayne was saying. He kept crying as he rambled on, jumping from one topic to another. Talking nonsense, really.

After about fifteen minutes or so, Wayne started settling down a bit and wanted to discuss their troubled past.

"Why did Dad treat us the way he did?" Wayne asked. "Why did our mom leave us? Nobody loves me or cares about me."

"Well, I love you," Rodney said. "I care about you. I mean, I'm here."

Rodney was not the crying type, but he was crying now, too. He didn't like to see his brother so upset. It made him a little emotional.

Then Wayne shifted gears and wanted to talk about cars, an interest they'd always shared. Rodney restored muscle cars as a hobby, and Wayne wanted to know what kind of motor Rodney put into a certain model, that sort of thing. But that topic lasted only five minutes or so before Wayne started weeping again.

Over the past year, Wayne, who worked as a long-haul truck driver, had come through Vallejo twice a month to see Rodney. Often, they'd meet up for breakfast, or Wayne would have a meal with Rodney, Janell, and their two daughters at their condo. But Rodney usually couldn't spend as much time with his brother as Wayne would have liked.

Wayne would always complain that his ex-wife Elizabeth wasn't letting him see their baby son, Max.

"I miss my boy," Wayne would say. "I can't see my boy."

Rodney had told Wayne not to marry Elizabeth in the first place, that she was too young and they weren't a good match. Wayne didn't take his advice.

Rodney had seen Wayne shed a tear or two since the divorce, but nothing like what he saw in the cabin that night.

After a while, the conversation took an unexpected turn. "I hurt some people, and I don't want to hurt anybody anymore," Wayne said.

"You hurt some people?" Rodney asked, confused.

"Yeah."

The two of them used to throw punches, wrestle around, and give each other bloody noses as kids, but Rodney always won. As an adult, though, Wayne often got into brawls when he drank. That was nothing new.

"Did you get in a bar fight, or did you break a guy's arm?" Rodney asked.

But Wayne wouldn't discuss the extent of his actions. He simply said he wanted some help, because he didn't want to hurt people anymore.

"I'm here to help," Rodney said. "I want to help you."

"I want to go to the sheriff's," Wayne said. "I want to turn myself in."

After working all day, quitting his job, driving for ten hours, and now having to deal with this, Rodney felt like he couldn't cope with another single thing.

Despite the surreal feeling that filled room zero, Rodney knew why he was there and what they had to do. But for the moment, all he wanted was to close his eyes and shut everything out for a few hours.

"Let's just go to sleep," he said. "We'll wake up in the morning, go get some breakfast, and work this out."

When they got up around 7:30 A.M., Rodney suggested they both shower and get cleaned up before getting something to eat. Wayne, who had been staying at a campground down the road for the past week, clearly hadn't bathed during that time.

Wayne seemed more like himself that morning. He was in a pretty good mood, in fact. He put on a blue knit cap, a pair of black combat boots, some faded jeans, a long-sleeved T-shirt, and a camouflage jacket over his six-feet-two-inch, two-hundred-pound frame.

They decided to go to the Denny's just off the highway in Eureka, where, over breakfast, Rodney tried broaching the subject again about the people Wayne had hurt.

"I don't want to talk about that right now," Wayne said. "I just want to spend the day with you. Let's go and look at the apartment where we lived as kids."

So that's what they did. Rodney drove them to the zoo and some of their other childhood haunts. They searched for the houses where their aunts and uncles used to live, went into a couple of motorcycle shops and checked out the bikes.

One minute Wayne would be fine, but then he'd start crying again, babbling about things Rodney couldn't understand. He just wasn't acting like the Wayne that Rodney knew.

Counting the night before, Wayne must have gone on six or seven of these crying jags, his mood shooting up and down like a yo-yo. Wayne had had a short fuse ever since the bad head injury he'd gotten in 1980, but this was different.

Rodney wondered what Wayne wasn't telling him.

"How did you hurt some people?" Rodney asked.

"If I tell you, you won't love me. You'll hate me."

"I love you," Rodney said. "I'm your brother."

"I hurt some people bad and they don't have to worry about anything anymore."

Rodney didn't like the sound of that at all. Did he mean it was too late to save any of these people from the danger they were in? Was anyone tied up or being held hostage? Or was it something worse? Rodney wondered what the hell his brother had dragged him into.

As they talked some more, they agreed that Rodney shouldn't be placed in the position where he would get into trouble for whatever Wayne had done. But by the same token, now that Rodney knew what he did, he wasn't going to let Wayne walk away—especially when Rodney could be viewed as an accomplice after the fact.

Aside from that, the two brothers had forged an unspoken alliance long ago, and Rodney intended to carry out his part of the deal.

"He knew that if I was involved, it would get done," Rodney said later. "He knew I would do what was right, regardless of the consequences."

This had been going on since Wayne was fourteen, when he broke into a sporting-goods store through the skylight and took $1,700 worth of merchandise, including a couple hundred shotgun shells and some fishing rods.

Afterward, he showed Rodney his stash, piled up in his bedroom closet. Wayne knew that Rodney would have to tell their father what he'd done. It was all part of the implicit agreement in their twisted brotherly version of show-and-tell.

Wayne even told his brother so, later on: "I knew you would make me follow through with it," he said.

This time, Rodney knew the situation was much worse, and his brother's emotions were far more complicated. Wayne kept talking about how screwed-up his life was, and how he was never going to see his son again.

"Why do you think you're not going to see your son?" Rodney asked.

Rodney was concerned because Wayne had tried to commit suicide a couple of years earlier during the divorce, and had been talking about killing Elizabeth, too. But that morning, Wayne assured him that Elizabeth and Max were okay.

Wayne wouldn't say much more than he already had. He still wanted to turn himself in at the sheriff's department, only he didn't seem to want to actually *go* there.

He was distraught, drawing out their day together as long as he could, to make the most of what time he had left with Rodney. Once he gave himself up, he said, he knew he wouldn't see Rodney anymore because he was never going to get out of jail—the only one who could forgive him was God.

"I don't want to live anymore," Wayne kept saying. "I don't want to live with myself. I deserve to die."

Later that afternoon, Wayne suggested they go to a movie, so they picked a vampire flick, a genre both of them liked.

It was quiet and dark in the theater, which gave Rodney a chance to think for a minute. By the time the movie came on, he was feeling pretty antsy. He knew he was too nervous to sit still for two more hours, given their peculiar day and knowing what was to come. He wanted to get this thing over with.

About fifteen minutes into the movie, Rodney leaned

over and said, "We need to go to the sheriff's. It's getting late."

"I don't want to go now," Wayne said, meaning not *right* now.

"Well, we're going."

Rodney led Wayne out of the theater, then drove them over to their grandmother's house. It was only a few blocks from the courthouse, which housed the sheriff's department and jail. He figured they could use a calm, relaxing walk before doing the deed, but he also didn't want the sheriff's deputies to impound his truck, mistakenly assuming that it had something to do with Wayne's crimes.

They were about ten minutes away when Wayne started to change his mind.

"I don't want to go now," Wayne said belligerently, meaning he no longer wanted to go, *period*.

"We have to go," Rodney said firmly. "There's no way that we're not going to go."

"I'm worried that if I go there, I'll never come out."

"What do you mean by that?"

Wayne described an incident that had occurred when he was a teenager, living in Redding with a woman named Melva Ward, a dispatcher for the Shasta County Sheriff's Office. He told Rodney that Melva came home one day and said a guy had killed someone and then hung himself while in custody.

"I think he had some help," Melva said, laughing. Wayne took her remark to mean that a correctional officer had killed the guy in his cell.

Trying to calm his brother's fears, Rodney said he would stay with Wayne as long as he could once they got to the station, but in the meantime, he would see what he could do.

"I'll call the FBI," he said. "I'll call whoever I need to,

to make this easy and make you feel better. We have to do this."

Rodney made a call on his cell phone around 6:00 P.M. to an 800 number he thought was the FBI's field office in San Francisco, although he later learned it was a private company known as Federal Prison Industries. He got a recording and left a message, which comforted Wayne enough to continue on to the sheriff's.

After entering the sheriff's lobby, Rodney picked up a wall phone, which connected to a receptionist sitting behind bulletproof glass. He explained that he and his brother needed to see the sheriff so that his brother could turn himself in.

"Why?" she asked.

"He said he hurt some people and he wants to be off the street."

The dispatcher ran Wayne's name and date of birth through the computer system, but nothing came up, so she asked to talk to Wayne. He told her the same thing his brother had.

She asked if he had any weapons and he said no, so she told him to have a seat and said someone would be out to talk to him.

As Rodney and Wayne were waiting on a couple of benches, Wayne said he wanted to go.

"No," Rodney said. "You're not leaving."

They waited for twenty minutes before Deputy Michael Gainey came out.

Memories vary about what transpired in that lobby over the next few minutes, but here is what happened according to law enforcement authorities:

Gainey approached the Ford brothers, then asked Wayne why he was turning himself in.

"I've hurt a lot of people," Wayne said.

Gainey told him that they needed to take one step at a time; he needed some basic information, such as where Wayne lived and what he'd done to warrant this trip to the sheriff's.

"I don't want to hurt anyone anymore," Wayne said.

Sergeant Michael Thomas joined them a couple of minutes later, thinking that Wayne looked anxious and unsettled. As he and Gainey explained that they still needed more specifics, Wayne motioned toward one of his jacket's front pockets.

"Once you see what I have in my pocket, you'll know," he said. "It's just the tip of the iceberg."

"What's in there?" Thomas asked cautiously.

When Wayne did not respond, the sergeant asked if he could look inside. Wayne started reaching toward the pocket, but Thomas stopped him.

"No, no, don't do that," he commanded. "We'll do that. Please, just for our safety purposes. We don't know what you have in there. Is there anything in there that'll hurt me or hurt us?"

"No, it's nothing like that," Wayne said, raising his arms to signal to Thomas that he could have unfettered and secure access to the pocket.

The sergeant reached down and lifted the external flap of Wayne's pocket and the deputy pulled it away from Wayne's chest. Inside, they could see what looked like a plastic Ziploc sandwich bag. So, not knowing what they were going to find, the officers each put on a pair of latex gloves. The deputy pulled out the pocket again while the sergeant reached in to retrieve the bag.

Wayne looked down at the ground as Thomas examined the bag, which contained something fleshy and was leaking fluid into his palm.

Thomas immediately recognized what he was holding: some fatty yellow tissue with a brown nipple.

It was a human female breast.

"Things are so screwed-up in my head now," Wayne said "I just want help."

Gainey told Wayne to stand up. Wayne started crying as he rose to his feet and asked if he could hug his brother. As they embraced, Rodney began to cry as well.

The officers told Wayne to turn around, placed handcuffs on his wrists, then Gainey walked him out of the lobby and across the street to the jail. Thomas asked Rodney to stick around and answer some questions.

Both officers testified later that Wayne was arrested on suspicion of aggravated mayhem—the unlawful removal of a body part—in the lobby before he was handcuffed.

In his initial incident report, Gainey wrote that Wayne "mentioned at the outset that he had wanted an attorney present while he had spoken about the tissue found," and repeated the request during a brief interview with him and a detective later that night.

In 2001, Gainey scaled back the urgency of Wayne's request, saying he remembered Wayne telling him in the lobby only that "Maybe I should have an attorney."

According to Rodney, he and Wayne discussed his need for an attorney in front of the officers and then Wayne explicitly stated that he wanted a lawyer.

Thomas went back to his office and called Detective Juan Freeman, who had been working tirelessly to solve a homicide case involving a young female victim whose body had been left in a waterway north of Eureka, known as Ryan Slough, about a year earlier.

It was an unusual case. The woman had been dumped after someone had cut off her head, arms, and legs. She was a Jane Doe, known more affectionately among local law enforcement as "Torso Girl."

Since then, Freeman had tried to identify her through more than one hundred missing persons reports nation-wide, but the trail had grown cold. He still had no idea who she was—and, until that night, had no solid suspects.

The sergeant explained to Freeman about the two brothers in the lobby and how he'd come to possess the plastic bag of human flesh that he was carefully guarding.

"We think it might have something to do with your torso case," Thomas said.

"That's a great guess," Freeman said. "I'll be right down."

During a series of shocking interviews over the next three days with sheriff's detectives from four California counties, Wayne would reveal a tale of rough sex, bondage, rape, torture, and sometimes death, involving dozens of women, most of them prostitutes. And, in a move that at-torneys would later wrangle over in court, he would do so without an attorney present.

PART I

CHAPTER 1

KAREN AND GENE

Wayne Adam Ford was born on December 3, 1961, in Petaluma, a relatively small and mostly white community in northern California, just off Highway 101 in Sonoma County.

Petaluma, ranked recently by *Money* magazine as the eighty-eighth best community to live in America, first earned a place on the nation's crime map when twelve-year-old Polly Klaas was kidnapped and killed after being abducted from her bedroom by a stranger in 1993. Also a lesser-known favorite for movie directors, Petaluma was chosen as a location for parts of *Basic Instinct*, *Peggy Sue Got Married*, and *American Graffiti*.

Wayne's German mother, born Karen Brigitte Danziger in January 1942, was a stay-at-home mom, albeit without the nurturing gene that most mothers possess. However, this particular parenting deficit was one that Karen openly admitted to having.

When she was growing up, Karen moved between

Germany and the United States as she was traded between her grandmother, who she'd thought was her mother until Karen was nine, and her real mother, Vera. Karen never played with dolls, preferring instead to walk in the woods or play with trains and string tops. She never pictured herself as becoming a mother someday.

Karen developed early, and by thirteen, she was already feeling the power that came with her shapely physique. She used her body and her precocious sexuality to tease her older male teachers. She got one of them so aroused that he tried to sneak into her room one night.

She liked older men. She felt they offered her the safety, the security, and the mature father figure that was missing from her life.

Wayne's father, on the other hand, had no choice but to learn parenting skills at an early age. As the eldest of eight children, Calvin Eugene "Gene" Ford began babysitting while he was still a child himself.

Born in Missouri in March 1938 to Murl and Myrtle Ford, Gene grew up in northeast California. But because his father worked in lumber mills, his family soon followed the work to the coast.

When he was almost eighteen, Gene and a group of friends decided to join the army in 1956, looking for new opportunities. His father had been a navy man, but Gene never cared much for the water. His entrance test results were so good—among the top 1 percent of inductees—that he was selected for intelligence work, which involved the interception of global radio signals.

When Gene met Karen in 1957, he was stationed at Herzo-Base in Herzogenaurach, Germany, about fourteen miles from Nuremberg.

Karen was just sixteen—and no longer a virgin—when she met Gene at a birthday party on the base shortly after she, her mother, and her stepfather, Billy Lane, had moved back to Germany from Texas. Karen and her mother had a slap fight on the voyage over, which Billy, an army tank commander who was ten years younger than Karen's mother, and twelve years older than Karen, had to break up.

Gene was four years older than Karen and physically mature for his age. Standing a sturdy six feet three inches and 235 pounds, and sporting a dark mustache, he reminded her of Rhett Butler. Karen, who liked to think of herself as Scarlett O'Hara, was smitten, and the feeling was mutual.

Karen, a petite five feet two inches and 106 pounds, went by the nickname "Kitten." Gene enjoyed watching her sing in the military version of the musical *Oklahoma*.

"I thought she was cute, but it was kind of a taboo thing, because she was an American dependent and I was a GI," Gene said.

Karen and Gene dated for about a year and a half, often sneaking away to the village of Höchstadt an der Aisch, where her grandmother lived. Karen later claimed that this was because her mother didn't approve of the relationship, but Gene never had that impression.

Karen wasn't getting along any better with her mother, whom she found overbearing.

"I was wanting to kill her," she recalled later. "I had thoughts about it because I was so desperate to get away . . . but it didn't go very far. . . . You know what kept me from pursuing the thought was I didn't want to go to jail."

Karen soon saw an opportunity: Why not marry Gene and escape from her mother's clutches?

One day when Gene was over, Karen announced her

intentions, only to have her mother decree that there would be no such marriage.

"Well, I'll just get pregnant and then we'll have to get married," Karen declared.

Later, Gene didn't remember this conversation, but said Karen might have been arguing with her mother in German. He'd always thought that Karen's parents wanted them to get married.

Whatever the reason, Karen felt something snap inside her, went into the bathroom, and impulsively stuffed her mouth full of her mother's pills.

"I swallowed them and went in the bedroom and lay down, waited to die, and after some time, they missed me. They came in and I was already out, [so they] called the ambulance and took me, pumped my stomach, and kept me there for two or three days."

Gene said Karen did not stay overnight in the hospital. Rather, he said, he followed the doctor's advice and walked her around her family's apartment on base for hours, until the drugs worked their way out of her system.

"She got mad because, if I recollect properly, I spent too much time talking to her father," Gene recalled. "She could not stand having to share her attention with anyone."

Karen later contended this was the only time she tried to kill herself, but Gene claimed Karen's parents told him this was her second suicide attempt—the first being while he was back in the United States on emergency leave, shortly before this incident, when Karen was scared he would not return.

Over the years and during interviews for this book, the perception of this and other events voiced by Wayne's mother and other Ford family members varied widely—and often conflicted dramatically as accusations of abuse, behavioral problems, and moral and criminal wrongdoing were exchanged in the recounting of events deemed relevant in evaluating Wayne's crimes.

When Karen and Gene were wed, she was two months pregnant with Rodney, although she didn't know it at the time. The ceremony took place in her grandmother's town, Höchstadt, presided over by the mayor. Karen wore a midcalf dress with a black-and-white floral print.

According to Karen, Gene's sexual behavior toward her began to change on their wedding night.

"I don't remember the details," she said later, only that Gene "was just going to do whatever he felt like doing, regardless of whether I wanted it, too."

In this case, she said, whatever he wanted to do wasn't mutually acceptable, let alone enjoyable.

"All I know is that I was very upset, and I locked myself in the bathroom, and I went to sleep on the floor that night," she said.

Gene said none of this ever happened. "We'd been having sex all along and our wedding night was no different."

Karen said the two of them made up afterward, but it wasn't long before she felt that Gene just wanted her around for sex.

"I realized that now I had married somebody very similar to my mother. He was totally dominating . . . I was his little girl. . . . I realized that I had jumped out of a fire into a bigger one."

When they were first married, Karen would want to go out dancing, and according to Gene, this caused some barroom incidents because she flirted with other men.

One night in particular, he said, he told her he needed to go back to the barracks.

According to Gene, Karen said, "You can go, big boy, but I'm staying."

So he picked her up, tossed her over his shoulder, and dumped her in the car. When a soldier on the street questioned his actions, Gene said he "punched him once and down he went."

Gene said Karen got physical with him on two occasions in those early months. One night, he said, Karen slapped him during an argument, drawing blood from his nose and mouth. Gene said he threw her on the bed with enough force that she rolled off the other side.

The next time she tried something like that, he wanted to make sure she understood it wouldn't happen again without consequences. She hurled something at him while he was reading, smacking him in the side of the head, so he took her by the shoulders and told her, "Don't ever do that again or I'll take care of it. You'll put yourself in the place of a man," he said, meaning that he would hit her back.

Karen said she acted like "a little puppy" and a "good German hausfrau" around Gene, trying to please him by lighting his pipe and bringing his slippers when he came home from work.

Yet, all she felt from him was indifference. She said he made decisions without talking to her and never gave her enough money.

Gene said he didn't marry Karen for sex; if that's what he wanted, he could have gotten it from any of the young women who wanted to hook up with a soldier. He married her because he loved her.

He said Karen was in charge of the household budget,

but he would pay the bills. That said, he acknowledged that he probably bought and sold a car without talking to her, but he noted they didn't have much money to begin with.

The prime emotion that Karen felt about being pregnant with Rodney was not joy, but fear. Fear of being trapped in a life she didn't want. On top of that, she was worried she would get fat, so she put herself on a nine-hundred-calorie-a-day diet and was on the verge of being anorexic after Rodney was born in Nuremberg on March 26, 1960.

Although Gene said he didn't remember Karen taking birth control pills, she claimed she took them because she did not want to get pregnant a second time. But for some reason she couldn't remember later, she said she was off the pill one weekend when Gene was playing in a football game out of town. She said Rodney had stayed home with his grandmother so she could join Gene in a hotel, where the couple got into another argument about sex. Karen later claimed that Gene raped her that night.

Again, Karen claimed not to remember all the details, but she said he climbed on top of her, spread her legs, and held her shoulders and arms down so that she couldn't move.

"Basically, he forced me, and I was screaming, and I was crying, I remember that. I was pleading, 'Please don't, don't,'" she recalled later. "Of course, in those days, that wasn't considered rape if it was your husband."

Karen said she sensed that she got pregnant that night, and she was right. She never said a word of this alleged incident to anyone until years later. However, the damage had already been done because, according to Wayne's defense team, Karen told him at some point that he was the product of rape.

Only she and Gene know the truth about what

happened that night, but when Gene recently learned of her accusation, he fervently denied it.

"She's fantasizing," he said. "I probably didn't want to have sex if she didn't want to. I don't want to be in bed with somebody who doesn't want to. . . . 'No' means *no* and I respect that."

He said he didn't remember arguing with Karen about sex—ever—and said they never stayed together in a hotel when he played football out of town.

When he heard that Karen told Wayne he was the product of rape, he said, "That's sad. That's really sad."

Curiously, when Karen's mother, Vera, gave an interview in Wayne's court case, she, too, said that she had been raped as a young woman. She also said that when she was pregnant with Karen, she tried to have a miscarriage for fear of what her mother would do. However, it's unknown whether she communicated that to Karen.

CHAPTER 2

FEAR OF PUNISHMENT

As a nineteen-year-old with two children, Karen felt so tied down that she feared she would never be able to get a divorce.

She thought there had to be more to life than being young and sitting home alone for six or eight months while her husband was away on classified intelligence missions. It didn't help matters that Karen didn't get along with the other military wives. In fact, she didn't like women in general—unless they were much older than she was.

Given the circumstances under which Karen felt Wayne had been conceived, she was determined *not* to love her new baby.

Nonetheless, she couldn't help but notice that Wayne had the most perfect little body, completely symmetrical and not in the least bit chubby. Wayne was such a good baby that she couldn't stop herself from softening to him, although she later admitted that she was never one to show love for her children.

Karen was more concerned with trying to cope with her own loneliness and misery over her lost freedom than she was with being affectionate to her boys.

"I just always assumed they would know that I loved them," Karen said later. "I feel bad about it because now, you know, looking back, I see I should have just not assumed. I should have shown them how I was feeling."

Gene said Karen would touch the boys, but not lovingly. When she changed their clothes, he said, "she was pretty rough on them."

Rodney didn't seem to need nurturing, but Karen thought Wayne needed it more than anything. Wherever she went, Wayne followed, content just to be leaning up against her or touching her in some way.

"He just liked to be near me," Karen said, "and, I mean, I liked having him near me. . . . It didn't take much to make him happy."

Wayne sought attention from his father, too. When he was three or so, he used to stand next to Gene while he was shaving, imitating his gestures with the razor. He also started singing country western songs, and by all accounts, he had a surprisingly good voice.

For years, Gene's family had no idea about his marital problems. In fact, Gene's brother Jimmy thought Gene and Karen had a very strong bond. While Gene was stationed in the early 1960s at Two Rock Ranch near Petaluma, Jimmy said, Gene liked to show Karen off.

"She was a nice-looking woman," Jimmy said later. "I think he put her on a pedestal."

Gene, a strict military man whose life was very structured, was always seen as the dominant partner in the marriage.

Jimmy looked up to Gene, who was ten years his

senior and was the brother after whom he patterned his own life. Gene commanded respect and authority, but even Jimmy had to acknowledge that he could be short on patience, just like their mother.

"[He] has a strong personality," Jimmy said, but added that Gene was never "overdomineering."

Still, despite Gene's stern, gruff exterior and Karen's lack of nurturing ability, they each had a softer side. They both drove buses for disabled children as a part-time job.

Growing up, Rodney and Wayne had their own room with bunk beds. One morning, the boys seemed awfully quiet. Then Karen saw why. Two-year-old Wayne had reached into his diaper and smeared feces all over his bed and the surrounding walls.

"Now, that day I got angry," Karen said later.

Rodney watched with amusement as she cleaned Wayne in the tub, then washed down the room.

Not long after this incident, Karen heard Wayne screaming outside their mobile home in Cotati. When she got to the front door, she saw that he'd fallen down the stairs and hit his head, right near the hairline.

"It scared the heck out of me because there was so much bleeding," she said.

She drove him to the doctor's office, where they gave him three stitches. They told Karen to watch him carefully and to make sure he didn't go to sleep, but he seemed okay.

When it came to minding their mother, the two boys couldn't have been more different.

Karen used to count to three, and by the count of one,

Wayne had already done whatever his mother demanded. Rodney, on the other hand, would wait until the very last second to make a move.

According to Karen, the boys' punishment was a matter of dispute between her and Gene.

"He would holler and he would get out a belt and I used to have fights with him over that. I would say, 'Don't do it, stop!'" Karen said.

She said Gene didn't do this frequently, but sometimes he hit them too hard, leaving welts on their shoulders. Karen said she would cry and sometimes he would stop the beating, and sometimes he wouldn't, which prompted the children to run off, screaming.

Many years later, Rodney said he couldn't remember Karen ever trying to stop Gene from hitting him or Wayne, nor could he remember any welts. But what he did remember was that Karen always left the discipline to Gene, saying almost daily, "Just wait till your dad gets home."

Gene said he'd always hated it when his own mother used to slap him in the face and when his father beat him and left welts. So when it came to his own boys, Gene said he sometimes used a belt, but mostly used his hand, trying "not to hit them anywhere but their butt."

He also said that he could never be sure whether the boys had really done something bad enough to deserve a spanking, as Karen repeatedly asserted, so he didn't do it very hard—and he didn't remember leaving any marks.

But of the two boys, Gene and Rodney later agreed, it was Rodney who took the brunt of his discipline.

Wayne and Rodney were close, but they also competed against each other. Wayne would later tell a psychologist that Gene used to make the boys put on boxing gloves and duke it out, but Gene and Rodney said that order actually came from the boys' grandfathers. Karen explained that her stepfather Billy thought it was a more gentlemanly way to settle their differences.

"I was a coward when I was a kid," Wayne told the psychologist. "My brother is a little heavier than me, but I could never beat him up, so I just got beat up."

Wayne said things eventually turned around. Although he and Rodney disagreed on the time frame, they both said that Wayne, as a young adult, was finally able to get the best of Rodney.

The contrasts between the boys also came out in the ways they took their punishment—often for fighting with each other.

"Rodney would just slough it off," the boys' uncle Jimmy recalled. "He knew that he screwed up and he should make sure that he doesn't do it again. Wayne handled it quite differently. . . . He would hold it in . . . maybe even to the point of holding a grudge for a long time."

One afternoon Wayne and Rodney had given each other a bloody nose and a black eye, rolling around in the gravel until two of Gene's employees broke them apart. Wayne knew that Gene would be angry, so he ran off and hid in an abandoned car.

When Gene came home, Rodney ratted out his brother's hiding place. Gene jerked open the car door and Wayne's limp body poured out. Wayne had been so scared of getting in trouble that he'd passed out, waiting for his punishment. Gene slung him over his shoulders, laid him on the sofa, and told Rodney to get his brother some water.

"Gene, myself, and my father are all good at that— putting the fear of God in without even touching a person," Jimmy said later.

Although Gene was brought up Protestant, he didn't go from church to church with Karen and the boys as she explored various religions. Karen was born Jewish, and, thus, so was Rodney, who later became very religious and joined the Seventh-day Adventist Church.

Rodney was far more social than Wayne. While he liked to play outside with the neighborhood kids, Wayne was happy to hang around the house with Karen or in the sandbox with his toys. But he didn't cry much as a child unless he hurt himself or got upset with Rodney.

While Rodney was even-keeled, Wayne displayed emotional highs and lows like his mother, held on to his feelings, and couldn't let go.

"He was defenseless," Karen recalled. "Everything got through to him. . . . It penetrated."

He was also very loving.

"There was a sweetness about him," she said. "He always had that little smile—not that ha-ha thing, you know? It was just quietly sweet."

Perhaps in an unconscious effort to overcompensate, Karen tried to do more for young Wayne then she should have. She finally realized this one day when she got a call from his kindergarten teacher.

"I want to ask you something," the teacher said. "Do you do everything for Wayne?"

"I don't know what you mean," Karen said.

"Well, the other kids are putting their shoes on and putting their coats on. He stands there and waits for me to do it. I'm thinking you must be doing all these things for him."

Karen said yes, she did.

"He should be learning to do these things himself," the teacher said.

* * *

Because of the nature of his intelligence work, Gene was sent all over the world on assignment—to Beirut, New Delhi, Tehran, Bangkok, North Thailand, and Okinawa—spending up to a year at a time away from Karen and the boys.

When he got word he was going to Okinawa, Gene decided to try once more to make his flailing marriage work, this time by bringing his family with him. The only problem was that Karen didn't want to go.

According to her, she threatened to divorce him if he made her go.

"Just let me stay here," Karen pleaded.

But Karen said Gene told her he would take the boys away from her if she left him. "'I'll turn into an alcoholic and I'll just do away with myself,'" she quoted him as saying.

Karen said that's when she stopped talking about leaving. She was miserable, but she didn't want the boys to grow up without their father.

Gene insisted he never threatened to harm himself or commit suicide. Rodney and Gene both said he wasn't the type—Karen was.

Nonetheless, the whole family did, in fact, go to Okinawa for a couple of years when the boys were in elementary school in the late 1960s.

Life was very difficult for Karen during that period. She felt as if she was about to have a nervous breakdown.

"Send me back to the States," she begged Gene. "I want to go back to the States. I can't do it anymore."

One morning eight-year-old Rodney came into the kitchen and saw his mother sitting in a pool of blood, with both of her wrists bleeding. Karen told him that she'd cut herself on the lid of a can, but Rodney didn't believe her.

"I was smart enough to know it wasn't an accident," Rodney said later.

Rodney said Karen had been taken away by paramedics to the military hospital by the time Wayne woke up.

Years later, a forensic psychiatrist would classify Karen's teenage incident of swallowing pills as a suicidal gesture and this incident in the kitchen as a genuine suicide attempt.

Karen claimed she got her wish to go home after she finally spoke to Gene's commander about her wishes, but Gene said he sent her back himself after one of his men broke down and told him that he'd been having an affair with her.

"Shortly after that, I started making arrangements to get her back to the States with the boys," he said.

Karen brought the boys back to Eureka, California, where she proceeded to have an affair with Gene's fifteen-year-old brother, Billy, who was still living with his parents.

"Evidently, she got lonely and decided that she liked the looks of my little brother and took up with him," Jimmy recalled. "[Billy] talked to me about it and he was scared to death. . . . He asked me what he should do, and I said, 'Well, Billy, there's not much you can do, and, hopefully, this thing will go away.'"

Karen told Gene about the affair when he returned, prompting him to buy her and the boys a house in Santa Rosa—220 miles away from Eureka and Billy—before he went back to Okinawa to finish his assignment. He was discharged from the army as a staff sergeant shortly thereafter, in 1969.

"There was rape committed, but not by me," Gene said later. "[Billy] was a kid. Now that's rape."

* * *

In 1970, Karen said, she and Gene had another argument about sex, this time at two in the morning while the boys were asleep.

Again, memories vary drastically among the Ford family members.

Karen told it like this:

She always kept a .38-caliber Magnum in the house, careful to hide the bullets in a separate place so the boys wouldn't shoot themselves. Karen said Gene got the gun out that night. "If I can't have you, nobody is going to," he said.

After trying unsuccessfully to wrestle the weapon away from him, she ran to hide the bullets—only, Gene got to them first. She was scared he was going to kill her, the boys, then himself, so she ran next door and asked the neighbors to call the police.

When she came home, she still didn't know if the gun was loaded.

"Don't do this," she told Gene.

Luckily, at this point, the police pulled up.

"I'm divorcing this man," she told them. "Take him right now. I don't want him in the house."

She said the police took Gene away, and when he came back a few days later, he said something Karen would never forget.

"You won," he said.

According to Gene, this description of events is another of Karen's fantasies. "That's quite a story," he said. "I've never been in jail in my entire life."

Gene said he'd bought a gun for Rodney to use, once Rodney was old enough to be responsible. And yes, he said, he kept the bullets in a separate place. After an argument at the end of the marriage, Gene recalled, Karen gave the gun to their next-door neighbor, saying she was afraid Gene was going to hurt her or somebody else.

He said he and Karen had sex one last time at her encouragement, but it wasn't enough to hold them together any longer.

"It's not working, is it?" Karen told him over breakfast the next morning.

"No, it's not working."

"How 'bout thirty days? Is that enough time for you to clean up your affairs and leave?"

"How 'bout today?" he replied.

Rodney said Karen gave him the news in the hallway that morning, saying, "Your father and I are getting divorced."

Both he and Gene said the police never came to the house.

CHAPTER 3

DIVIDED ATTENTIONS

Within days of his parents' split, Rodney said, Karen's new friend Steve Shurtluff came over to the house. Rodney and Gene later shared the belief that this relationship had been going on long before the breakup.

Karen, however, said she didn't meet Steve, a twenty-four-year-old Vietnam veteran and postal carrier who was seven years her junior, until a year later. She said she introduced him to the boys after they started dating, and they all seemed to get along well.

After about six months, she said, Steve started talking marriage, but she wanted to live together for a while first. They ended up getting married, anyway.

During this time, Gene would take one or both boys to his house in Healdsburg, in Sonoma County, for his weekends with them, often fighting with Karen when he picked them up.

Rodney said he and Wayne always looked forward to those weekends, when Gene would teach them construction skills or take them flying. After leaving the military, Gene had begun buying fixer-upper apartment complexes and remodeling them. He would move into the worst unit while he worked on the others. He'd rent out the finished units, fix up the one in which he'd been living, then sell the whole complex.

One year, Karen said, Gene was supposed to pick up Wayne for his birthday, but he never came.

"Wayne was sitting out on the front doorstep, waiting for his dad, and his dad never called and never showed and [Wayne] was very depressed," Karen said. "It was a really sad moment for Wayne. It really hurt. His dad was always making promises and letting him down."

Gene said he didn't remember doing that, but it's possible that he could have missed one of Wayne's birthdays if it fell on one of the alternate weeks that Karen had the boys.

In Steve's view, Wayne was a nice, shy kid who didn't know how to express his feelings in a positive way. Rather, he would throw temper tantrums, leave class, or skip school entirely. Steve said he and Karen never talked to Wayne about why he behaved this way; Karen had no ability to communicate about private, intimate things.

Wayne didn't understand the dance between the sexes, so he was put off when girls would tease him because he couldn't figure out whether they liked him.

One day, a girl gave him a card at a school party that said, "Wayne, you have too much kindness." He brought the card home, embarrassed, not understanding why a girl would do or say something like that.

Steve recalled that Karen showed no emotions toward the boys and never hugged them. If one of them got hurt, she would simply try to talk them through it.

* * *

By the time the boys were teenagers, Karen and Steve could see that Gene favored Rodney over Wayne, and Wayne could feel it.

"I never saw Gene outwardly shun Wayne or anything like that, but I knew that he didn't quite understand Wayne," Karen said. "He didn't have the rapport with Wayne that he had with Rodney."

Gene later said that he and Rodney were a lot closer in many ways because they were so much alike, but he always paid more attention to Wayne so as not to hurt his feelings.

"He was a pretty envious or jealous person, as was his mom," Gene said. "If anyone was treated unfairly, it would have been Rodney, and he never complained about it."

Rodney, who always felt that Wayne got more attention, often called him a mama's boy. "If we were both in the same spot and trouble happened, I'm the one that got it," he said.

Karen's separation from her sons—when Wayne was twelve and Rodney was fourteen—is another example of contrasting perceptions of events among family members. Wayne, Rodney, and Gene have always felt that Karen abandoned her sons, and yet Karen said this accusation amazed her.

According to Gene, twelve-year-old Wayne called him up in tears one day, saying, "Dad, can you pick me up? Can I live with you?"

"Of course," Gene said. "When do you want me to come get you?"

"Right now."

"What do you mean?"

"Well, I'm on the porch with my bag. She threw me out."

Gene said that when he talked to Karen about this, she told him, "I just can't control him anymore. I don't want him around me."

Rodney said he stayed behind to try to ease the tensions between family members and please his mother, but Karen soon kicked him out, too. He said he was fourteen when he came home one night to find the front door locked.

"Let me in," Rodney said.

"Nope, you're not getting back in this house," she declared.

Rodney said Karen told him he was uncontrollable and that "I was just like my dad and she wasn't going to have me around anymore."

Rodney went to live with a couple of families in the neighborhood, a few nights here and a few nights there, but that only lasted until his father found out. Gene decided Rodney should come and live with him, which didn't go over very well with Wayne. Gene said Wayne started acting out because he no longer was the sole focus of his father's attention.

Gene expected the boys to help with his construction projects when they came home from school. If they didn't do what they were told, Gene came down on them—and hard.

Not surprisingly, the brothers handled this differently. Rodney enjoyed learning everything he could, while Wayne struggled. He couldn't do what his father and his teachers wanted and take care of his own needs at the same time.

At a loss for how to handle Wayne, Gene approached his friend Keith Hale, saying Wayne had totally shut down. He asked Keith to talk to Wayne and see what he could do.

Keith found Wayne in his room with the shades drawn, sitting in the middle of a heap of clothes, schoolbooks, and papers. Wayne was rubbing his feet.

Keith asked what was going on and Wayne replied that his feet hurt.

"When he took his socks off, his feet were covered with open sores that had become infected," Keith later recalled. "He said it had been months since his last shower or even a change of socks."

Asked if he would like to move into Keith's house for the summer, Wayne said yes.

"He went to work with me most days," Keith said. "He got stronger and things were looking good. At the end of the summer, he went back to his dad's."

Gene said Wayne was fine until Gene met the woman who would become his wife in 1976. Wayne didn't like his new sister or Gene's new wife.

"That upset him, that changed him," Gene said later. "He didn't like getting the divided attention, just like way back when, with his mother."

Keith said there was never a doubt that Gene loved his sons. He just expected them to work as hard as he had growing up. "The big difference I see is that Gene's family was solid. What he was able to provide the boys was anything but."

Time periods seem to blur together for this family, so it's difficult to tell how long Wayne stayed where, but he was traded back and forth between his mother and father and his uncle Jimmy before heading off on his own to Redding when he was about fifteen.

* * *

Karen had an entirely different take on Wayne's adolescent and teenage years.

According to her, Wayne had problems with some of his teachers, with whom she and Steve had met several times. One said that Wayne seemed angry and that he was taking it out on them by being aggressive and belligerent.

When Karen and Steve tried to talk to Wayne about this, he denied there was a problem and refused to discuss the matter further.

Then, Wayne came to her one day and said, "Mom, I want to go live with my dad."

When she asked Wayne why, he said that his father would teach him how to fly and they could work construction together. So she thought about it for a few days, then told him to go ahead, even though she figured Gene would ultimately let Wayne down.

A few months later, she said, Gene told her that he was having issues with Wayne.

"[He] called me and said there was some problem with Wayne having broken into a store and there was a gun involved and he was pretty angry with Wayne. And he said, you know, 'He's an idiot, blah, blah, blah.'"

After that incident, Gene was able to work out an informal arrangement with some friends in the police department so that Wayne would wash police cruisers every day after school for six weeks as punishment. Soon afterward, Wayne stole a car and went joyriding, causing the punishment to be extended by four weeks. Gene said Wayne would not only wash the cruisers, but also rewire them so they didn't work properly.

Karen said Wayne called to say he wanted to come back to live with her because he was upset with his father. He claimed that Gene had promised to pay him for his work but never did; he felt used.

After Wayne came back, it all went downhill from

there. He started staying out late, prompting Karen and Steve to drive around looking for him so he didn't get picked up by police for breaking curfew. When he'd finally come home, he wouldn't tell them where he'd been. He only grew more and more defiant.

Then one of his teachers called to complain that Wayne had hit her—an offense worsened by the fact that she was pregnant. She advised Karen to get Wayne some counseling. The incident earned Wayne a weeklong suspension, but Wayne refused to see a counselor.

The tension peaked when Wayne grabbed his mother in the garage during an argument over his behavior. For the first time, Karen felt scared of her own son.

"Don't ever do that again, Wayne," she recalled telling him. "Next time, I'll get up on the chair and I'll punch you out."

Years later, Karen would acknowledge that perhaps Wayne felt neglected because she and Steve went out so much; she was having fun for the first time in her life. She said they tried to include the boys when they went bowling or to baseball games, but neither one usually wanted to go. Rodney had his friends and Wayne was involved in wrestling.

Nonetheless, Karen was at her wit's end, so she called a lawyer for advice on what to do with her out-of-control son. Karen was told that as long as he was living at home, she would be legally responsible for his actions. She didn't remember whose idea it was, but Wayne went to live with his uncle Jimmy in Eureka.

Jimmy remembered his teenage nephew as a loner, always so deep in thought that he could be quite uncommunicative. Wayne also had pronounced mood swings and could get very upset at times.

Wayne would tell Jimmy that neither of his parents loved him, that "nobody cared for him at all," Jimmy recalled. "I'm sure that after he left my place that he probably felt the same way about us."

Jimmy bought him a motorcycle, and Wayne took out his anger on the machine.

"He'd beat it up, physically kick and beat the motorcycle because it wouldn't start," Jimmy said.

By this time, Wayne's feelings about punishment had evolved in an unusual way. One day he decided to run away, so he headed north, but he turned around and came back once he reached Arcata, California. Instead of returning to his uncle's house, however, he went straight to Juvenile Hall.

"They wanted to know why he's turning himself in, and he says, 'Well, I was trying to run away,'" Jimmy said. "And then I had to go up and get him out of Juvenile Hall and bring him home. . . . He wanted punishment because he had the thought of running away, and he felt that he needed to be punished for that."

Jimmy was baffled by this, so, he said, "I didn't hammer on him for it."

In another incident, Jimmy and his wife went away for several days, and when they returned, Jimmy could sense that something wasn't right with his Camaro.

They were sitting around the house when Wayne broke into tears and confessed to Jimmy that he'd taken the car.

The next night, the doorbell rang, and Jimmy opened the door to find a police officer with Wayne on the doorstep. Apparently, the officer had caught Wayne trying to steal a battery from another car to put into the Camaro because he'd killed the battery by leaving the lights on.

"He couldn't handle doing something wrong and not

being punished for it," Jimmy said. "He has such a strong sense of justice, even today, about things."

When Wayne was sixteen, Karen said, Gene called to complain that he was upset with their younger son.

"We decided maybe the best thing for him would be to go in the military to get him off the street and get some discipline," she said.

Wayne would later claim that he got the idea to join the U.S. Marines after seeing the movie *The Boys in Company C*, but because he was still a minor, he needed parental consent.

"Dad, will you sign papers for me to go into the Marine Corps?" he asked Gene.

Gene was ecstatic. "Yes, where do I sign?"

Rodney said Wayne lied about his age to the recruiters, but no one noticed because he was big for his age. He had just turned seventeen by the time he entered boot camp in January 1979.

The marines would train Wayne—like every other recruit—to be a lean, mean killing machine.

CHAPTER 4

KELLY AND THE
HEAD INJURY

Around Halloween in 1980, Wayne met Kelly Dick, a pretty, petite blonde, on a blind date. They were introduced by one of Wayne's coworkers at Shakey's Pizza in Irvine, who also worked with Kelly at a bank. Wayne was still in the marines and Kelly was in college, living in an apartment on campus.

Kelly liked the macho silent type, so she was attracted to Wayne, who seemed a bit standoffish and indifferent at first. He would go without calling for a week, saying he'd forgotten her phone number; then, curiously, he would walk fifteen miles to see her from Marine Corps Air Station El Toro, where he lived on base. She couldn't figure him out—or if that was his intent—which kept her intrigued.

On their way back from dinner in late November, they saw a two-car accident at the side of the highway. Wayne asked Kelly to stop so he could see if anyone was injured.

One of the passengers was bleeding from the neck, so Wayne told Kelly to go find a pay phone and call for an ambulance.

Kelly drove off in search of a phone, but because it was dark and she wasn't familiar with the industrial area, it took about twenty minutes before she could get back.

She saw fire trucks, police cars, and rescue workers, but no sign of Wayne, so she approached a firefighter and tried to describe her missing date: "Big, tall marine. Have you seen him? You know, a jarhead. You can't miss the haircut."

But no one had seen him. They just kept asking if she'd seen the third car.

"Well, I was the third car."

"No, the red car."

Kelly didn't learn until later that they were referring to a red car with a drunk driver who had swerved off the highway, hitting Wayne and another person, then sending them nearly forty feet down an embankment.

She drove around until 3:00 A.M., looking for him, tracing the route he would have taken if he'd walked back to the base.

It was the next morning, and she was at Shakey's, talking to the friend who had introduced them, when one of her roommates called to say that Tustin Community Hospital had phoned. Wayne was in the hospital and wanted her to come.

At the hospital, she learned he was in the intensive care unit, which had a big sign that said RELATIVES ONLY. She wondered why they'd called her if she wasn't allowed to visit him.

"Are you Kelly?" the nurse asked.

"Yeah," she said.

"Get in there, all he's been doing is repeating your

phone number, over and over and over and over again, till we promised him we'd call you."

Wayne looked as if he had landed right on his face, which was swollen to twice its normal size. His face was black and blue around the eyes. The fall had ripped off most of his lip, requiring stitches to sew it back together. His four front teeth were shattered and his jaw was broken, but he was conscious.

Considering that he couldn't seem to remember her phone number before the accident, Kelly wondered how he'd managed to do so after taking such a pounding.

When she returned the following morning, Wayne's mother was at his bedside.

Karen was still living in Santa Rosa when she got a call from an ICU nurse.

"We have your son here, and if you can come, it would be a good idea because he's been in a serious accident. He has serious head damage."

"How serious?" Karen asked.

"Well, his teeth are knocked out and he's got damage to his mouth, and we think he has a concussion."

Karen asked the nurse to tell Wayne that she was on her way. She called Rodney to see if he wanted to fly down with her, but he said he wanted to go by himself.

Wayne was conscious, but in pain, when Karen arrived. His primary injuries, as far as she could tell, seemed to be in and around his mouth.

"Thanks for coming, Mom," he said, complaining about his missing front teeth. "I'm going to look terrible."

"You can get teeth," she said. "Nobody will even know that they're false."

Karen only stayed for a couple of days, leaving Kelly to take care of Wayne for the rest of his nine-day stay.

Rodney said Karen called him after she first heard from the ICU, saying, "You need to come and see your brother. I don't know if he's going to make it."

But he and Gene later said neither of them felt the need to go to the hospital because Wayne's commanding officer told Gene that Wayne's injuries weren't serious, that he'd only gotten "a couple of teeth knocked out," and Gene had passed that assessment on to Rodney.

Neither of them learned the severity of Wayne's head injury until much later.

Years later, Wayne told a psychologist that he'd been pressing his hand against the wounded driver's neck to stop the bleeding when he was thrown down the embankment. Apparently, he knew quite a bit about the arteries in the neck.

"A drunk swerved off and hit me. Killed me," Wayne said.

"Killed you?" the psychologist asked.

"Yeah, they revived me. I woke up three days later. . . . The whole one side of my body just didn't work very good and my head was all swollen up, and it was a pretty tough time."

Wayne wasn't able to go back to work right away, and because Kelly's three roommates had gone home for the holidays, she offered to let Wayne stay with her so she could nurse him back to health. They grew closer over the next week or two, and once he was feeling better, they traveled to northern California to visit his mother, Rodney, and some other relatives.

They flew up and drove back in a 1953 Chevy that Wayne bought from his brother.

Kelly noticed a change in Wayne's behavior after the accident—he seemed much friendlier to her and paid her more attention.

In February, Wayne was about to leave for a couple of months of training in Alabama. He told her he would earn a bigger salary if he was married, so they decided to get hitched on the sly, while Kelly was still in school. She would go home for the summer; then they would have a big wedding in the fall.

They eloped in Las Vegas that May. However, their plot was foiled by Kelly's sister, who found out their secret and told Kelly's mother all about it.

Kelly noticed another change in Wayne's behavior, about two weeks into the marriage. The two of them were talking over some wine when Kelly asked Wayne about his family and what it was like growing up; she'd gotten the feeling that he hadn't been treated very well. When she pressed for more information, Wayne clearly didn't want to talk about it, but she wouldn't let up. That's when Wayne got physical.

"He wasn't actually aiming for me, he was just trying to swing at me, to tell me to shut up, and he ended up hitting a stud in the wall and broke the knuckles in his right hand," Kelly said. "It just shattered all the knuckles, so he ended up going to Alabama with a cast on his hand."

Something had changed in Wayne since they'd said, "I do." He'd become more demanding and domineering. His whole attitude toward her had shifted. And it only got worse.

Some of Kelly's complaints about Wayne's behavior sound somewhat similar to Karen's complaints about Gene. Regardless of what may have happened in the Ford family house when Wayne was growing up, it would be typical for him to model his expectations of how a wife should act and be treated based on his perceptions of his parents' marriage.

While Wayne was in Alabama, he called Kelly, ranting that the money she'd sent him hadn't arrived on time. She was hurt to find out that he'd hocked his wedding ring to go out drinking beer with his friends. He, in turn, wasn't happy to learn that she was pregnant.

When he got home, she said, "He basically told me that . . . he wasn't about to have kids right now and I had to have an abortion. I told him I didn't want to have an abortion and he said, 'Well, I'm leaving then.' And I felt like I had no choice."

At the abortion clinic, a woman asked Kelly if anybody was forcing her to have the procedure.

"What if I say yes?" Kelly asked.

"Then we couldn't perform the abortion."

Kelly walked out of the interview room, past Wayne in the waiting area, and out into the hall, where she started to cry.

Wayne followed her. "What?" he demanded.

"I don't want to do this," she said.

Wayne grabbed her by the arms and shoved her toward the waiting room. "Get back in there," he said.

After the abortion, Kelly said, Wayne became abusive, saying the only reason he married her "was for a steady piece of ass." (Wayne had started having sex when he was fifteen and slept with eight women—primarily those with large breasts—before Kelly.)

When she didn't want to have sex, Wayne wouldn't take no for an answer, so Kelly started giving in just to stop the "mental torture" for a few hours. Otherwise, he would keep her awake, sometimes until 4:00 A.M., until she relented.

But after a while, even that didn't work.

"It was like my whole life at home had to do with sex,"

Kelly said later. "If I was a nymphomaniac, it might've been a great situation for me. But I'm personally not that sexually motivated."

Wayne made it known that he wanted her to remain naked around the house. If she sat down to watch TV, she said, he would "feel free to come up and start suckling on a breast. I mean, it was just a constant barrage of this, like that's all I was there for, that I was an object for his pleasure."

When they went out together, he would ask her to wear shirts that were so see-through, she felt she wasn't even wearing one.

Things got so bad that she started crying at her desk at five o'clock because she knew she had to go home. He expected her to cook elaborate three-course dinners—more often than not while she was in the buff—and he wouldn't accept plain vegetables. They had to be doused in cheese sauce.

"If it wasn't perfect or right, he got angry," she said. "The thing was, I could never get angry back at him, because then I'd get in trouble."

In January 1982, Wayne took a trip to Big Bear with some other marines. He asked Kelly to go, but she couldn't, so he went without her. Before he left, Kelly told him not to lose her good towels, and also not to screw around.

"I already had the idea that he wasn't going to be able to go five days without having sex, so it was like, half-joking, but half-serious," she said later.

Two days after he left, one of Wayne's friends phoned.

"Kelly, has Wayne called you?"

"No."

"If he calls, tell him to come back."

Kelly wondered what was going on. "Come back from where?" she asked. "What happened?"

"We can't tell you. Just if he calls, tell him to come back."

At the time, Kelly was playing cribbage with a young gay friend, who had overheard the conversation. He was so scared of her husband that he ran out of the apartment in case Wayne showed up.

When Wayne called that night around eleven, she was amazed to hear his story. Not only did he think that he'd done nothing wrong, he also didn't seem the least bit embarrassed to tell her about it.

"He just knew he was going to get caught, and that's why he'd run," she said later.

Wayne told her that he and the guys had met these two young girls roller-skating, and he and one of his friends had invited them over to the cabin the next day. Wayne said they slipped off their wedding rings and had oral sex with the girls, who turned out to be only fifteen.

When Wayne's friend went to take the girls' home, they stopped to help a young guy whose vehicle had broken down. The guy turned out to be the boyfriend of Wayne's date, who immediately got out of the truck and screamed that she'd been raped. When the police came to the men's cabin, Wayne took off, out the back door. He made it through ten or fifteen miles of woods before he finally found a pay phone to call Kelly.

Wayne was eventually arrested for attempted rape and an arraignment date was set, but it kept being postponed. Kelly said this went on for six or eight months, which she remembered being "a very tense and stressful time for Wayne."

Today, Wayne's rap sheet says only this about the case: "Victim unavailable/decline prosecution." Whatever court records there might have been about the incident no longer exist.

* * *

In April, Kelly and Wayne moved to Santa Ana, where he got a job managing their new apartment complex.

Wayne's mother had gone to India for a while and had come back with an Indian boyfriend. Karen and her new man lived with them for a couple of months, which gave Kelly a break from the nonstop sexual pressure.

But that didn't stop Wayne from being demanding in other ways. Wayne had a pool party one Saturday, during which he insisted that Kelly iron his uniforms and spit-shine his shoes. After she'd finished doing the chores, he told her to put on the new bathing suit he'd bought for her. It was white, with a gold patch at the crotch, and as long as it wasn't wet, it wasn't too revealing. So, of course, Wayne made her get into the pool so that everyone could see her in full glory.

After a mix-up with the rent checks, the landlord got upset with Wayne, so they all had to move. However, Karen and her boyfriend got their own place because Wayne kept making racial slurs about the boyfriend being unclean and unfit to handle their food.

Kelly got a new job working with thirty men in a warehouse, so Wayne switched gears and made sure she wore baggy clothes when leaving the house each morning. He also started trying to entice her into incorporating bondage into their sex acts.

While he and Kelly were walking around Hollywood, they stopped at a sex shop, where he bought a deck of cards featuring women from the neck down or the knees up. The cards were specifically focused on the breasts, which were generally wrapped or tied up.

Wayne got the idea that Kelly should imitate these

women's poses during sex. He had her dip her breasts in wax so he could make molds of them. He also told her he'd like to cut holes in a sheet, then cover her up so that only her breasts were exposed.

Kelly felt as if she was losing herself amid all this kinkiness. "During this whole time, basically because of the verbal abuse . . . I had to have . . . such a tight rein on my emotions, so that I just didn't totally have a breakdown. . . . I was just like a walking zombie."

Her salvation came in the form of a coworker named Bob, who, like her, was unhappy in a bad marriage. Bob became her confidant, and he began telling her that her home life "was not right."

Kelly's breaking point came a couple of weeks before Christmas in 1982.

Wayne was a total grinch. They'd spent two Christmases together, but they'd never gotten a tree, and he wasn't one much for gifts. Kelly somehow persuaded him to let her put up a tree that year.

One night, she came home from work, and as she always did, got on tiptoe and peered through the glass pane in their front door before she opened it. She could see Wayne inside, wrapping a big stack of presents he'd bought her. But after he saw her, peeking inside, he dragged her through the door and made her open every one of them. He was furious that she'd ruined her own surprise.

When Kelly finally got up the guts to tell him that she was leaving, Wayne became apologetic and contrite. After Christmas, he even called her up at work and asked if she'd go to marriage counseling with him. She agreed.

The therapist was a woman, who talked first to Wayne alone for half an hour, then to Kelly alone, and finally to the couple together. As she conveyed Kelly's concerns to Wayne, Kelly could see the veins throbbing in Wayne's neck.

At the end of the session, the therapist pulled Kelly aside and said she'd have someone drive Kelly home. "I don't want you going home with him," she said.

Wayne had never hit Kelly before—only grabbed her by the arms and shook her occasionally—so she wasn't all that concerned.

"No, no, I'll be fine," Kelly said.

Kelly had seen Wayne get violent only once, when a kid in the video arcade had bumped Wayne and caused him to lose his game. Wayne hauled off and hit him so hard that he broke the kid's nose, embedded his eyeglasses in his face, and split the skin above his eye deep enough that he needed stitches.

After the counseling appointment, Kelly and Wayne went to the movies and discussed the therapist's suggestions, one of which was to live apart for a week—him on base and her at the house. So that's what they decided to do.

The next day at work, Kelly told Bob what had happened and he suggested they go to dinner with some coworkers. Kelly had taken the bus to the warehouse, so Bob drove her home afterward. As they were approaching the house, Kelly could see a truck belonging to one of Wayne's friends parked in the driveway, a sign that Wayne had brought a friend home when he was supposed to be staying on base.

"Don't stop," she told Bob. There was no way she was going to walk into the house at 10:30 P.M. if Wayne was there waiting for her.

Bob drove her to a nearby pay phone, where Kelly called her sister.

"Can I come to your house?" Kelly asked.

"What is going on?" her sister replied. "Wayne's been

calling here, like, every ten minutes for the past three hours. He's drunk and he's waiting for you to come home."

Kelly's sister agreed to let her stay the night. Later, Kelly found out that Wayne had come home with two dozen red roses, hid the car, and waited for her to show up. But as the hours passed, Wayne drank more and more beer, growing increasingly angry. At some point, he put on his camouflage uniform and waited in the bushes with a bow and arrow to shoot her and whomever she'd been out with.

Wayne was still phoning Kelly's sister's house at 1:00 A.M., ranting and raving, so Kelly finally took his call.

"I'm not going to talk to you tonight," she told him. "I'll see you tomorrow."

Kelly went home the next night, but Wayne took out his anger and jealousy on her for days.

On January 13, 1983, Kelly hit an emotional wall as she was ironing.

"I want a divorce," she finally told him.

Surprisingly enough, Wayne didn't seem angry.

"Okay," he said. "Would you mind staying, living with me, until I find somebody else?"

Kelly was a bit frightened by the strange calmness that had taken over her volatile husband. "No, I don't think that would work out too well," she said.

They proceeded to discuss how to split up the furniture, TV sets, the car, and their two motorcycles. Wayne was fine, until Kelly said she wanted to keep her bike.

"Why?" he said.

"Because I have friends that ride."

Wayne blew up, dragged her to the phone, and

demanded she call her friend. She did as she was told and dialed Bob's number.

"Wayne wants to talk to you," she said, feeling bad about putting her friend in the middle of all this.

"What happened?" Bob asked. "Are you okay?"

"I'm fine, just Wayne wants to talk to you."

Wayne invited Bob to meet them for breakfast at a restaurant down the street in forty-five minutes. Bob agreed, so Kelly went to change out of her pajamas, taking Wayne at his word.

But, of course, it wasn't going to be that easy. While she was getting dressed, Wayne came into the bedroom and raped her, leaving bruises on her back and wrists. Then he told her to get dressed and they walked down to the restaurant. Just like that.

When they got there, Kelly sat speechless—in the silence of the surreal—as Wayne asked Bob if he knew any girls he could introduce Wayne to, preferably ones with large breasts.

"Bob's just, like, flabbergasted," Kelly recalled later. "He's sitting there, like, 'Well, gee, I don't know, Wayne. I don't know of anybody offhand, but I'll keep my eye out.'"

After breakfast, Bob turned to Kelly and said, "Drive [my car] to your house and get some clothes and I'll take you away." Then he took a stroll with Wayne, assuming that he had called Bob there to punch him out.

"So you want to fight?" Bob asked.

"Oh, no, man," Wayne replied. "I'm happy for you."

Bob was confused as he and Wayne walked back to the house, where Kelly had already packed a bag. Wayne did nothing as she left with Bob.

Wayne moved out a few days later, but he didn't stop calling Kelly, who had moved to Pasadena. Within a couple of weeks, she started dating Bob, whose wife had kicked him out of the house. Eventually, he and Kelly moved in together.

"I had made it clear to Bob, at the beginning, that I still loved Wayne, but it was just a difficult situation," Kelly said later.

Meanwhile, Wayne was stalking her. Every day he would call and report that he'd seen her driving down a particular street, kissing Bob at a certain traffic light, and having dinner in a specific restaurant.

Because he worked during the day, he was only able to follow her in the evenings, but that changed when he showed up at her office one afternoon. He grabbed her by the arm and dragged her outside, where he yelled at her in the pouring rain, their wedding rings pinned to the front of his jacket.

Kelly kept glancing around for Bob, who was scheduled to pick her up around that time.

"Are you looking for him?" Wayne demanded. "If he comes here, I swear to God I'll kill him. He better not even come anywhere near."

Bob drove up, as if on cue, then walked up the ramp toward them.

"You got a problem?" Bob asked Wayne.

But Wayne backed down. "No, I just . . . thought maybe we could get a cup of coffee or something and talk."

So the three of them went out for a while. Wayne described to Bob in explicit detail the sex acts he and Kelly had performed together, but Bob would not give Wayne the satisfaction of reacting. He just let Wayne talk until he was finished.

Later, Wayne came to Kelly's apartment and wrote messages on her windows, reinforcing the fact that he knew where she lived.

Kelly and Bob finally moved to Cathedral City, near Palm Springs, to get away from Wayne. Shifting his focus, he tried to harass Kelly's sister into giving him Kelly's new address.

Kelly began divorce proceedings, hoping that Wayne wouldn't fight her move to finalize the divorce in six months, around the fall of 1983. Wayne waited five months and twenty days before he made a showing, so the six-month clock had to start all over again.

During this period, Kelly lived in constant paranoia. She and Bob were at a sporting-goods store in Palm Springs one morning when she looked across the street and—to her horror—saw her estranged husband.

"Oh, shit, it's Wayne," she said.

"No way."

They got in the car, drove around the block, and, sure enough, it was Wayne, so they headed back to their trailer.

Wayne found them within three hours. Somehow he'd learned that they were living in a trailer park near Palm Springs, so he went methodically to every single one in the area until he figured out which was theirs.

Kelly never saw him again. He held up the divorce for a while longer, but he finally gave up. Or so she thought. The divorce ultimately became final in August 1984, which allowed Kelly to marry Bob.

But Wayne would still not let go. He showed up at Kelly's grandparents' ranch in Chino in 1985, telling her uncle that he was an officer for the Norco Police Department (which did not exist), and asked to use the phone to report a car accident he'd witnessed. He attempted once again to get her address, but Kelly's relatives pretended they didn't know where she was.

Looking back, Kelly described Wayne as extremely narcissistic.

"He did not, from my view, comprehend that there are moral rights and moral wrongs, as long as it felt good to . . . him."

Rodney didn't see much of Wayne while he was in the marines and married to Kelly.

Rodney joined the navy in 1983 and was assigned to the Seabees construction battalion. He stayed in the service until 1990.

When the two brothers finally spent some time together after the separation, Rodney noticed that his brother was acting aggressively and self-destructively.

"He'd come unglued, throw a fit, leave. If it wasn't his way, it wasn't going to happen," Rodney recalled.

At the time, Wayne told Rodney that he was driving very fast on his motorcycle, missed a turn and hit a guardrail. He said he also wiped out while doing a wheelie several months later.

Once Rodney learned more about his brother's head injury from 1980, he attributed these incidents, along with Wayne's increasingly aggressive behavior and hair-trigger temper, to that. Before the accident, Rodney said, Wayne had gone four-wheeling and rode his motorcycle, but always within safe, reasonable limits.

CHAPTER 5

"DANGER TO HIMSELF, OTHERS AND GOVERNMENT PROPERTY"

Wayne's military records provide a revealing look at his state of mind, as well as his view on life up to that point.

At 7:30 P.M. on April 8, 1983, several months after the separation, Wayne was admitted to the naval hospital's psychiatric ward in Long Beach, where he'd been sent from the marine base in El Toro after complaining of depression and problems adjusting to work. He blamed the difficulties on his split with Kelly.

On his patient questionnaire, Wayne gave a few short but succinct answers about his mental condition: "No hope, constant failure, lost will to live."

Asked what he knew about his mental problems, he wrote, "I know the answers, but I can't put them to use."

He said he'd had no significant health issues other than being hospitalized in November 1980, when "I was run over on the freeway."

Under allergies he listed, "penasillin (you spell it)," yogurt and pot, adding that he vomited when he smoked marijuana.

He described his alcohol intake as "couple of beers weekly," and stated that he smoked 1½ packs of cigarettes a day.

Under vision/hearing/speech, he wrote, "When I was young, everyone had trouble hearing me. People said that I mumble and talked to [sic] soft. It has come back."

He checked every box available for emotional difficulties: anxiety/nervousness, tension, restless, depression, irritability, and other.

During his intake interview, Wayne told the nurse that he was seeking treatment for depression and low self-esteem.

"If you send me back to duty, I'll just find another way out," Wayne said.

Wayne told the nurse that he'd been pretty happy until he was seven and his parents got divorced.

"I lived with my mother until she could not control me and then I moved in with my father," he said. "I got involved in sports and started lifting weights to carry a macho image, but my parents never went and watched me, they just bought the necessary equipment. I did well in school until I was thirteen years old. When I got a little older, I got involved with the Hells Angels and got into trouble. I joined the Marine Corps . . . [and] also got involved in weight lifting and kickboxing. . . . After I graduated, I used to kick ass every day. I got into NBC (Nuclear, Biological and Chemical Warfare) preparedness school and became an instructor in that. I did well in that—I received meritorious advancement to corporal.

I was really happy there. I also got instructor of the month for thirteen weeks. . . . I worked alone and did not like that I was expected to do everything, and slowly I started to make mistakes. I would put on a false front by smiling, and feeling bad about myself inside. I got no gratification from it. . . . I would get an occasional pat on the back, but not at the unit. While this went downhill, my marriage started to go downhill. One time I was at an arcade and this one guy was giving me some shit, so I kicked his ass and put him in the hospital. This scared my wife. She was intelligent but had no common sense. She refused to pay bills, and at times I would hit and kick holes in the wall, and I think she was scared of me from then on. Finally I just gave up on her and now she is in the process of getting a divorce. Well, I think a lot of my problem is a lack of self-discipline with some laziness. Mainly, I just have no self-gratification. I live alone, sleep alone, and can't stand being alone."

A drug screen on April 9 showed that Wayne had no recreational or prescription drugs in his system, as was the case in subsequent hospitalizations.

On April 10, the same nurse noted that Wayne was being passive aggressive.

"If they send me back tomorrow, they might as well send me to the brig," Wayne told him. "I don't think talking with some jerk for an hour is going to change the way I feel. What I need is to talk to a psychologist about my problems. I know what is going on, but I still don't know how to put the tools into action."

During group therapy, Wayne said he knew he needed to be on the unit, but he also made inappropriate comments and laughed when other patients were speaking. When Wayne was told he couldn't leave the ward, he threw kicks into the air next to a patient and had to be told twice to stop.

The doctor's summary stated that Wayne had a "recent history of alcohol abuse. Past history of explosiveness. . . . Mental status exam revealed an angry Caucasian man in fatigues. . . . Patient stabilized quickly on ward without meds."

The doctor recommended that Wayne be returned to full duty, but to follow up with outpatient group therapy.

"I don't want to go back to duty," Wayne said. "I'll come back here."

One nurse noted that Wayne's motivation for continued treatment was poor, and so was his understanding of his own illness.

Wayne was released on the morning of April 11. There is no record that he pursued group therapy.

In May 1984, Wayne was seen by a psychiatrist as an outpatient at the El Toro base, where he was diagnosed with adjustment reaction with mixed features and a personality disorder with explosive and immature features. Nonetheless, he was returned to full duty once again.

"He is energetic, industrious and extremely able to complete tasks assigned," Wayne's supervising officer wrote in a July 1984 evaluation, adding that Wayne too often allowed "outside personal problems to [affect] his military professionalism."

Wayne had quickly risen to the rank of sergeant, E-5, while teaching NBC, but after separating from Kelly, he was written up for a number of infractions and demoted to corporal, E-4.

Wayne's demotion came after a dispute with his supervising officer, who had flunked Wayne's unit during inspection. Wayne was also cited and disciplined for conduct unbecoming and failing to report to the Camp Pendleton firing range. After going AWOL for two days, he was disciplined for impersonating an officer over the phone as he tried to excuse his own absence.

Shortly thereafter, he was transferred to the base in Okinawa, where he was hoping to "get his stripe back."

But he soon experienced more mental problems. On September 27, Wayne was found sitting in "a catatonic-like state" in his barracks. Even while he was being removed from the area, he refused to speak.

He was taken to the hospital on base, where, during a physical examination, he became violent and ran out. He had to be forcibly returned to the hospital, where he became so agitated that he had to be placed in four-point restraints in a locked room and given shots of Haldol, a psychotropic drug often used to treat schizophrenia. Among its side effects are involuntary muscle spasms and twitching, followed by muscle stiffness.

"I can't remember what happened today," Wayne told the nurse. "Last night . . . I was awakened to do field duty and I just went off. I was really pissed."

On September 29, Wayne denied that he had tried to hurt himself or hospital staff the day before, but he did acknowledge that this was his second psychiatric admission.

"Will my admission affect my chances of being an attorney?" he asked. "I want to try to go to law school."

Wayne said he didn't understand why he was on suicide watch. "I never said I would hurt myself, and I know I'd never try."

Later that night he told another nurse, "I'm a real likable person. I wouldn't think of hurting myself and I wouldn't hurt anyone else unless I was cornered. I was seeing a psychiatrist about a week before I came here, though, for a suicide attempt. My mother was a manic-depressive. She's living in India now."

"I can play like I'm having a catatonic break if I have to," he said. "But mostly, I play like I'm normal."

The next day, Wayne exhibited paranoia. "Do you put anything in the food here before we eat it?" he asked the nurse. Once he was reassured that his food had not been drugged, he ate all of his meals.

On October 2, Wayne was back with the rest of the patients and in a better mood, doing sit-ups and push-ups by the afternoon.

"I have a positive attitude about getting out of the Marine Corps—I know I will do well," he said.

A nurse noted that his talk of becoming a lawyer seemed rather grandiose, given the situation. She wrote in his treatment plan that he should be encouraged to verbalize his feelings, "but toward a more realistic goal."

Ninety minutes later, another nurse noted that he was exhibiting the potential to harm himself or others and had become abusive.

"I've been hearing gossip that I'm trying to seduce a sixteen-year-old girl," Wayne said. "If anybody tries to accuse me of that, I'll break their fucking head."

Six and a half hours later, Wayne was cheerful, happy, and optimistic about his future again.

"I am being administratively discharged from the service. It's just what I was hoping to hear," he said.

On October 3, Wayne said he was feeling "some pain and hurt" for the teenage girl because he knew what she was going through.

The next day in group therapy, Wayne seemed upset and was having trouble controlling his anxiety. One of the nurses wrote that Wayne complained the staff was trying to "control his mind and that we (staff) were out to get him. Reassured patient that no one was here to hurt him. Received feedback from female patient who assured him that the staff wasn't controlling anyone's mind or out to hurt anyone."

Wayne was restless during group therapy, cracking his

knuckles, pulling threads off his clothes, and playing with the flame of a cigarette lighter until it was confiscated.

Later that night, he told a nurse, "There comes a time in every Christian's life when he must make a sacrifice. From now until this is over, I won't touch food or water, and no word to another human being shall pass my lips."

He swore that he wouldn't hurt anyone, but he grew agitated and increasingly angry.

"Go ahead, give me the shot—you can't hurt me physically," he said. "That's what you're doing now, hurting me physically."

He was given some medication, but when he refused another dose, he was placed in seclusion, where he wouldn't eat or speak and began singing, praying, and pacing. He was placed in four-point restraints and was given more Haldol.

After five days of being medicated and restrained, Wayne was no longer aggressive. Depressed and tearful, he complained about the Haldol's side effects, saying his muscles were stiff and sore.

By October 7, he was acting more cooperative, so staff reduced his four restraints to two.

"I'm in control of myself," he told the nurse. "I wouldn't hurt myself or anyone else. I would like to get out of here, if possible."

Wayne was released from locked seclusion the next afternoon. He seemed appreciative, his mood bright and alert.

On October 9, Wayne expressed anxiety about his future again. "Now I won't be able to work where I want because of my hospitalization," he said.

Ultimately, the doctor diagnosed Wayne with Borderline Personality Disorder, "severe and chronic," noting that he'd recovered from the episode of "acute decompensation."

* * *

Wayne called his uncle Jimmy in the middle of the night from Okinawa—4:00 A.M. California time—saying he was coming home.

"[He] told me that he had messed up, that he went in and tore up the commanding officer's headquarters—or the office—and they were going to kick him out. I think that's what he was after at the time, but he wanted to come home and go to school . . . and try to become an attorney," Jimmy recalled later.

"Well, that's not a problem," Jimmy told Wayne. "You can live here. How about finances?"

"Oh, I'll have that all squared away," Wayne said. "I just need a place to live."

"Okay, that won't be a problem."

But when Wayne got back to California, Jimmy said, he didn't "have a nickel to go to school on."

After three and a half weeks in the Okinawa hospital, Wayne was flown by medical plane to Letterman Army Hospital at the Presidio in San Francisco. He was supposed to go to San Diego but ended up in the Bay Area "due to an apparent lack of inpatient beds" in southern California.

When he arrived at Letterman on October 21, his medical records had been lost in transit. The admitting doctor's initial impressions: "No evidence of a psychotic disorder presently. The etiology of this problem is unclear . . . an underlying personality disorder is likely, though uncertain."

But before Wayne was discharged, he received a very different diagnosis: "1. Borderline Personality Disorder, severe as manifested by intense and inappropriate anger and lack of control of anger, marked shift in mood from normal to depression, irritability and anxiety. Depression when alone and a chronic feeling of emptiness or boredom. 2. Atypical psychosis manifested by frequent psychotic breaks, unmarked by hallucinations or affixed delusional system, not caused by a mind altering drug. 3. Rule out schizophrenia. Rule out paranoid disorder."

The hospital staff arranged to transfer Wayne by ambulance to the Oak Knoll Naval Hospital in Oakland. Wayne didn't want to go there because he was worried they would give him a sedative, a likely reference to his dislike for Haldol. He began "expressing feelings of religiosity and was seen playing his guitar on the ward," one doctor wrote.

Wayne was admitted briefly to Oak Knoll on October 23, then was transferred to the naval hospital in San Diego on October 25.

Still without his records, he said during his intake interview that he'd been hospitalized in Okinawa because he "was working fourteen hours a day, seven days a week, without breaks, and so I broke."

He also reported that he'd been admitted to the Long Beach naval hospital in 1983 for "homicidal ideations."

"I found my wife in bed with another man and I wanted to kill them both," he said. "I have been separated from her for two years. I'm not bothered by the incident anymore."

At the hospital in San Diego, Dr. M. J. Foust Jr. and Dr. R. J. Forde recorded their impressions about Wayne, noting that he was not a "reliable historian" about himself. Forde also wrote that he had "serious doubt" that the head trauma Wayne suffered in 1980 was contributing to his current psychiatric issues.

"He describes his mother as a very religious person, who later went to India to live and work with Mother Teresa," Foust wrote. "He left his mother to live with his father because 'the grass is always greener.' He lived with his father for one year, after which time his father gave him his own apartment to live in at the age of thirteen. The patient states that he became a 'juvenile delinquent,' engaging in car theft, burglary and truancy. He was arrested at least twice and spent some period of time in Juvenile Hall on detention. At the age of fifteen, he bought a car and traveled around the country. He was then taken in by a woman of middle age and lived with her until the age of seventeen when he joined the US Marine Corps . . . , worked in electronics and did poorly and then became a truck driver, which he quickly became bored with. He became interested in NBC, liked it and became 'the model Marine.' He quickly progressed in rank to sergeant. He did well until his wife abandoned him for another man in 1982."

Foust wrote that Wayne's aggression and manipulation of fellow patients supported the diagnosis of Borderline Personality Disorder.

"He appears to have recovered fully from his previously decompensated and psychotic state and further hospitalization does not appear warranted at this time," Foust wrote.

That said, the doctor stated that Wayne was not in any mental condition to continue on in the marines.

In a recommendation that was approved by Forde, the Psychiatry Department's inpatient director, Foust wrote: "This patient will be discharged to Marine Corps Liaison with the recommendation that he be expeditiously administratively separated from the US Marine Corps due to a newly diagnosed and documented personality disorder of such severity that he can no longer render useful service to the Marine Corps. Until such administrative separation is effected, it is our opinion that the patient remains at risk of another decompensation and could become a danger to himself, others and government property."

On January 31, 1985, Wayne was discharged from the military for "the convenience of the government, character, and behavior disorders."

CHAPTER 6

ADAM AND WADAD

After Wayne was kicked out of the military, he drove delivery trucks for Sears and Wards. His uncle Jimmy also got him a job repairing boats at a fishery in Eureka. It was dirty work, Jimmy said, but paid good money. Wayne soon quit and moved back to southern California.

"He didn't like that because the work was too demeaning," Jimmy recalled later. "Wayne always had this attitude that he was better, not than anybody else—well, he did have a very high opinion of himself for some reason, and that type of work was beneath him."

Following in his mother's footsteps, Wayne started calling himself Adam, his middle name, around this time. (His mother had already begun going by her middle name, Brigitte; his father and brother also went by their middle names, but they had always done so.)

In 1986, he landed a job as a driver's helper, loading

trucks at American Delivery Service in Garden Grove. There, he met a nice Kuwaiti girl named Wadad Radwan, who was in her late teens and worked in the customer service office. Wayne asked her out for coffee and their relationship progressed from there.

He never held any one job for very long. In addition to delivering papers for the *Orange County Register*, Wayne sold cars at two dealerships, worked at a motorcycle shop, and drove a school bus for disabled children in San Juan Capistrano. He also worked as a tow truck driver and security guard.

By the same token, Wayne never lived in the same place for very long. Given this pattern of behavior, it's not surprising that Wayne's six-year relationship with Wadad was very off and on, marked by breakups, sporadic periods of living together, and a passing engagement.

Not long after they began dating, they got into an argument and split up for a couple of weeks. Wayne moved in with his friend Dave from the marines, back with Wadad, in with Dave again, then back with Wadad.

Wadad, who just wanted Wayne to be happy, lived with her mother during the in-between times.

"Whatever he did, he was never challenged enough," Wadad, who knew Wayne as Adam, said later. "He was too smart for his own good, I think. He'd get bored too quick. He was always depressed. . . . I wanted to see him happy because I believed in him."

Similar to his relationship with Kelly, Wayne's sexual practices with Wadad seemed normal at first.

Initially, he asked her to give him oral sex, but she said no.

"I can't do something like that if I don't love you," she said.

Wayne seemed pretty upset by this, but he didn't take it out on her, perhaps because things changed soon enough.

It wasn't long before Wadad fell in love with Wayne, so she was more willing to do what she needed to please him—that included letting him put a safety pin in her nipple during sex.

"I loved him a lot and I thought, well, you know, I'll try that," she said later.

Even though it hurt, she let him stick her on four separate occasions. He never pushed the pin all the way through, he just pricked her with it and pulled it out when she complained of pain. (Wayne later told a psychologist that he'd administered diabetic injections to one of his teenage girlfriends, and over time, the needles became sexually arousing to him.)

Wayne would ask Wadad to bite his nipples and he would bite her breasts as well, hard enough to leave teeth marks, but not enough to make her cry. Wadad knew he liked this, so she went along. She also didn't object to him setting up a camcorder so they could watch themselves while having sex.

But Wadad had her limits. She drew the line when he said he wanted to bring another woman into their bed. It made no difference that he said an ex-girlfriend let him watch while she had sex with another man.

"I thought about it, but then I thought . . . it wasn't in my heart to really do something like that," she said. "I'm just not like that, and so I never—thank goodness—I never did something like that, because I would've regretted it."

She also refused to have anal sex with him after they experimented once or twice because it hurt too much.

Unlike with Kelly, Wayne never forced Wadad to have sex when she didn't want to. On the other hand, Wadad said, "I never said no to him, so I don't know how he reacts to that. But he never . . . coerced me or anything."

* * *

Years later a woman named Janice Hawkins said she'd met Wayne at a karaoke bar in Vallejo in October 1987, and she let him live with her for a time. During that period, she said, he asked her to pinch his nipples so hard that she feared she would pinch them off. She also said she hit her once while they were having sex, and masturbated in front of her teenage daughter.

In 1989, Wadad said, she and Wayne were living in a two-bedroom house in San Clemente. They both knew their relationship was not going anywhere and that they weren't good for each other, so they started to break up. Again. But then Wayne had an idea.

"Why don't we just break up slowly?" he said. "I'll sleep in the other bedroom."

As usual, Wadad agreed to go along. She had no other immediate plans.

So Wayne moved into the other bedroom and they lived largely as roommates, although they were still occasionally intimate. This went on for a year, while Wayne was supposed to be looking for another place to live. Wadad said she wanted to keep the house because she had a dog.

Around this time, Wayne told his brother he'd started taking prelaw courses at Saddleback College, a community college in Mission Viejo, with the hopes of becoming a criminal defense attorney someday. (Wayne never got past the tenth grade in high school, but he ultimately earned his GED.) A Saddleback spokeswoman confirmed he attended courses there from 1990 through

1992, although she couldn't confirm which classes he had taken or whether he'd completed them.

One day, Wayne came home, crying, but he wouldn't tell Wadad what was wrong. "I don't want to," he said.

"Tell me," she said. "Tell me what happened."

"I don't know exactly."

He finally explained that he'd been walking along the sidewalk when he came across a girl, grabbed her purse, threw it up on the roof, and bit her breast. Wadad didn't understand why Wayne would do such things, but she didn't press him for an explanation because he was crying.

There were other strange incidents around this time as well. While he was working as a tow truck driver and helping some people on the road one night, a young teenage couple from out of state approached him. They said they had no money and needed to buy gas, so Wayne brought them back to the house.

It was summertime and Wayne was on break from driving the school bus, so he sat around the kitchen table, playing cards with these kids. Wadad came home from work one evening and saw Wayne, sitting at an angle and facing the girl, who was about fifteen. He was shirtless and was wearing cutoff shorts with no underwear, so his testicles were hanging out the bottom. Wadad tried to signal him to tuck himself in, but he remained oblivious.

Finally, she had to say something.

"Why don't you cover yourself?" she asked.

"What's the big deal?" he replied.

Wadad felt he was being disrespectful, but later she realized he must have liked watching the girl react to his exposed genitals.

Also during that time, Wadad and Wayne rented the second bedroom to a young woman whose pretty cousin came to stay with them. Wayne told Wadad he saw the cousin, through the window, sleeping naked on her bed.

"What were you doing looking in the window?" Wadad asked.

"Well, her blinds were open."

It didn't hit Wadad until later that there was no other reason for Wayne to be outside her window except to stare at the girl. Their yard was such a mess that they never even used it except to let the dog run around.

Finally, at long last, Wayne announced he'd found another place to live.

"Where?" Wadad asked.

"Right there," he said, pointing to the house next door, which was also adjacent to his former employer, B&M Towing.

Wadad was outraged. "You can't do that to me," she said.

She soon realized that she would have to move because even after he was living next door, he was still coming and going from her house as he pleased. She found a studio in San Clemente and left her dog behind.

Wayne was drinking quite a bit and going out at night, singing karaoke. He and Wadad were still intimate off and on until the end of 1992, when he told her that he'd been with somebody else. That was the end for Wadad.

"I told him I didn't want any part of him after that," she said.

In September 1992, Wayne applied for a job with the U.S. Border Patrol. In his application, he claimed to have supervised more than thirty-five employees at a time in the marines, writing that he left the military because "as a career I was not interested."

During his time in the marines, he wrote, "I was responsible for maintaining high standards of appearance, mental and physical readings. I was an expert with the

M-16 A2 rifle and .45 pistol for most of my six years. I was promoted to sergeant after my 20th birthday."

He listed the skills he'd developed as: "map reading and navigation math with logarithms"; first aid for chemical, nuclear and biological injuries; radio communications; use of radiological equipment; "survival in harsh environments"; "nuclear blast reporting; use of weather data; and many other classified and unclassified skills. I learned teaching, leadership, and the ability to speak and write clearly and concisely."

He omitted mention of his demotion and discharge, but perhaps the description he gave for his job after the marines spoke for itself: "As a security officer I was responsible for ensuring the security of some 35 pools, Jacuzzis, tennis courts and two small lakes. . . . I was also responsible to cite violators of the association rules and regs (the strictest imaginable). During my employment with Woodbridge, I developed or maintained the following skills: radio communications, crisis situation management, abnormality observation, public relations and rating of situation reports."

Wayne didn't get the position with the Border Patrol, which, as a federal law enforcement agency, may have had access to the details of his separation from the Marines.

In March 1993, Wayne called Rodney to say he'd been arrested on suspicion of firing a weapon and cruelty to animals.

"What happened?" Rodney asked.

Wayne explained that the two Dobermans belonging to the owner of the B&M tow yard next door were barking constantly and trying to get under the fence between their two properties, apparently wanting to get hold of Wadad's dog. Wadad had asked Wayne to keep the fluffy, mild-mannered white creature when she moved into her new apartment.

Wayne told Rodney that he had repeatedly warned the owner about what he would do if the dogs got into his yard.

"You need to fix the fence," Wayne said he told the owner. "If they get in here and hurt my dog, I'm going to kill them."

Eventually, one of the Dobermans did get past the fence and got into a fight with Wadad's dog. Wayne told Rodney he tried to separate them, but he finally gave up. So he went inside, got his shotgun, and killed the Doberman.

"I would probably have done the same thing," Rodney said later.

Ultimately, Wayne was sentenced to five days in jail for cruelty to animals, but it's unclear if he served any time.

Although Wayne and Wadad were engaged for a while, Wadad never really thought about a wedding or having kids with him. Looking back years later as a wife and mother, she tried to make sense of why she stayed in their relationship for so long.

"I think I was just waiting for him to make the right move in his life, but he never did it," she recalled. "I waited till I was twenty-six and I woke up that morning, on my birthday, and thought, 'What am I doing here?'"

After living away from Wayne for a while, and evaluating how she should be treated by a man, she decided that he hadn't respected her at all.

"I just don't think he respects women, period," she said.

But Wadad didn't seem all that angry at him. She said she figured the way he turned out had something to do with his relationship with his mother. Wayne had told her that he'd been very close to Karen, hanging on her dress in the kitchen as a child; then one day, "she just looked at him and said, 'I don't want to be your mother anymore,' and she left. She just left."

Rodney agreed with Wadad's assessment. "Something happened when he got kicked out of the house [by our mother]. He didn't trust women anymore," Rodney said. "That's as far as I can see when he started having problems with women."

Rodney described Wadad as a very nice person, "one of the best people I ever met." She always got along well with Rodney's wife, so well that the four of them often went to car shows together.

"We just loved her to death," he said. "Wadad was the best and healthiest thing that ever happened to my brother."

But Wayne didn't seem to appreciate what he had in Wadad until years later.

"He used to browbeat her, treat her terribly," Rodney said.

The ironic part about all of this is that Wayne would later look back on these years and describe Wadad as the love of his life.

CHAPTER 7

ELIZABETH AND MAX

In early 1994, Wayne was working as a disc jockey at Taka-O, a Japanese sushi restaurant and bar in San Clemente, where he ran the karaoke machine.

His friend Dave was dating a pretty twenty-one-year-old named Elizabeth Ault, but after they broke up a few months later, the slender blonde started coming to the bar just to see Wayne, who was a dozen years older than she was.

They started dating at the end of May and got close pretty quickly. In the beginning, Wayne brought her flowers. Within a couple of months, they were living together, and soon after that, they were talking about getting married.

Elizabeth was working at Lane Bryant, a clothing store in Orange County. Wayne, who was still going by the name of Adam, was working at an auto repair shop with his friend Scott Hayes, a mechanic he'd met when the two of them worked at B&M Towing. Scott was married to a woman named Linda, and the four of them often socialized together.

Before Wayne and Elizabeth had a chance to set a wedding date, she got pregnant. This time, Wayne left the decision about having an abortion to his girlfriend, and because they weren't married yet, Elizabeth chose to have the procedure.

On October 15, 1994, the two of them were married in Las Vegas at the Tropicana Hotel, once known as the "Tiffany of the Strip," and home of the city's longest-running showgirls production, *Folies Bergere.*

Right before the ceremony, Rodney, who was Wayne's best man, made his feelings known about the impending nuptials, while the bride's father and brother stood silently by. Elizabeth's father, who worked for the Las Vegas Metropolitan Police Department, eventually was promoted to deputy chief and commander of internal affairs.

"You shouldn't marry her," Rodney told Wayne. "She's too young. She's too volatile. You've already had problems and I don't see it getting any better."

But Wayne didn't listen and stubbornly married his young bride anyway.

Wayne stopped working at Taka-O after the wedding, because, Elizabeth said, it wasn't the kind of "scene to be working in when you're married."

But that didn't stop the two of them from going there together. Wayne liked playing darts and the two of them often entered tournaments.

They were talking one day, asking each other questions about their past lives.

"Have you ever killed anyone?" she asked, wondering about his time in the marines.

Wayne said no, but he did tell her about the night in

1992 when he hurt a girl pretty badly in a bar in San Clemente. He said someone had jumped on his back, so he turned around and reflexively decked the person, only to see that it was a young Latina woman whose jaw was dangling from his punch.

He said he ran out of the bar and took off in his red Jeep. He went over to Scott's house and told him he needed to paint his vehicle blue because the girl he'd hurt was part of a Mexican gang and he didn't want her fellow gangsters to track him down by his car and take revenge.

Just as in his previous relationships, Wayne started asking to expand their sex life soon after the wedding: he wanted to watch Elizabeth have sex with another man.

Initially, she said she didn't want to, but she changed her mind after he fought and argued with her, making her life a living hell.

"I can't even put it into words," she said later, crying as she recounted a part of her life that she had since tried to forget. "He would just make life so bad that I thought, if this will make him happy—and it's stupid on my part, you know I've made some mistakes in my life—and I just thought maybe it would get [our life] back to normal."

Elizabeth wanted to make her husband happy and get past this fantasy. So one night, she got drunk enough to feel emotionally numb, then the two of them picked up a marine from a bus stop and went back to the barracks. The three of them had sex, but the men didn't touch each other.

The next morning, Wayne was very proud of Elizabeth. "You were great last night," he said.

Elizabeth looked at him and said, "I can't believe I did that. I never want to do it again."

Nevertheless, she agreed to do it two more times, and each time, Wayne's afterglow only lasted about a week.

Finally, Elizabeth said she couldn't do it again, and meant it.

"It's awful," she told him. "I don't know why you would want to do that to me."

"Well, don't you want to make me happy?" he replied.

But sometimes it was hard to make him happy—especially when he was sulking. If Wayne didn't get eight hours of sleep, he blamed Elizabeth and refused to go to work. She would toss and turn before she went to sleep, and he needed to lie still, so Elizabeth slept on the couch most of the time.

By March 1995, Elizabeth was pregnant again.

During the pregnancy, Elizabeth hadn't really felt much like eating until the evening. But one morning in August, she was unusually hungry, so she made herself some eggs, bacon, and toast. She settled in on the sofa to eat her breakfast while she watched some TV, but Wayne decided that he wanted to eat her food rather than cook something for himself. He also wanted to have sex.

"What he expected of me as a wife was to cook his breakfast, and cook his lunch and cook his dinner," Elizabeth said later. "If he had to go to work without his breakfast, he was pissed at me . . . whether or not I was sick."

But this time, he took his anger out in a different way. "He just took control of me and he—he raped me. . . . It was bad. I didn't want anything to do with him. I just wanted him away from me and he took a belt and wrapped it around my neck and told me to suck his dick. And I wanted to bite it off, but I didn't want to get killed or anything. That was the only time I was really frightened of him. . . . He hit me with the belt. . . . He got on top of me [and] I felt like I was going to die."

Elizabeth ran out of the apartment naked, screaming, and into the laundry room, where she grabbed a towel and wrapped it around herself. Wayne got scared and called her back inside and told her it would be okay.

"No, I'm not going back in there," she told him.

Elizabeth looked around in case anybody was watching, and she saw a young boy. She went back into the apartment so that she didn't cause a scene.

She took a shower and then let Wayne have sex with her. She lay there, lifeless, letting him do what he wanted, hoping it would make things better. Afterward, she cried.

They were supposed to drive up to see Rodney and his wife and kids that day in Pomona, so they could all go to a classic-car show. They went as planned, as if nothing had happened.

A week later, they got into an argument and she took off to see her family in Las Vegas, but came back the next day after she and Wayne talked on the phone. Looking back, Elizabeth knew that she should have stayed away, but she wasn't ready at the time.

Other than the rape, Wayne was never violent with Elizabeth—not even the time she hit him during an argument over whether she should visit her mother in Vegas. Strangely enough, he wanted her to go and she didn't. He was standing on her purse and bending over to reach inside for her mother's phone number when she smacked him in the face. He called the police, but by the time they arrived, he'd calmed down enough to talk them out of taking her away, because she was pregnant.

* * *

Wayne had seemed pleased about the baby once he found out that it was a boy. Elizabeth didn't know what they would've done if it had turned out to be a girl.

When it was time to go to the hospital, Elizabeth said, Wayne seemed very put out that he had to go along.

On December 10, 1995, their son was born and they named him Max.

Not long after the birth, Elizabeth's father suggested, as he had in the past, that the young family move to Las Vegas, where there would be great job opportunities for both of them.

They made the move that February and stayed with Elizabeth's mother until they could get their own apartment in the same complex the following month.

Once they were on their own again, Wayne started asking Elizabeth to talk to him about being a prostitute. Since she'd never been a prostitute, she didn't quite understand his new sex game and refused to tell him what he wanted to hear.

Wayne started working as an apprentice for the electricians union, but he decided he would rather drive a cab.

Meanwhile, Elizabeth stayed in their two-bedroom apartment, taking care of Max. She kept the house clean, did the laundry, and cooked for him, just like he wanted, but she began to detach herself emotionally as the sex games continued to escalate.

Elizabeth let Wayne tie her wrists together once, which she considered "normal kinky," but she wouldn't do it again because she didn't like feeling confined. On several occasions, Wayne put his hands around her neck as he was reaching climax. He wasn't forceful about it, so Elizabeth never said she minded, although she didn't say she liked it, either.

Still, Wayne wasn't happy. He was constantly depressed, holding on to things and not letting go of them. In addition, he started making her drink vodka straight from the bottle until she threw up. He talked about putting a padlock on her vagina so that no one else could get inside and started asking to pierce her breasts with safety pins.

She figured if she let him do it once, then he'd be satisfied and move on. But that didn't happen. If she didn't let him poke her, he would become morose. So sometimes she would let him, just for a minute.

"That really hurts, I don't want to go through this, Adam," she would tell him. Sometimes she would cry, saying, "Why would you want to do this to me? I don't like it."

More and more, this odd behavior seemed to be something that Wayne needed, and also something that Elizabeth could not withstand. She didn't like the way he was constantly masturbating on the couch, either, particularly when she caught him in the act.

In June 1996, Elizabeth decided she couldn't take all of this anymore, so she and the baby moved upstairs to her mother's apartment for a week.

Wayne pleaded with her, promising that things would be different. But Elizabeth was starting to build up her own life—and her confidence. She was working with her mother in a catering company, and in just a matter of days, she had the car insured and was able to put Max in child care. Wayne called it "baby prison," but he didn't object to it enough to take care of Max himself. In fact, she later said, he never seemed to take much interest in their baby at all. He would never bathe or feed Max and he rarely changed his diaper.

Finally, Elizabeth gave Wayne an ultimatum: he had two weeks to prove that he could change.

"The way you live is not right and I am going to work,"

she told him, referring to his previous opposition to her getting a job. She also told him that he wasn't going to have his meals on the table whenever he wanted, because she had other things to do.

"I don't know what's wrong with you, but I'm not going to live like this," she said.

Wayne tried to meet her demands for a day or two, but once he saw that she was serious about working, and not being his domestic slave, he went back to acting depressed.

On July 4, 1996, Wayne and Elizabeth went to a party at the top of the Stratosphere Hotel and Casino, and two days later, she left him for good.

Elizabeth moved in with her mother because she didn't have enough money for a down payment on her own apartment. The following month, she met a man and went to stay at his place in Green Valley.

"I mean, here I am with a six-month-old baby and I'm thinking nobody's ever going to want me again," she recalled later.

Her father disapproved of her new living arrangement. So in October, she and Max moved in with him.

At that point, Wayne had Rodney and Gene pick him up in a motor home and take him back to California, towing his broken-down Jeep behind them. Wayne lived with his father in Napa for a few months before he moved south.

Wayne was working for a karaoke company when he met a woman at the Blue Rock Inn in Vallejo. After they dated for a couple of months, he moved into her trailer in the waterfront community of Benicia, which is next to the Carquinez Strait, and is part of the San Francisco Bay.

While they were living together, Wayne told the woman

that his ex-wife "destroyed their family" when she left him for another man. He talked about wanting to kill Elizabeth and often told her, "I know I'm going to hell," but he didn't elaborate.

He lived with the woman, whom he slapped once during sex, until he moved to his grandmother's house in Eureka in September 1997. After that, they began dating long-distance.

One night in January 1998, the woman's nephew got "pretty wasted" with Wayne on rum and Coke, and Wayne said he "hated women, that his wife took his kid away from him, and that he wanted to 'cut them up,' 'dismember' them and 'hide everything that would identify them.'"

The nephew later admitted that he'd been intoxicated at the time, so he wasn't sure if Wayne was talking about what he wanted to do to women, or if he was confessing about something he'd already done. Nonetheless, he subsequently told his aunt that Wayne was evil and she should stop seeing him.

The woman ended the relationship during a visit to Eureka the following month, when Wayne told her that he was in love with her twenty-year-old daughter and wanted to have a child with her.

Two months later, Wayne showed up in Benicia and argued with the woman at the trailer. She never heard from him again.

Sometime after his split with Elizabeth, Wayne started calling his mother, who was now going by her new married name, Arora. After moving back and forth to India, Brigitte was living in Austin, Texas.

Wayne always called pretty late at night. According to Brigitte, the first conversation went like this:

"I'm sorry, Mom, I'm calling you so late," he said.

"It doesn't matter. I'm just glad you called. How are you and what are you doing?"

Over the next ninety minutes, Brigitte said, the two of them cried as they talked about his feelings that she didn't love him and that she had "deserted him."

"Wayne, I love you," she said. "I'm sorry that I didn't show it more."

"You abandoned me," he said.

"Wayne, you're the one who wanted to leave. I didn't want you to leave," she said. "I don't even remember how we came to that. I love you."

"Really?" he said. "You never told me."

"Maybe I didn't and I'm sorry. I just assumed you would know."

Wayne told her how lonely he was and how people were hurting him.

"Whenever I open my heart," he said, "whenever I'm honest with people, whenever I more or less reach out to them, they stab me."

Brigitte could see that he was feeling sorry for himself, but she didn't say anything because she didn't want to scare him off after their estrangement. She wondered whether he was having a psychological breakdown.

Brigitte had just started a new job and couldn't leave town, so she asked if he wanted to come visit her for a few days.

"No, Mom, I can't," he said.

"Why?"

"I just can't."

Brigitte told Wayne he could call her collect again, anytime. She also tried calling him, but nobody ever answered.

It was several months before she heard from Wayne again. Just like the first time, it was at midnight or 1:00 A.M., and Wayne was crying.

This time, Wayne said he was angry that people were persecuting him, but he wouldn't give any specifics. He complained again that he was lonely without a girlfriend.

"Mom, I really want a family," he said.

"Wayne, you have to go out there and make friends," she said. "There are nice people out there and it doesn't particularly have to be a girlfriend. Just go out and meet people. There's a girl out there for you."

Looking back later, Brigitte realized she may have sounded idiotic to Wayne, but she had no idea where his mind had taken him.

In December 1996, Wayne returned to Las Vegas with some relatives to see Max for his birthday, saying he was proud that the two of them shared a birthday in the same week.

Wayne brought Max a tricycle with a big helmet, which Elizabeth thought was ridiculous, considering their son was only a year old and could barely walk.

Elizabeth felt torn. When she called Wayne to encourage him to take part in his son's life, all he wanted to talk about was getting back together.

"Max doesn't have a mommy and daddy anymore," Wayne would tell her.

"Yeah, he does," she'd reply. "It's just that you have to make an effort to be in his life, that's all."

"It just shouldn't be like this," he'd say.

"Well, it is and you just have to make sense of that, instead of trying to go back, 'cause that'll just never happen."

Wayne always blamed Elizabeth for his not being in Max's life, reminding her that she was the one who left.

"So he frickin' moves to California and makes it completely impossible to have a normal relationship," she said later.

* * *

At some point in 1997, Wayne called to tell Elizabeth that he was coming to Las Vegas to see Max. So they came up with a plan for Elizabeth to drop Max off at the child care center, where Wayne could spend some supervised time with his son. She always feared that Wayne might abduct the boy.

Elizabeth had hoped to avoid running into Wayne, but he was there when she arrived with Max, so she suggested they get something to eat at a nearby McDonald's while Max got used to being with his father.

Wayne's eyes welled up with tears as they sat in the restaurant. "I just miss you," he said.

Elizabeth didn't want to get into it, and since Max seemed fine with Wayne, she told him to go ahead and take Max for the day, then drop him off later at child care.

Later on, Elizabeth went for sushi with her boyfriend, then called the center to make sure that Wayne had already come and gone.

"Did Adam drop Max off?" she asked.

"Yeah, but Max didn't want to stay, so [Wayne is still] here," they told her.

Eventually, Wayne left Max inside, but he sat outside in his car, ruminating, for quite some time.

On October 14, 1997, Elizabeth and Max met up with Wayne in Arroyo Grande, just south of San Luis Obispo, so that father and son could have a visit mediated by Wayne's friends Scott and Linda Hayes.

The three of them took a trip with the Hayes family to the pumpkin patch known as Avila Barn, then spent the afternoon at Avila Beach, where Wayne and Max went for a half-hour stroll along the shore.

Scott thought Wayne seemed excited to see his son, and although Wayne was cordial to Elizabeth, he could see Wayne's lingering disappointment about the separation. Wayne also told him he wasn't happy that Elizabeth had shaved Max's head bald.

Wayne left in a funk after the six-hour visit with the family he'd lost. But no one would know just how much the visit upset him until more than a year later.

PART II

CHAPTER 8

"Torso Girl"

The coastline of Humboldt County curves northwest into the Pacific Ocean and back again, ending about fifty miles below Oregon. The economy of this rural region depends on seasonal fishing, lumber, and the tourists who flock there to see the famous redwood forests. More artists live in Humboldt, per capita, than anywhere else in the state.

The greater Eureka area, which has more than forty-two thousand residents, is the largest metropolis for three hours in any direction. A network of tributaries, which flow through and around the city, is fed with salt water by the tides and freshwater by the rain. Known as sloughs, they run from the bay inland, creating a brackish environment that supports fish, shrimp, and crabs.

In 1997, Wayne was working three days a week at Arcata Readimix, a cement and gravel-mining plant on the Mad River, seven miles north of Eureka. Because he was also working in Vallejo with a karaoke company, he lived part-time on his father's property in Napa and part-time with his aunt Doris and other Ford family members in Eureka.

At the Ford family homestead, Wayne's cousin Robert Johnson tried to engage Wayne in conversation, but it was hit-and-miss. As long as they were discussing race cars, it was fine. But, Robert said, "If you tried to talk about any other subject, family or whatever, he just kind of wouldn't say anything, or get up and walk out of the room."

One day, for example, Robert saw Wayne sitting in his room, staring at a ceramic slab imprinted with a child's hand and the name "Max."

"What's that?" Robert asked.

Wayne looked up with a lost expression, then closed the door without a word.

"What's wrong with Wayne?" Robert asked his mother, who was also living there.

"I have no idea," she said.

Another time, Robert went to Wayne's room to get him for dinner.

"I'll be right there," Wayne said.

It was fifteen minutes before he joined them in the kitchen.

"What took you so long?" Robert joked.

Wayne gave him a strange look, ate his dinner quietly, went outside to smoke a cigarette, then retreated to his room.

Wayne and his relatives used to go out together to bars, where Wayne liked to drink and sing karaoke. He also used to enjoy playing his guitar and singing to them at the house, but he gradually stopped performing, even when Robert asked him to.

Wayne went out one night with his cousin Leslie and met her friend Candy, a schoolteacher.

He came home afterward, laid his head on his aunt

Ginger's lap, and told her about his immediate attachment to Candy.

"Aunt Ginger, I really love her," he said as she stroked his hair. "I want to go out with her."

Ginger, who used to babysit Wayne and Rodney, felt Wayne's mother never gave him the upbringing she should have, hiding him away in the house with the shades drawn all day. Ginger thought that Wayne had always felt different and needed attention. He wanted so badly to fit in.

Wayne's aunt Vickie also thought Karen had seemed peculiar, sleeping around with other men while she was married to Gene. Vickie later said she thought Wayne resented his mother because of these other men and for abandoning him as a teenager. His ex-wife Elizabeth reminded Vickie of Wayne's mother.

Vickie would later recall how Wayne used to walk around the house in a silk robe, like Hugh Hefner. He also would walk around downtown with a briefcase, dressed in a suit and tie for no reason in particular.

As a result of his continued remarks about "needing space," his aunt Doris suggested that he buy her trailer and move into it somewhere private. He accepted her offer that July and moved into the Town & Country Trailer Park in Arcata.

Arcata has a fluctuating population that expands to twenty thousand when Humboldt State University is in session. It gets about forty inches of rain, mostly between November and April.

Wayne's trailer was only a few feet from a fence separating the park from Arcata Readimix. Because he had no garbage service, he would dispose of his trash at his aunt's house.

* * *

The afternoon of October 26, 1997, was sunny but seasonably cool when photographer Bob Pottberg and a few friends put their kayaks into the frigid Freshwater Creek. Pottberg liked to go canoeing a few times a year, but he'd never explored Freshwater Slough, which connects to Ryan Slough, both winding waterways with muddy banks surrounded by marshland.

The plan was to spend a few hours meandering down to the boat ramp under Samoa Bridge, where they had left a car to drive home.

By 4:00 P.M., the air was starting to grow even cooler. Pottberg was coming around a bend to a wider portion of the canal when he saw a white object ahead on the north bank, unnaturally stark against the lackluster green and brown landscape.

As he paddled closer, he thought he could make out buttocks, and wondered, *is that a mannequin—or is it a body?*

At that point, Pottberg thought it would be better if his friend, Lynne Sarty, who worked at a local hospital, checked it out. But she declined.

"No, it was your idea, you go poke it first," she said.

Sarty was trying to be playful, but she, too, was nervous that it might actually be a body. Her husband, who had their four-year-old in his kayak, had the same concerns, so he paddled ahead without them.

As Pottberg drew nearer, he told himself that it had to be a mannequin because it was missing its arms, legs, and head. The yellow areas had to be stuffing and the white covering had to be fabric or plastic.

He got close enough to tap it with his paddle. Only he didn't get the sound of wood against hard plastic that he expected. Instead, the figure, which would have been facedown, was squishy to the touch, and he could see that the yellow material was actually fatty tissue, where body parts had been surgically removed.

Pottberg was horrified.

"This is real!" he called out.

Whoever had cut up this poor soul, the gender of whom he could not determine, had done so with precision. There had been no hacking involved.

"At this point, I freaked, turned around, and [went back] to where my friends were," Pottberg recalled later.

Pottberg's hands shook as he fumbled for his cell phone and punched in 911. After going through dispatch, he arranged to meet a Eureka police officer downstream at the municipal airport, Murray Field, a fifteen-minute trip by kayak.

The sky darkened and the air grew chilly as Pottberg and his friends waited near the airport for almost an hour before the authorities arrived.

Pottberg tried to explain what he'd found, and initially they were almost blasé about his discovery, saying they found several bodies in the slough every year. Pottberg, who was still thoroughly disturbed by the experience, tried to make them understand that this was different.

"This isn't just a body," he told them. "This is *no* body, so to speak."

The officers finally got the point, once Pottberg detailed the surgical cuts.

"Oh," one of them said.

Once he'd described the exact location as the north bank, the authorities determined that the Humboldt County Sheriff's Office should handle the case because the Eureka Police Department's jurisdiction covered only the south bank.

So sheriff's Lieutenant Frank Vulich, Deputy Coroner Charlie Van Buskirk, and a California Department of Fish and Game officer went by boat to collect the torso from the slough near the end of Park Street, in the neighborhood known as Myrtletown, where they were met by a deputy and the sheriff himself.

The next day, Vulich, commander of the sheriff's detective bureau, assigned Detective Juan Freeman to be the lead investigator on the case. The torso, as it turned out, was also missing its breasts, so the victim was identified as Jane 194-97 Doe. Freeman called her "Torso Girl."

Freeman had started working for the sheriff's department as a correctional officer in the Garberville jail and substation in January 1977. By 1988, he'd transferred into the detective bureau, where he started investigating child abuse cases and eventually progressed to major crimes, many of which were homicides.

As a hobby, Freeman restored hot rods, classic and custom cars. He and his wife, Lynn, were nicknamed "Dagwood and Blondie Bumstead," after the comic strip characters, because Lynn always wore her blond hair in a ponytail. Although he and his wife reportedly carried "the Bumstead curse" for the misadventures they experienced on their car trips, Freeman didn't look anything like the cartoon Dagwood. He was bald, stood a sturdy five feet ten inches and weighed 220 pounds.

By the time Freeman got the torso case, he'd already worked a couple dozen homicides, but this one was a first for him.

"I was pretty sure I had the work of a serial killer in front of me," he said.

All of his homicide cases got to him, but he'd never tried to solve a case where he had no face, teeth, or specific characteristics to help identify his victim and catch his killer.

"I've never encountered body parts where I had to build a victim," he said.

In conjunction with visiting the area where the victim was discovered, Freeman's first task was to compile a list of "identifiers," such as approximate height, weight, hair color, and race. This would be done during the autopsy, which was scheduled for October 29 in San Joaquin County; Humboldt had no pathologist of its own.

Accompanying Humboldt's coroner, Glenn Sipma, and his deputy, Charlie Van Buskirk, Freeman left Eureka at 3:00 A.M., with Jane Doe's body in the trunk, starting the six-hour trip to the morgue in French Camp in a county vehicle with no air-conditioning.

"It was a nasty trip all the way there and back," Freeman said.

Also present at the autopsy were San Joaquin's pathologist Robert Lawrence, Charles "Butch" Cecil, a forensic anthropologist and skeleton expert from San Francisco, and Joe Herrera, a sheriff's deputy who worked in the coroner's division.

The autopsy took about two hours and the subsequent findings of Dr. Lawrence and Dr. Cecil were remarkably consistent: Jane Doe was white, with possibly some Hispanic background; she was between eighteen and twenty-five years old and had given birth at some point; she was five feet three or five feet four inches tall, weighed 120 to 125 pounds, and had brown or auburn hair; and because she had a low level of carbon in her lungs, she came from an area with little air pollution and was likely a nonsmoker.

They counted twenty-seven stab wounds on the right side of her back and buttocks, all but one of which appeared to have been inflicted after death. All eleven of her bruises, however, were made before death. Three of the bruises were the size of fingertips, patterned like grasp marks on the back of her right shoulder; the rest were on her lower left back.

Some of the stab wounds looked as if they'd been made with a small double-edged blade, and others, including the premortem wound, by a single-edged knife. Ranging in size from a ½-inch to 9/16-inch, they all looked as if they had been cut with a jerking, hesitating motion. The method of limb removal, however, varied. Some bones looked as if they'd been sawed cleanly in half, while others appeared to be half-sawed and then smashed or broken, as if the killer had grown frustrated with the time and effort it was taking.

The head was severed at the neck below the voice box, between the C-5 and C-6 vertebrae. Her breasts had been sliced off and pared down to the rib cage. Her torso had been slit down the center to the pubic area, and her pubic mound had been cut off. Given that her vagina had also been sliced out—and that her body had been lying in the slough for some time—it was no surprise that the pathologists found no trace of semen in or on her body.

Although the Humboldt County Coroner's Office initially estimated that the torso had been in the water for "less than a week," that calculation was later amended to the lower range of two to twenty-four hours because of the lack of "animal action" on the body.

The cause of death, however, could not be determined.

On Halloween night, Wayne had dinner with the Ford family at his aunt Doris's house.

The topic of the well-publicized torso case came up in conversation, and one of his aunts asked, "Who would do such a thing?"

Doris later recalled that Wayne said nothing. He just looked down at his dinner plate.

* * *

In the days after the autopsy, Freeman and two teams of investigators, each with a boat and a cadaver dog, searched the water and both banks of the slough system for any other remains belonging to Jane Doe. Both dogs showed strong interest in the area where the torso was recovered; the handlers believed that porous pieces of driftwood may have retained the body's scent. After fanning out a mile in either direction, the dogs found no more missing limbs.

Freeman, who prayed every day with his wife for God to help him solve this case, submitted the victim's basic identifiers to the Department of Justice (DOJ) Missing and Unidentified Persons database, which was tied into the FBI's National Missing and Unidentified Persons System. Initially he asked for a run of young women who were reported missing between October 20 and 26.

He also submitted the data to the state DOJ's Violent Crime Information System, to the FBI's violent crime database, and to a database in Washington State that cross-referenced MOs for violent criminals, known as the Homicide Investigative Tracking System. In addition, Freeman contacted profilers with the FBI and the state DOJ in Sacramento and conducted his own research by sending out a national all-points bulletin, asking other agencies with similar cases to contact him.

Within the next year, Freeman developed about a hundred leads on missing women who could have been his victim. Although he came close several times, the DNA never matched.

"I scratched the ground until my fingers bled," he said.

* * *

On November 25, Karen Mitchell, a nice girl from a nice family, went missing five days before her seventeenth birthday. Karen had been living with her aunt Anne and uncle Bill Casper, who was the head criminalist at the state DOJ crime lab in Eureka, which undoubtedly contributed to the media's and law enforcement's close attention to the case. Karen was last seen leaving her aunt's shop at the Bayshore Mall and walking along Broadway to the Coastal Family Development Center, where she took care of children.

Freeman and other authorities immediately suspected that her disappearance was related to the torso case.

On December 5, Wayne walked into a mental-health clinic in Eureka.

During the intake interview with psychiatric social worker Todd Flynn, Wayne said he had suffered from severe depression for most of his life and described his crying spells, thoughts of suicide, multiple aches and pains, feelings of hopelessness and agitation, and recurrent insomnia.

Flynn wrote in his notes that when Wayne became depressed, he would abruptly leave his job and had problems maintaining relationships.

"Patient had been using alcohol more, binged while he was singing in bars," Flynn wrote.

Apparently minimizing his alcohol problems, Wayne said he drank half a beer every few weeks. He also said he'd been obsessively focusing on his thoughts, which disrupted his sleep and judgment. To Flynn, he seemed negative and sad, describing activities that were clearly doomed to fail. However, he never mentioned killing or wanting to kill anybody.

Flynn's diagnosis was dysthymia, a low-grade depression

that could possibly be more serious, with histrionic (displays exaggerated emotional responses), dependent (allows other people to meet his needs), and narcissistic (uses other people as objects to meet his needs) features.

Flynn referred Wayne for a psychiatric evaluation. But after the staff psychiatrist talked with Wayne, he decided that Wayne should undergo counseling before trying medication.

Wayne made an appointment for December 18, but he never showed up.

On December 18, 1997, Freeman met with two profilers from the state DOJ he'd contacted. The profilers, Sharon Pagaling and Richard Sinor, had also come to Eureka to check into the Karen Mitchell case for the Eureka PD.

Freeman toured Ryan Slough with the profilers before they went to the police station to review the Mitchell file.

Pagaling and Sinor told Freeman that they, too, thought the two deaths were related. They said the killer likely was a white man in his forties, who had killed many times before and, generally, did not intend for his victims to be found. In the torso case, however, they believed the killer was especially proud of his handiwork with the knife, so he put Jane Doe into the slough—where someone would find her.

They believed the killer also weighed the risk of being caught while transporting the body from his home, where he felt it was safe to commit his crimes. They figured he worked a regular job, because the body was dumped on a weekend, and that he lived nearby, was a frequent visitor, or had lived there before. His knowledge of the area would be crucial, they said, because he needed to park close enough to the slough that he wouldn't have to risk being seen while carrying the body.

Pagaling and Sinor suggested that Freeman try to determine what was in the victim's stomach because, as he was well aware, these types of killers rarely had sexual intercourse with their victims; they usually forced them to perform oral sex and swallow the semen.

Freeman already knew what had happened to the stomach contents. During the autopsy, he'd seen Lawrence, the pathologist, dump them into a strainer, looking for pills. Lawrence had found a few beans, which he rinsed with water, thereby disposing of the gastric fluid. Sipma told Freeman that if he'd done the autopsy, he would've saved the stomach contents as a matter of routine.

"I was very disappointed at that," Freeman said later. "Very disappointed."

The profilers also requested that Freeman try to determine where the victim had been actually thrown into the slough, because it was possible that more body parts could be found in a sunken container or a barrel nearby. They suggested he pick a day when the tides were similar to the weekend the body was found and put some weighted bags near the estimated location to see where the current took them. If any of the bags ended up where the body was found, the bottom at the dump site should be searched.

On January 29, 1998, two people cutting driftwood at the beach in McKinleyville, a town north of Eureka, pulled an arm out of the surf.

It was a left arm, sunburned and dried out. Freeman ordered DNA tests to look for a match with Karen Mitchell or his Jane Doe. The hand was sent to the DOJ lab in Sacramento to see if it could be rehydrated enough to take a set of usable fingerprints.

The next day, a team of investigators searched the shore from Clam Beach south to the Mad River, which flowed from the mountains through Arcata, emptying into the ocean near McKinleyville. No other body parts were found.

By mid-March, Freeman learned that the arm's DNA matched the torso's. The arm also appeared to have been sawed partway through, which was consistent with the marks on Jane Doe's left shoulder.

After hurting his back at the cement plant, Wayne went on workers' compensation leave on November 21, 1997. He believed the company was stringing him along because they wanted him to quit rather than fire him, so he went next door to Edeline Trucking and asked for a job in February.

He was assigned truck #60, which had a forty-five-foot flatbed for transporting freight, and he started driving that night. Because he didn't own a car, he essentially lived in the sleeper portion of the cab, driving it over to the trailer park to do his laundry.

Meanwhile, Freeman talked to Kay Rhea, a psychic he'd used on previous cases. Many of the details she provided turned out to be true, even though she'd offered some of them in the wrong context.

"Kay asked me to describe the general location where Jane Doe was found. I did this and Kay told me the victim had dark brown hair, but not black hair," Freeman wrote in an investigative report.

Rhea told Freeman that Jane Doe had lived with the killer, who was at least forty-five years old, hardened, drawn, and wore a beard that was at least two inches long, untrimmed and graying.

She said he lived in a small house or cabin deep in the

woods and up a dirt road, outside Eureka city limits—i.e., within the sheriff's jurisdiction—where marijuana was being grown. He owned a short pickup truck with a camper shell, "possibly a Ford," which rattled and had traces of dried blood in it.

Rhea said he may have worked with wood, or was a logger, but he waited each month for his disability or veteran's check to arrive. His right arm was covered in tattoos, including a large one that ran from the elbow down and had something to do with the marines.

She said he would rather drink coffee and smoke than eat. He also took drugs and drank a lot of alcohol. In fact, he was in a drunken rage when he killed Jane Doe. The man was not clear-headed much and often felt sorry for himself.

"He also reverts back to how he was treated as a child," Freeman wrote. The killer got angry at Jane Doe when she said she was leaving. She was getting her things together when he knocked her down and bashed in her head.

Rhea said the killer had scattered body parts and she was surprised that a leg hadn't shown up. She felt the legs were near Trinidad.

She said she could see the killer having sex on a blanket with the victim, who had an irregular nose, brown eyes, and an upper right tooth with metal in it, possibly gold. She was not tall, had known the killer for two or three months and had traveled with him. Nineteen or twenty years old, she may have had some Indian in her.

"Kay said that he now regrets killing her," Freeman wrote. "Sometimes he wishes she were back. Kay also said that it is not like his conscience is bothering him. It is he misses the things she did for him."

"Kay said this person is not a serial-killer-type guy. She said his ability to have sex is low because he has a small penis. He gets very mad if someone laughs at him about his size. . . . Kay said she sees the victim lying in a pool of blood around her head. He uses the 'F' word a lot. Kay said he wakes up and says, 'F***, f***, f***, what did I do now?'"

Freeman attempted to carry out Pagaling's request to float objects in the slough to see where they ended up, but the exercise had to be canceled in December, January, and February due to bad weather.

He and Deputy Roy Reynolds, who had researched the area's tidal patterns, attempted a floatation experiment on March 16, when they filled about eighteen burlap sacks with enough wood chips and empty plastic bottles to equal the torso's weight. They started placing the bags intermittently along the slough, but they had to abort the exercise because they ran out of time.

Meanwhile, the coroner's office quietly buried Jane Doe's remains in Potter's Field, an indigent section of Ocean View Cemetery in Eureka.

Freeman and a larger team of deputies conducted a second floatation experiment on May 5. This time they filled thirty-one gunnysacks with wood chips and plastic bottles, placing them in four parts of the slough where they thought the body had most likely been dumped.

Bag 14 was placed near the Park Street Bridge and came to rest about one hundred feet from where the torso was found. Bag 18, placed near the Devoy Road Bridge, about one and a half miles downstream from Bag 14, ended up where the torso was found, but it took three complete tide cycles to land there.

Because the torso was thought to have been in the water less than twenty-four hours, Freeman decided that the Park Street Bridge was the more likely dumping site. If the killer had placed the torso there at dawn on October 26, he and Reynolds decided that it would have moved to its final resting place by the time the tide went out that evening.

In the year after Jane Doe's death, Freeman came up with a half-dozen possible suspects by comparing notes with various agencies and investigators all over the country, some going back a decade or more. But none of them turned out to be his guy.

"What I found out during this investigation is that a lot of people do really weird things," Freeman said later.

It bothered him that he still didn't know the victim's name.

CHAPTER 9

THE MONEY COW

On April 15, 1998, Wayne and Elizabeth's divorce, custody, and visitation agreement became final. Wayne was allowed to visit Max for one week every three months, on the child's birthday, on Christmas in even-numbered years, and for the month of December in odd-numbered years. However, Wayne never exercised those rights.

As part of the settlement, Wayne had agreed to start sending child support payments: $200 each month.

In late May, Elizabeth heard some strange clicks on her answering machine. She figured it was Wayne calling and hanging up. The following weekend, she and Wayne talked for the first time in a while. They had a surprisingly decent conversation and communicated well for a change.

"I was in town this weekend," he said.

Elizabeth was upset that Wayne, who had only come to Las Vegas two or three times to see his son since they split, hadn't called ahead to arrange a visit.

"Why didn't you let me know?" she asked.

Once they got past that topic, Elizabeth proudly told him that she had bought herself a new car and had landed a great job. She and Max were doing well. But, as usual, the conversation came back around to the failure of their marriage.

"It's kind of your fault because you left me," he complained.

They also talked about why Wayne didn't see much of his son.

"You have a choice of being in your son's life or not, and you're choosing not to," she said.

"It's hard," he said.

"That's not my problem."

At that point, Elizabeth heard the beep of someone calling on the other line, so she clicked over, then came back to Wayne.

"I've got to let you go," she said.

"No, I'm not done yet."

Elizabeth talked to him for a few more minutes before they hung up.

It would be five more months before Elizabeth would learn exactly what Wayne had been doing in Las Vegas that weekend in May.

In July, August, and September, Wayne left messages on Elizabeth's answering machine, apologizing for sending his $200 check late.

"I'm sorry, I'm on the road and I just forgot. I'm sending it off now," he'd say in that "woe is me," melancholy tone of his.

The check always came about two weeks late and Wayne had taken to writing "The money cow" in the top left-hand corner where the return address would normally go.

The last time he left such a message was in September, when his check arrived on the twenty-eighth day of the month.

In October, Elizabeth didn't receive a check at all.

CHAPTER 10

TINA RENEE GIBBS

The California Aqueduct is one of those necessary parts of life that southern Californians generally don't think about when they take a bath or drink a glass of tap water.

The water takes seven days to flow down this 442-mile, concrete-lined conduit, coursing from the Sacramento Delta through wide open stretches of farmland, under bridges and beneath freeways to the desert at Lake Perris, about twenty miles past Riverside. The canal splits into two branches in northern Los Angeles County near Gorman, where the water is diverted into various reservoirs, to treatment plants, and on to homes and businesses.

But what most people probably don't know—and what the California Department of Water Resources doesn't go out of its way to publicize—is that the canal has been an unwelcome repository for less than savory items since it was built in the 1960s. Many of these foreign objects aren't found until that particular portion of the aqueduct, which is divided by intermittent gates and pumping plants, is drained for cleaning and maintenance.

Slippery and slimy with green algae, thirty-two feet at its deepest point and 110 feet across the surface at its widest, the aqueduct has been host to guns, phone booths, pipe bombs, stolen cars, semitrucks—and, sadly, the decomposing corpses of infants and adults.

Some cases have been publicized more than others, such as the body of a fifty-seven-year-old, fully clothed gold dealer who was murdered and dumped there in August 1980, his ankles and left wrist shackled to a large steel chain. Or the body of screenwriter Gary DeVore, who had been missing for more than a year when he turned up in his Ford Explorer in July 1998, submerged in mud where the Antelope Valley freeway crosses the canal. Investigators believed DeVore swerved off the road during a long, late-night drive home from New Mexico.

State water officials say ten corpses were found in the aqueduct in 1996 and 1997, combined. Although some such deaths are deemed homicides, many are thought to be drownings, despite the bold black-and-white signs posted on the gated entrances, cautioning: STAY OUT OF AQUEDUCT. YOU MAY DROWN.

Cotton is the number one crop in the tiny farming community of Buttonwillow, where more than two-thirds of the population of 1,266 was Hispanic at the time of the 2000 census.

"The only thing Buttonwillow seems to be in the middle of is nowhere," Matt Phillips wrote in the *Bakersfield Californian*.

Nonetheless, it is still an important point as "nowhere" goes. Buttonwillow earned a claim to fame and distinction in 2000, when the California Land Surveyors Association declared it the state's "center of population," meaning that the town—or a field thereabouts—was the most easily accessible point on average for all California residents.

It's unknown why four men who worked for a Bakersfield construction company were in the Buttonwillow area on the evening of June 2, 1998, but around six o'clock, they reported finding the nude and badly bloated body of a woman hung up on the steel cable of alternating red and white buoys that spanned the aqueduct. After the discovery was confirmed by two sheriff's patrol deputies, the homicide team was called in.

The woman appeared to have been in the water for a while, so authorities were initially unable to identify her, and little publicity was given to her death. At that point, she was just another Jane Doe.

Gary Rhoades, a thirty-six-year-old detective with the Kern County Sheriff's Office, was off-duty at his house in Bakersfield, with his wife and three daughters, when he got the call just before 7:00 P.M. Rhoades, who started with the department as a deputy in 1981, had been working homicides for less than a year.

Knowing that he was going to be investigating a crime scene in or near water, Rhoades purposely dressed down in jeans and a polo shirt, something he wouldn't mind getting dirty.

It was just getting dark when he met up with his partner, Ron Taylor, the lead detective, and their sergeant, Don Ferguson. The patrol sergeant and commander and a coroner's investigator also showed up to join the two patrol officers who had initially responded.

The woman's body was about forty feet downstream from the Highway 58 bridge, which crossed the canal and was surrounded by flat fields as far as the eye could see.

The rope line was meant as a safety device for people who had inadvertently fallen into the cold water. But given that the woman's body was nude and facedown, Rhoades figured she hadn't fallen in accidentally while fishing.

"You automatically think it's some kind of rape or murder, or something like that," he said later.

Rhoades and Taylor walked both sides of the bridge and both banks above the cement canal, searching by flashlight for shoe or tire tracks, pieces of clothing, or any other evidence. But they found nothing.

The investigators gathered on the west bank of the aqueduct, just south of the bridge, and lowered a boat into the water so that Rhoades could take a look at the body. Seeing no obvious signs of foul play, such as a gunshot wound, he took photos of the victim, then pulled her by the arm to the shore, where she was placed in a body bag.

By about 9:30 P.M., he and the other officers had tied ropes to the bag, hoisted it up the embankment, and lifted it into the white van of the private company contracted by the coroner's office. This Jane Doe was five feet five inches, weighed about 125 pounds, and had blue eyes and reddish blond hair.

The next day, Taylor and an evidence technician went to the morgue in Bakersfield to try to roll a set of fingerprints, but her skin was too decomposed.

The department also sent out teletypes, distributing her description to agencies throughout the state, with the hopes of identifying her as a missing person.

On June 4, Rhoades and Taylor returned to the morgue for the autopsy, where Dr. Donna Brown noted that the victim had premortem, dime-sized bruises to the left side of her jaw along the cheek, a triangular mark underneath her neck, bruises to the right side of her neck, and scrapes on her temple and chin. Her neck was fractured and circled with a linear mark, as if she'd been strangled with something. Under the skin, Brown found deep bruising in the cheek and in the voice box area.

They took a sexual assault kit—anal, vaginal, and oral swabs; hair from her head and pubic area, and a blood sample—to try to match the DNA with a suspect once they found one.

The victim wore five rings on her left hand. On the web between her thumb and first finger was a tattoo of the letters "JJ," encircled with a heart. She also wore a ring on her right ring finger.

The pathologist removed her hands, then soaked the skin in a chemical solution to improve the chances of obtaining fingerprints. They were finally able to take a usable set of prints, which they entered into the state DOJ's Western Identification Network and the FBI's databases.

Meanwhile, Rhoades and Taylor searched the missing persons' files to see if they could find any leads. But they came up empty.

On July 29, their victim got a name.

Rhoades got a call from Sharon Pierce, a sheriff's evidence tech, saying that she'd gotten a fingerprint match with a Tina Renee Gibbs from Tacoma, Washington, who had a criminal record as a prostitute there and also in Las Vegas.

But even then, the death of the woman, listed as a Tacoma resident, warranted only a three-paragraph brief inside the local news section of *The Seattle Times*. It noted the lack of suspects in the homicide case, but it did not mention how she made her living. No major newspaper in California appears to have noted her passing.

"The body of Tina Renee Gibbs, 25, was found floating in the water June 2 near Buttonwillow, a small town about 30 miles west of Bakersfield," the *Times* story said. "She was strangled before her body was left in the aqueduct, Kern County sheriff's coroners said."

According to the *Times*, John Douglas, a former FBI serial killer profiler, referred to the Pacific Northwest as "America's killing fields," because that's where serial killers Gary Ridgeway, Ted Bundy, John Allen Muhammad, and Robert Yates Jr. all came from.

But at the time, Rhoades and Taylor had no real leads on how Tina's body ended up in Kern County.

"It was just anybody's guess," Rhoades said. "We talked about pimps and every option you could think of, really," even the theory that the killer was a truck driver. "We were pretty much open to anything at that point."

Using information from the coroner's office, which was part of the sheriff's department, Rhoades located Tina's father, Carlos Gibbs, in Fayetteville, North Carolina.

Carlos didn't express much emotion at the news.

"I'm guessing that's because he didn't even know his daughter," Rhoades said later.

Asked if he knew how to contact Tina's mother, Carlos said Tina had told him she was dead.

Tina and her mother, Mary, had left Carlos when Tina was about eighteen months old. He didn't hear from either one of them until Tina called him out of the blue in 1990. She called him again around Christmas 1997, saying she was with her boyfriend "Boo" in Las Vegas.

Rhoades asked Carlos for names and phone numbers for Mary's relatives, which ultimately led him to find Mary—remarried and very much alive in Blair, Oklahoma.

* * *

Tina was born in Fayetteville on April 20, 1972.

When Mary left Carlos, she took Tina to Georgia.

Tina was about seven when her mother began dating Ron Sharp, an army police investigator, and within a few months, Tina was already calling him "Daddy."

Ron soon married Mary and made it official. Biology aside, he was Tina's father.

Tina was a happy-go-lucky child who loved going to the beach and singing what her mother called "oldies but goodies." She played quietly with her cat and wondered at the beauty of a butterfly.

She also liked to go fishing. Even if she wasn't all that fond of baiting the hook with a worm, she appreciated the overall experience. She enjoyed going to carnivals and the circus, particularly watching the trained animals perform.

Ron taught Tina to swim. She wasn't very coordinated with her feet, so he would hold her up in the water while she kicked. About every third kick, Tina would thump Ron in the side of the head, but he stuck with it until she could swim on her own.

"She caught on pretty good," Ron said later. "Whenever we got close to water, she wanted to be in it."

Ron also taught her to play softball. He coached her team for about seven years until she got tired of the sport, in which she played short center field, the tenth position on a softball team. She may have been an average player, but Ron thought she was fantastic. She hustled around the field and didn't seem to mind getting bruised.

Tina alternated between being a girly-girl and a tomboy, so she and her mother would also fix each other's hair, crochet, go shopping, and cook together. Her diet of favorites was pretty all-American: strawberries, ice cream, and hamburgers.

As she grew older, the Sharp house became a hangout for teenage Tina and her friends, a comfortable place to just be. Like many teenagers, she played pool and listened to music.

The family stayed in Georgia until Ron left the army and moved to Oklahoma for six or eight months, but Ron got bored with the slow pace and wanted to get back into police work, so they moved to the state of Washington.

When Tina was sixteen, the family went on a road trip along coastal Highway 101, heading south down into California, where they camped on the beach, and drove through the redwood forest. They continued on to Lake Tahoe and Reno, where the Sharps couldn't seem to get Tina out of the Circus Circus hotel and casino.

Tina was eighteen in 1991, when Ron and Mary wanted to move to Oregon, and this time Tina decided to stay put. She'd fallen in love and wanted to be on her own.

Mary instinctively knew that Tina was using drugs and had fallen in with the wrong crowd. Ron, on the other hand, thought she'd grown up and was "ready to rule the world."

"She called me one day and asked me if—if I would come and pick her up so she could come home," Mary later recalled, "and that's when we found out that she was messing with drugs. We were her sole support. Anything that she wanted, we gave it to her."

Mary and Ron tried to get Tina counseling and off drugs, but they weren't successful.

After they moved to Oregon, they heard from her only a couple of times a year. After they moved back to Oklahoma, they lost touch with her altogether.

The last time Mary remembered talking to Tina was in 1994, possibly on Christmas Eve.

Either way, Mary recalled one thing very clearly: "I was begging her to come home," she said.

Tina agreed to come home, but she never followed through.

For years afterward, Mary tried to track down Tina through her friends. She kept hoping that Tina would get her life together one day, knock on the door, or give her a call.

Police records in Tacoma show that Tina was arrested more than a dozen times, five times for soliciting prostitution, in 1995 and early 1996, before she relocated to Las Vegas.

Tina seemed to know her way around the streets by the time of her final arrest in Tacoma, the night of January 11, 1996.

She was standing in front of Jack in the Box on Pacific Avenue, wearing jeans and a blue jacket, when undercover Officer Kelstrup decided to go after her. He pulled his unmarked car into the restaurant parking lot, where Tina walked over, opened the door, and got in.

"What are you doing?" he asked as he drove through the lot and headed down Pacific Avenue.

"I'm working," she replied.

"You mean like prostitution?"

"Yes. Are you a cop?"

Kelstrup said no, so Tina told him to prove it. He asked her what she meant, but she didn't answer.

"What sex act will you do?" he asked.

Tina looked at him and replied, "What do you want?"

"Just a blow job."

"How much [money] do you have?"

"Twenty dollars, I guess."

Tina said she needed $40.

"That kind of seems like a lot," he said.

"Well, I really need forty."

Kelstrup agreed to the price, then gave a prearranged arrest signal to a fellow officer, who stopped them on

Fawcett Avenue in his marked patrol car. Tina was arrested and booked for soliciting prostitution and several outstanding misdemeanor warrants.

Rhoades didn't check into Tina's life in Tacoma, but he did contact the police department in Las Vegas, where a homicide sergeant confirmed that Tina had been a working girl there, too.

"The sergeant told me that all of her last addresses and places where they'd last contacted her were parts of the city that were known for prostitution at the time," Rhoades recalled.

Tina had lived for a time in a Ramada Inn on Boulder Highway, but her last known address was a motel on South Boulder Highway.

Her violations, which started in November 1996, ranged from soliciting prostitution to trespassing, unlawful possession of drug paraphernalia, obstructing traffic, driving without a license and insurance, and failing to heed an order to stay out of an area where she'd been previously arrested for prostitution.

Tina was last cited by police on May 6, 1998, less than a month before her body was found, for giving false information to a police officer, but her records show that the charge was dropped "per negotiations."

Tina was sentenced numerous times and ordered to spend anywhere from ten to 180 days in jail, but it's clear from the dates of her arrests that she didn't serve out the longer sentences because she was arrested again in short order.

Court officials said the detailed court records for her crimes no longer exist, so the specifics of her lifestyle and activities in her final years could not be determined. However, judging by the available records and most recent booking photo, it's obvious that she was an attractive but troubled young woman, using drugs and selling her body for money.

When Rhoades got a copy of her booking photo, he couldn't believe how different she looked in death.

"I would've never guessed in a million years that was the same person," he said.

In early August 1998, Tina's mother came home from work to find her husband standing just behind the front door, as if he were waiting for her to arrive. Ron never did that, so Mary instantly knew that something was wrong. Horribly wrong.

Ron had gotten a message to call the coroner's office in Kern County, California, that afternoon. They told him what they could, which wasn't much. Mostly, they needed to know what to do with Tina's remains. That left Ron with the hardest job—telling Mary that her daughter, her only child, had been murdered.

Ron said he needed to talk to her and sat her down on the couch.

"There's no easy way to tell someone that a loved one is dead," he said later. "I've done it a number of times as a police officer. . . . You just got to say it."

Ron delivered the news in the gentlest way he could, but he couldn't stop Mary from feeling what she described as "the most gut-wrenching sorrow that a mother could feel."

Mary ended up in the hospital the next day, her body overcome by grief.

"She fell apart," Ron recalled nearly a decade later. "I've been trying to hold her up ever since."

When Mary called the coroner's office, they told her she shouldn't come to see Tina's body because of its condition, so a cremation was arranged. Soon afterward, Tina's ashes arrived in a little plastic brown box, her rings wrapped in a piece of cloth.

Ron crafted a beautiful oak urn to hold them, which Mary kept on top of the dresser, surrounded by the earthly things that Tina cherished.

"It's got a little music box on it," Ron said. "It hasn't been wound up forever, but you can walk past it and it will start playing."

But from that point on, Mary couldn't focus anymore. She was so emotionally devastated that she couldn't face going to work.

Before they'd moved to Oklahoma, Mary had worked as a nurse in a nursing home, where sometimes Tina would tag along with her. Mary would also bring Ron's German shepherd for the elderly residents to pet. Once they moved to Oklahoma, Mary worked at a construction warehouse similar to Home Depot.

After Tina's death, Mary couldn't do much of anything, not even putter around in the garden the way she used to. The mental anguish paralyzed her so much that she had to be hospitalized on five occasions, for four to six weeks at a time.

At first, she would try to return to work, but she eventually realized she couldn't handle it. She became medically disabled, and according to Ron, she would never be able to work again.

CHAPTER 11

THE ONES THAT
GOT AWAY

On June 16, 1998, Wayne picked up a prostitute in Anaheim, California. Later dubbed "Orange County Doe" by authorities to keep her identity confidential, she told police that she was working at the corner of Beach and Lincoln Boulevards when she approached Wayne in a gas station parking lot.

She said Wayne paid her $40 to sit in his truck while he masturbated. She also told authorities that she agreed to perform oral sex for $35. Either way, once she got in his truck, she learned he had other things in mind.

Wayne told her to climb into the sleeper, where no one would see them, and they both removed their clothes. Wayne directed her to get on her hands and knees in front of him, then grabbed her arms and tied them behind her back with one end of a nylon rope; he tied the other end around her neck. Next, he took another rope, pushed her knees to her chest, and bound her wrists and ankles together.

Wayne told her not to struggle because it would only make things worse. He then proceeded to gag her, burn her breasts and vagina with a cigarette lighter, poke her genitals with a sharp instrument, and sit on her face. He took a break to drive around for a while before returning to the sleeper.

Then he raped her. Four separate times during sex, she said, he choked her with a rope until she fell unconscious, bringing her back each time with CPR.

Afterward, he rifled through her purse and took all her money. As he dropped her off, he told her she was lucky because the others had not survived.

On August 21, Wayne showed up at Scott and Linda Hayes's house at 4:00 P.M., a day Scott would remember well because he'd had a vasectomy.

Wayne stayed a couple of days, during which time he talked Scott out of his favorite knife—a hunting knife in a special case.

Wayne wouldn't let anyone go near his truck until he cleaned it. He initially tried to trade his mattress for one of Scott's, but after learning that Scott couldn't get rid of the old one, Wayne changed his mind, saying the new mattress wouldn't fit in his sleeper.

Linda Hayes noticed that Wayne drank a lot on that visit. He also didn't change his clothes or bathe for three days. Other than that, he was the same guy.

After he left, they never heard from him again.

Twenty-two-year-old Rachel Holt lived in Vallejo, but she worked the streets of Santa Rosa, often at a Motel 6.

On August 23 at 11:00 P.M., she was standing in front of the Monte Vista Motel on Santa Rosa Avenue with a couple of other prostitutes when she saw a big, shiny, and dark truck pull up.

Wayne reached over and pushed open the passenger door, which Rachel took as an invitation.

"What's up?" she asked. "Do you want a date?"

"Yeah," he said. "I got a hundred bucks. Jump in, let's go."

Rachel, who had been a working girl for five years, was only four feet eleven inches tall, so she had some difficulty climbing up onto the steps and into the passenger seat. Wayne gave her the money, which she tucked into her sock.

They drove for a little ways, looking for a place to park his massive truck. Rachel suggested the Friedman Brothers parking lot, which was large and would be empty at that time of night. Sure enough, it was, so Wayne parked in the middle of it.

He introduced himself as Adam and she told him her nickname, "Unique."

Rachel pulled her shorts down to her knees, but left her nylons on, because she had cut out the crotch for easier access.

After Wayne took off his pants, she put a condom on him and they proceeded to try to have sex. The problem was that Wayne wasn't too aroused, so it wasn't working very well.

Rachel didn't understand why he was so nervous, twitchy, and distracted. He kept looking around and was paying little attention to what they were doing. Meanwhile, Rachel tried to get him more excited, but he still wasn't hard enough to penetrate her.

"Why are you so nervous?" she asked. "Try to relax."

Wayne grabbed at her breasts more forcefully than she

liked. "Take it easy. Slow down," she told him. "You're being too rough."

"I apologize, I'm having a hard time here," he said.

But even then, he didn't let up, which made Rachel uneasy. She had a weird feeling in her stomach that something wasn't right.

They messed around for fifteen more minutes, but Wayne was still too soft.

"Let's switch positions," he said. "This isn't working for me."

Rachel turned over so that she was on her hands and knees, but the new position didn't seem to work any better. Wayne said it would turn him on if she put her hands behind her back and grabbed her butt, so she obliged him. But as soon as her hands were behind her, he grabbed and bound them together with a rope.

They hadn't talked about doing any S/M. Rachel did not like the direction in which things were heading. What was this guy doing?

She started to panic.

"Somebody help me!" she yelled. "Why are you doing this?"

Wayne ordered her to shut up. "If you scream, I'll kill you," he said. "I'll knock your teeth down your throat."

Rachel was crying now, but that only seemed to make Wayne angry.

"Shut up! Shut up!" he said. "I'll give you something to cry about."

Wayne started removing the rest of Rachel's clothes, pulling off her nylons, shoes, and socks. When he got to her shirt, he realized he couldn't get it off without untying her hands, so he undid them, but only long enough to get her naked.

"If you try to run or scream or anything, I'll kill you," he said.

By this point, Rachel had stopped fighting him. She didn't want to die. So she let him put her into whatever position he wanted. He moved her onto her back again, with her hands tied together underneath her. But she couldn't stop crying.

She just lay still, too scared to move.

Wayne had taken off the condom, but because he still didn't have an erection, he was barely penetrating her. As he continued to yell and threaten her, he seemed to be increasingly frustrated that things weren't going the way he wanted.

He told her to bite his nipples, but she didn't do it hard enough to please him.

"I can't even feel anything," he said. "Let me see how hard you can bite."

When Wayne figured out that her mouth couldn't really reach his nipples in her current position, he picked her up so that she was on her hands and knees again, and untied the rope from around her neck, then forgetting what he was intending to do, he tied the tie around her mouth. He lay on his back and told her to masturbate him and pinch his nipples.

Again, Rachel did what he told her. "He somehow wanted me to act like I was turned on by the whole thing, so I tried to play the part the best I could," moaning as if she were enjoying it, she later recalled.

Wayne moaned, too, but his penis still wasn't responding.

Wayne continued to glance nervously toward the front of the truck, as if he feared someone was about to come find them. Finally, he decided he'd better move the truck.

But first, Wayne tied Rachel's feet together, told her to pull her knees to her chest, then tied the remaining part of the rope around her neck so that if she moved, she

would choke herself. He retied her hands behind her
back and sat her on the baseboard of the truck so that
the back of her neck was on a step. As he started driving
down the highway, he had her facing forward, so that
she could see up into the sky. It was an incredibly uncomfortable position.

"Shut up. Don't scream. Don't cry," he said. "Don't
make any noise or I'll kill you."

Anytime she made a sound, he used his free hand to
punch her—hard—in the genitals, keeping his other
hand on the steering wheel. When she cried, he punched
her even harder or hit her with a leather belt with a
buckle. The rest of the time he was either drinking coffee
or masturbating her.

Rachel thought it was about an hour before he pulled
over, apparently somewhere north on Interstate 101.

Her hands were really hurting now. The rope was so
tight that they were losing circulation.

"Are my hands okay?" she asked. "Are they purple?
Are they white?"

"Yeah, they're all right," he said, untying and rearrang-
ing the rope around her neck so that she wouldn't strangle herself if she moved. He picked her up and put her
in the sleeper.

She had no idea where they were, but one thing was
clear: when he penetrated her this time, he was far more
aroused.

This had stopped being sex for money many miles
ago—this was rape.

"Don't look at me," he said. "Don't look at me."

He tied a man's necktie around her mouth, like a gag,
so she couldn't talk. But because she kept opening her
eyes and looking at him, he also used a tie as a blindfold.

As he penetrated her, he tightened the tie around her

neck until she lost consciousness. When she came back, he was giving her mouth-to-mouth resuscitation.

A few minutes later, he'd start it all over again. This must have happened four or five times. Rachel lost count.

Wayne seemed to be getting turned on by this, but he was still acting frustrated and nervous.

He forced her to give him oral sex, then turned her over and raped her anally. After one of the times that he revived her, he lit a match and burned her genitals with it, leaving a blister mark that later turned into a scar.

"I fantasized about doing this to someone, but was turned off afterward," he told her. "It wasn't as good as I thought it was going to be."

The ordeal lasted for hours. No matter how long or hard she cried, he just kept at it.

When she said she had to go to the bathroom, he put on a pair of latex gloves, and took out a Baby Wipes container. He handed her one of the wipes and had her urinate into the container, which had the condom in it from earlier that night.

Later, it was difficult for her to remember what happened in what order, but that didn't really matter. She knew she had been raped, vaginally and anally, forced into unconsciousness, and brought back repeatedly. It was more terrifying than words could describe.

When Wayne had finally had enough, he allowed her to get dressed. He seemed strangely calm by then—calm enough for them to have what seemed like a normal conversation. He almost seemed like a regular guy, even after everything he had put her through.

She asked why he was doing all this and he pulled out a photo of his ex-wife and son.

"He said his ex-wife took off with his son and he was trying to get revenge," she said later. "And he broke down and he cried right in front of me. And he . . . gave me a pretty strong human-being hug."

"I'm sorry I did this to you," he told her, saying he'd chosen her over her girlfriends because she was smaller and would be easier to control.

"Because you gave me a shoulder to cry on, I'm going to let you go."

He pulled her jacket hood over her head, and tied it nice and snug.

"It's pretty cold out there," he said "I don't want you to get cold."

He stopped the truck at the side of the freeway, walked her down the hillside a bit, and then hog-tied her, pulling one of his neckties around her neck. He went through her purse, removed $400 in cash, and gave some of it back to her—she later couldn't remember whether it was a $20 bill or her original $100 fee for sex—so that she could get home.

"Once I set you down, don't be trying to get out of them [the ropes] real fast," he said. "I don't want you to get up off the side of the hill and see my license plates."

Ironically, he tied the rope so loosely around her hands that Rachel had already gotten them free by the time she was out of the truck. She waited until she heard him pull away before she removed the rope from her ankles and scrambled partway up the hill. When she saw it was safe, she climbed the rest of the way up to the freeway.

A trucker saw her, pulled over, and drove her to the next freeway exit, where she called her pimp and then dialed 911. She made the calls from a pay phone outside a market in Cloverdale, which is at least twenty miles up Highway 101 from the Friedman Brothers parking lot.

When a Cloverdale police officer arrived at the market, Rachel was still clutching the rope and necktie.

Once the officer realized that the rape had occurred

in the Sonoma County sheriff's jurisdiction, he turned her over to a deputy, who took her to Sutter Hospital. While she was waiting to be examined, sheriff's Detective Dennis O'Leary, from the domestic violence and sexual assault unit, interviewed her.

Joan Kazmar, the nurse who examined Rachel, later said that out of 175 rape victims she'd seen in her career, Rachel was the most severely injured of them all.

Rachel cried but was cooperative throughout the four-hour examination, which started at 5:45 A.M. She cried and held her face in her hands as she recounted the night's events to Kazmar, who took a vaginal swab that later matched Wayne's DNA.

The nurse made note of Rachel's injuries, which included bruises on her face, right breast and neck, where she also had tenderness and swelling; a cut on her lip; swelling on the side of her face; linear red marks and swelling on her wrists; rope burns on her ankles; abrasions to her outer labia; and a burn mark on the inner labia. She noted that Rachel was too sore to let Kazmar complete a rectal exam. She also complained of wrist pain and was unable to move her bruised thumb because it hurt too much.

About a week later, Rachel gave a description of her rapist to a sketch artist. A couple of months later, after Wayne turned himself in, she identified him from a photo lineup.

Authorities later dubbed Rachel as "Sonoma County Doe," because she wanted to remain anonymous during his court proceedings. However, she agreed to let her real name and photo be used in this book.

In early September, Valerie Rondi was hitchhiking on Broadway in Eureka.

Wayne pulled up in his grandmother's Neon sedan and introduced himself as Adam. "Do you date?" he asked.

"Sometimes. Why, do you want to date me?"

Wayne said yes and Valerie told him it would cost $60. They went to his grandmother's place, where he said he was house-sitting, and had sex in Wayne's room. He asked her to pinch his nipples as hard as she could, but it still wasn't hard enough for him.

Apparently, the experience was over faster than Wayne would have liked.

"Since I just gave you all that money, the least you could do is sit here with me and talk for a while," he said.

Valerie agreed to stay for a bit, while they talked about his childhood and how he raised himself because his parents could've cared less about him. He told her about his ex-wife, how she wouldn't let him see her son, and that he drove a truck for a living.

"That must be fun, getting to travel all around," Valerie said.

"It is, but it gets awfully lonely."

He asked if she wanted to see his truck, which was parked out front. As he let her sit in the driver's seat and start up the motor, Valerie noticed that the interior was immaculate.

"He said his truck was the nicest one they had and the reason he got to drive it was because his boss knew from his other boss [at Readimix] how neat and clean he kept all the trucks they let him use," she said later.

Wayne asked if she wanted to go on a road trip with him to Santa Rosa. After he promised to get her back the next day, she agreed. Valerie was a heroin addict and would get sick if she didn't get her daily fix; she had only one bag with her.

They set off the next morning, and as they were driving, Wayne talked some more about his second ex-wife and son. He said he'd met his first ex-wife while singing in bars, claiming she was the actress who played the character of Felicia on the soap opera *General Hospital.*

"He said they had open sex, because it's what made her happy," Valerie said later. "It didn't do much for him, but he played along."

That night, they stopped at a truck stop in Ukiah, where Wayne attempted to get into his sleeper's lower bunk with her. She told Wayne not to get any ideas about having sex for free, but Wayne tried, anyway, and got snippy when she told him to stop. Wayne eventually left her alone and climbed into the top bunk, where she could hear him masturbating.

The next day, they made chitchat as they drove to a lumberyard in Santa Rosa. Wayne left the truck for a few minutes and came back, saying the dispatcher had sent him to the wrong place. Turned out, he was supposed to have dropped the load in Escondido, so that's where they had to go next.

"Where's Escondido?" she asked.

"A little past L.A.," he said. (Escondido is in northern San Diego County, a couple of hours south of Los Angeles.)

"L.A.!" she said. "We can't go there. You promised we'd be back to Eureka today! I don't have any more stuff and I'm already sick. I can't go all the way to L.A."

"Don't worry," he said. "We're going to get your stuff at one of the stops along the way, I promise."

Valerie tried to get him to take her to a bus station, but he pleaded with her to stay. "No, don't go," he said. "I'll find your stuff. Please? I really do like your company."

They drove all day and night until they reached a truck stop that was so big it seemed like a small city. Valerie went to take a shower and buy herself something to eat.

When she got back, he was already in the lower bunk. He asked her again for sex.

By this time, Valerie was going through withdrawal and refused to do anything with him. Wayne offered to pay her, but Valerie held her ground.

That's when Wayne started yelling at her. "Do you know how it feels, begging a prostitute to have sex with you, for money no less, and having her say no? It feels f***ed. It doesn't make me feel worth a shit. You should be offering to give it to me for free just for bringing your ass along."

Valerie started to speak, but Wayne interrupted. "Shut the f*** up!" he screamed.

Scared into silence, she thought she'd better be careful this far from home. So she climbed into the top bunk and heard Wayne masturbating again before he went to sleep.

The next morning, Valerie apologized. She was worried that Wayne was never going to take her home, so she figured she'd better do whatever he wanted.

They stopped at a store down the road, where Wayne bought two 12-packs of beer.

"Do you want me to put them in the icebox?" she asked.

"No, I'll do it."

Between Gilroy and the Grapevine, a long steep stretch along Interstate 5 between Los Angeles and Bakersfield, Wayne drank eighteen beers and Valerie drank most of three before he put the remaining three in the fridge.

Wayne suggested that he drop her off in San Clemente so she could find herself some heroin, but Valerie said no. She didn't want to be dumped in a strange town, sick as a dog, without enough money to take a bus home.

After dropping off the load in Escondido, Wayne

announced he had to drive farther south to Chula Vista, a city just north of the Mexican border.

By this point, Valerie was freaking out.

"Why are you lying to me?" she asked.

Wayne said he wasn't lying; he couldn't help where his dispatcher sent him.

"You never told me this was going to be a weeklong trip," she said. "Can't you see that I'm sick? You have to take me back north. Please!"

"Quit whining and shut up," he snapped.

After Chula Vista, he said, they'd start heading north again to drop the new load in Fremont. Then he'd take her home.

"Thank you," Valerie said, crying now.

By nightfall, they were driving north, but they were still nowhere near home, so Wayne pulled into another truck stop for the night.

This time, Valerie let Wayne do what he wanted. He'd bought more beer, and after drinking all day, he was drunk. It didn't seem to bother him that she was crying, afraid, and sick.

He told her to take off her shirt, so she did. She lay there while he had sex with her, following his orders to pinch his nipples. By the time they finished, Wayne was out cold.

The next day, Valerie was vomiting and could hardly sit up. When they finally got to Fremont, Valerie saw another Edeline truck in the lot where they'd stopped. Wayne got out and announced another change of plans when he came back. They were going to Nevada.

Valerie cried and begged him to take her to the nearest bus station so she could get home. Wayne continued his verbal abuse, but finally agreed to talk the other Edeline driver into taking her back to Fortuna, the next major city south of Eureka. Valerie ended up having to pay the driver's girlfriend to take her home.

A few days later, Wayne called and asked if she made it okay.

Valerie hung up on him.

CHAPTER 12

LANETT DEYON WHITE

Locals of the San Joaquin Valley say they can smell the change in weather come September, when the mornings and evenings are cool, but the afternoon temperatures still get up in the 90s. The air smells fresh, cleaner than the summer when it's filled with dust from the fields. Some say the autumn morning dew must cleanse away the mustiness.

The afternoon sky was a clear blue on September 25, 1998, when three men in a red Chevy truck, towing a cattle trailer, pulled over to change a plug wire in a gravel turnout along Highway 12, near Lodi.

They stopped on a two-lane road just west of Interstate 5, surrounded by vineyards, and raised the Chevy's hood. The men soon found more than they bargained for— a woman's naked body floating in an irrigation ditch parallel to the road.

One of them scooted over to the industrial building across the street and asked someone to call 911, but by the time the Delta Fire Department arrived, he and his buddies had taken off.

Once the sheriff's deputies got there, they told the firefighters to back out their engine the same way they'd entered the turnout so as not to disturb the death scene any further. With that, a deputy and a sergeant cordoned off the area with yellow tape so the homicide team could begin its work.

San Joaquin County, which spans approximately 1,400 square miles, is known as the nation's "salad bowl" and is home to many people who work in Stockton or the Bay Area, but can't afford to buy a home there.

Every year the valley sees a number of dead prostitutes, transported by their killers from San Francisco or Livermore and dumped in the waterways or on one of the islands within the Sacramento–San Joaquin River Delta.

So, at first, news that a woman's body had been found in a ditch didn't seem all that unusual to Detectives Joe Herrera and Mike Jones, or their sergeant, David Levesey.

After Levesey got the call around 12:30 P.M., he directed Herrera, Jones, and two of their colleagues—Antonio Cruz and Bruce Wuest—to meet him at the crime scene in their unmarked vehicles. Their office, housed in a building in French Camp, was only half an hour away by freeway.

Herrera, who'd grown up in nearby Stockton, just south of the state capital in Sacramento, knew the area surrounding the death scene well. It was right near the two giant silos that were once part of the old Stagi & Scriven sunflower seed plant, which now housed a company called Ehlers Elevators, Inc.

Heading west on Highway 12, the detectives stopped at the gravel turnout, which measured about forty feet from the road to the muddy bank of the ditch. The body was floating in shallow water near a large walnut tree—its trunk so big that a man spreading his arms could reach only halfway around.

Levesey told Jones to take the lead, named Wuest as the second, and told Cruz and Herrera to process the crime scene for evidence.

The woman's body was faceup in the 60-degree stagnant water, bloated and discolored. But curiously, her face, upper chest, and one shoulder were black and swollen. Being in the cool water probably slowed the decomposition, but this uneven pattern of lividity—the dark purplish color on the skin where the blood settles after the heart stops beating—was unusual. She was red around the middle as if she'd been bent or folded in half after her death.

Initially, Jones thought that the decomposition in the blackened areas of the body might have been caused by being in the sun for a long time, with part of her shaded by the walnut tree, or possibly was accelerated by exposure to a man-made heat source. He also figured she'd been turned upside down and on her side after she died because her lips were swollen.

But Jones, who had been a homicide detective for three years, didn't want to get locked into one theory about how she died. As the adrenaline flooded his body, he preferred to keep an open mind and let his thoughts go where they might.

As he wondered who she was and how she got into that ditch, he theorized that perhaps she was killed by an ex-boyfriend who'd gotten angry after they'd had sex. He wondered if the killer had stripped her body to make her death look like a rape. Or maybe, he thought, she'd died accidentally, scaring a friend into dumping her at the side of the road.

But most important, he wondered if they would

be able to identify her. Without a name, she was just another Jane Doe, lost in the world of women who had gone missing.

The investigators collected about fifteen items from the scene, including a brown leather glove and a plastic royal blue tarp, both of which were floating near the body. They couldn't be sure the glove was tied to the case, though, because all sorts of debris turned up in ditches.

They collected a white plastic bag that had blown and come to rest against some weeds about thirty yards away. It was marked with what looked like blood and the logo for Flying J, a national chain of truck stops. The bag was a good clue that the killer might've been a truck driver, a lead supported by the tire tracks left in the gravel. Given the rough and uneven surface, however, the tracks weren't clear enough to identify the tire pattern by brand.

A brown-and-tan-plaid shirt, rolled up and turned inside out, was also found on the north bank, about six feet from the body.

Herrera saw a pattern in the soft dirt as if a burst of truck exhaust had scattered clumps of the victim's auburn hair around the area, where investigators collected a yellow Bic lighter and some fallen leaves, also covered with a red substance that later proved to be the victim's blood.

Because she was in the water, investigators had to call in the sheriff's boat crew, who waded into the ditch in hip boots, slid the metal rescue basket underneath her, and pulled the gurney up the embankment by tying a rope around a tree. As they removed her body from the water, more clumps of her hair came off.

The body had no major visible wounds or bruises, which, after spending a year observing autopsies, struck Herrera as unusual for a woman who had been dumped, naked. He figured she'd probably been strangled.

She had a number of distinctive tattoos on her chest, right shoulder, and right ankle, but they were difficult to read because of the decomposed state of her skin.

The one over her right breast was written in cursive and spelled out "Ignacio."

The tattoo over her left breast, which also was in cursive, clearly spelled out the name "Debra." Above it, encircled with a squiggly design, some additional letters spelled *"Mi madre,"* which, in Spanish, means "my mother Debra."

Finally, the victim had a tattoo of a ribbon going through a heart on her right shoulder, and some initials tattooed on her right ankle, which said "mi" in small letters and "NAC" in big cursive letters.

They bagged her hands to protect them for fingerprinting, loaded her body into the van about 4:50 P.M., and transported her to San Joaquin County Hospital for full-body X-rays. After that, they took her to the county morgue.

Jones and his wife, Vonda, had had plans to go to a friend's party that night, so he called her from the car on his way back to the office to tell her to go on without him. It was already after 5:00 P.M. and he knew how things went with a case like this. Better to be safe than sorry where the wife was concerned.

Back at the morgue, investigators were able to roll a set of fingerprints from the victim and enter them into the California ID system, which, on a good day, can take only thirty to sixty minutes to get a hit. Generally, these are people with criminal records, but the database also includes everyone in law enforcement, security guards, people with special security clearances, and even some journalists who have been issued press passes.

* * *

The autopsy was conducted the next morning by pathologist Dianne Vertes.

Dr. Vertes removed a silver ring with a heart pattern from the victim's right index finger, a gold chain from her neck, and a friendship bracelet made of yarn from her right wrist, all of which she booked into evidence. She also took three vials of blood and a rape kit.

The victim had an abrasion on her right side near the rib cage and the skin of her neck was marked with a chain-like pattern that could have been made by the necklace, although there was no internal hemorrhaging underneath. Vertes also found an injury on the back of the victim's head, but she couldn't immediately tell if it was old or if she'd been struck or dropped there more recently.

Unfortunately, the autopsy didn't change the fact that they still had no specific idea of how this young woman died, which was disappointing.

"We were hoping for something, a stab wound or something that said, yes, it was a homicide," Jones said.

Nonetheless, he and his team still treated the case as a homicide, given the evidence at the death scene. The state of decomposition could have masked some findings, and they hoped the cause of death would become clearer once the toxicology tests came back. But until she knew more, Vertes preliminarily deemed it "homicidal violence of unknown ideology."

In this case, the detectives were lucky that the victim had a criminal record; otherwise, she might have remained a Jane Doe.

Her prints came up as twenty-five-year-old Lanett Deyon White, who had been arrested for forgery, commercial burglary, being under the influence of meth, public intoxication, and vandalism, starting in 1994.

* * *

Lanett was born on November 11, 1972, in Upland, California, the first of two children to Debra and Bill White. Debra had a difficult pregnancy with Lanett, who weighed nine pounds at birth.

At the time, the family was living in a duplex in Ontario, where Bill worked construction. Debra, who is part Cherokee, was born in Tennessee, and Bill, who is full-blooded Shawnee and Cherokee, was born in Oklahoma.

Debra stayed home to take care of Lanett, who, in her mother's eyes, was a wonderful child, albeit a bit fussy.

As she grew up, Lanett liked the circus so much she even dressed as a bearded lady for her kindergarten class when it performed a mock circus.

Athletic from an early age, Lanett ran track at her elementary school and practiced karate for two and a half years, earning a third-degree brown belt. She quit before she earned a black belt, however, after losing a tournament fight to a boy. She didn't think it was fair, girls having to compete against boys.

Bill and Debra used to take Lanett fishing at Guasti and Puddingstone Lakes almost every weekend, where her biggest catch was a two-pounder. She didn't like to take the fish off the hook because she was scared it would bite her.

Lanett's brother, Bill Jr., was born when she was thirteen, and she liked to play mother to him—dressing him up, cutting his hair, and fashioning it into pigtails. As they got older, the relationship took on a more typical sibling dynamic—fighting one minute and best friends the next. But they were always there for each other.

The family used to go to SeaWorld in San Diego and to drag races together. Lanett loved riding in her father's hot rod, boating on the lake, and sometimes went to work with him, where she helped put up the drywall tape.

As Lanett grew into a teenager—reaching five feet ten

inches and weight ranging from 130 to 165 pounds—she stopped going to school around the ninth grade, choosing instead to go to her aunt's house or ride her bike. And, like a typical teenage girl, she got a little boy crazy, though perhaps a bit more enthusiastic than most.

In November 1988, the day after her sixteenth birthday, she had a daughter named Amanda, with Robert Dewester. Then, almost a year later, she had Carlos, named after his father, with whom she also had Michael, who was born in March 1995. Finally, she had David with Ignacio Herrera in January 1998.

Lanett liked to cook for her children, particularly Mexican food.

"She was really fun. Instead of a mother, she was more like a friend," her daughter, Amanda, said later.

Lanett lived off and on with her parents, but no matter what, Debra later told authorities, she and Lanett remained best friends. Lanett would always be her precious little baby.

Lanett surely loved her family, but she also loved to have a good time. And she needed a way to pay for it.

She was twenty-one when she was first arrested. Chino police booked her into the West Valley Detention Center on September 28, 1994, for trying to cash a stolen check for $500 at the Vineyard National Bank.

Lanett initially told Officer R. Planas that she'd gotten the check from a woman she'd worked for named Mary and asked a friend, Araceli Aguilar, to cash it for her. After Planas took Lanett in for questioning and read her her rights, Lanett changed her story and said she'd gotten the check, already signed by a Christopher Gourlay, from a woman named Robin, who owed her money.

In October, Mary Gourlay called Chino police Detective

K. Devey to report that another two stolen checks, totaling $816, had been cashed from her account. These were made out to Adriana Gallegos, again with the forged signature of Mary's husband, who claimed he'd lost his checkbook and wallet several months earlier.

Adriana, who turned out to be the sister of Lanett's ex-boyfriend Carlos, said she got the checks from Lanett, who had lived with her brother for about four years. The couple had been evicted from their apartment and had $2,000 in debts, which Carlos asked Lanett to share. Carlos asked Adriana to cash the two checks, allegedly payment from Lanett's job, and then give him the money.

Lanett's family said she had parties to sell home interior products, but police records show her as unemployed.

"It was so unusual for Lanett to have any money, as she never worked and didn't have any means of obtaining a check," Carlos's other sister, Dulce, told police.

Devey tried unsuccessfully to reach Lanett by phone in January 1995, and again in early February, when he went to the apartment she shared with her parents in Chino.

On February 7, Devey put a "stop and hold" on Lanett and she was arrested by 4:00 P.M. Police deemed Adriana and Araceli unsuspecting accomplices and didn't arrest either of them.

Lanett was ultimately charged with two counts of commercial burglary, two counts of forging checks, and one count of being under the influence of methamphetamine. Through a plea bargain, she was sentenced to 120 days in jail and three years' probation, but she was allowed to serve her time in a weekend program, from 7:00 P.M. Friday until 7:00 P.M. Sunday.

A month before she was to start her jail time in November 1995, she was arrested again for being under the influence of meth by an officer investigating a hit-and-run collision involving a black Camaro, which Lanett's boyfriend said he'd loaned her.

During her arrest on the night of October 13, she admitted that she'd snorted "a little line" earlier that day. She was ineligible to enter a drug diversion program because of her prior conviction.

On Friday night, April 5, 1996—when she apparently should have been in jail—Lanett was arrested for public drunkenness outside Studebaker's bar in Chino, where she'd been kicked out for attempting to hit her boyfriend. Lanett was crying and mumbling to herself when police arrived.

"It appeared as if White had a hard time focusing on my face," the officer's report stated. "She would glance up towards my voice and her eyes would immediately fall back down towards the ground."

While she was being arrested, she was identified as the woman who had caused $1,700 in damage to a Chevy Beretta, belonging to the Studebaker's DJ, earlier that night. Lanett had walked on the hood and scratched it with her heels, mangled the windshield wipers, and destroyed the wipers' motor. She'd also broken off the antenna, which she used to hit the windshield until it cracked.

The officer, who took her to jail, wrote that she was too drunk to understand her Miranda rights, so he didn't even try to read them to her.

After being late and not showing up for her weekend jail program in 1995 and 1996, her probation was revoked in April 1996. A bench warrant was issued and her bail was set at $50,000. By the time Lanett was killed, she had five outstanding warrants to her name, with bail amounts totaling $127,500.

In July 1998, the San Bernardino County District Attorney's Child Support Division filed a complaint against

Lanett, seeking a monthly $370—her "presumed income as provided by law"—as support for Amanda, who had received $5,180 in welfare payments over the past fourteen months. The DA also asked the court to make sure that Amanda had health insurance.

Clearly, Lanett was a young woman in trouble, caught in a downward spiral.

The last time Debra White saw her daughter was September 16, 1998. Lanett had brought her mother a birthday cake, saying she'd return three days later on the actual day to celebrate. Debra said this was so typical of Lanett, who was always thoughtful, particularly on special occasions.

Debra got a call from her sister Judy on Tuesday, September 22, saying that Lanett had gone to Baker's restaurant to pick up a check on Sunday and never came back.

Three days later, an Ontario police officer notified Debra and Bill at their apartment that Lanett might have been "involved in a homicide." He told the Whites to contact the San Joaquin County detectives working the case, so Bill and his son went to a pay phone down the street to make the call. Debra later said she immediately went into shock, not understanding or wanting to accept the news.

Detective Mike Jones took the call.

"Do you know why she might be up in northern California?" Jones asked.

"Why?"

"We're conducting an investigation."

"No, I don't know why she'd be up there," Bill said.

Jones asked where Lanett was living and Bill gave him an address in the 10000 block of Catawba Road in Fontana, where Lanett and her two youngest children had been staying with her cousin Charlotte Bailey.

The detective could detect some concern in Bill's voice, but wanted to get a sense for whether he could be a suspect before giving him any real details. Normally, everyone who had contact with the victim, including family members, was considered a potential suspect. Jones would eliminate them, one by one, as he interviewed them.

"With a homicide, everybody's a suspect until you know different," Jones explained later.

Figuring that he needed to conduct the murder investigation in Lanett's home city, Jones decided to hold the specifics until he could talk to the Whites face-to-face in a couple of days. In the meantime, he went ahead with the official notification.

"Sir, well, I have some bad news for you. We found a young female in a waterway, deceased, near Lodi. We have tentatively identified her by fingerprints and it is Lanett," Jones said.

After the call, Bill and his son went back to the duplex and told Amanda about her mother's death. Almost ten, Amanda was old enough to understand and promptly burst into tears. They decided to wait until later to tell Amanda's three younger siblings.

When it came time to make arrangements, the Whites didn't have much money, and because of the decomposed state of Lanett's body, they decided to cremate her. As soon as they got the box of her ashes, they held a service for her at a local mortuary.

"I had to take my baby out of there [in a box], holding her like that," Debra said later. "I never . . . thought I'd ever have to go through something like that. Your kids, they go from an accident, car wreck, stuff like that. But something like this, there's no excuse for it. No excuse in this world for it."

* * *

On Monday, September 28, Jones made the ten-hour drive down to Fontana with Detective David Claypool. Knowing they would start their interviews with Lanett's parents, Jones called the Whites when they were about an hour away.

The city of Fontana is built on a flat area surrounded by mountains, ringed by a yellow layer of smog blown in from the urban metropolis of Los Angeles.

The sun was starting to go down when the detectives pulled up to Debra's sister Judy's house in the 9000 block of Beach Avenue, around 7:45 P.M.

Debra talked softly, crying off and on, as Jones questioned her about Lanett and her lifestyle.

"I was pretty confident that she wasn't involved, even though I didn't think there was a very close relationship between the two," Jones said later.

As they were talking, Debra said that Lanett had lived with her and Bill until the first part of September, when they had to kick her out. She didn't elaborate.

After Debra said Lanett's ex-boyfriend Theo Flores had sprayed Easy-Off oven cleaner on Lanett's trailer, and also tried to kill her, Flores moved to the top of Jones's list of suspects.

Jones spoke with Bill next, taking him out to the car to show him a photo of Lanett's tattoos so that he could confirm her identity. Jones wasn't going to show Bill any shots of Lanett's face or breasts, given their decomposed and blackened state. Even so, he still tried to warn Lanett's father about what he was going to see.

"I'm going to show you a picture of her back," Jones said. "The picture is not pretty."

Bill Sr. was devastated by his daughter's death. A

macho guy who never showed his emotions, Bill cried after seeing what had happened to his only daughter.

"He's a pretty brave man and I think it's messed with him ever since then," Debra said in 2006. "It's like he never used to cry very much, but now, I always see him crying. I mean, he tries to act like he's not, but I know when he's crying. And it's just like, you know, a heartbreaking, awful, terrible thing for someone to have to go through."

That same night, Jones spoke with Charlotte Bailey, Lanett's cousin, who seemed pretty honest, given that she admitted to smoking a dime bag of crank ($10 worth) with Lanett the last day she saw her alive. Charlotte said she, her sister Sharon, Lanett, and their seven children had all been living in her tiny unit on Catawba Road in Fontana for three or four weeks before Lanett was killed.

Crank is another name for methamphetamine, an extremely addictive stimulant that can be snorted or smoked, causing an unnaturally high euphoria that could last for hours, followed by a deep fall into withdrawal, which causes users to keep on using.

As was typical with what Jones described as "cranksters," he quickly determined that Lanett, her cousin, other members of her family, and some of her friends and acquaintances belonged to a community that had a different lifestyle and sense of time from mainstream society.

"[Charlotte] gave me a bunch of leads to start from there," Jones said.

Alcohol, drugs, and sex ran rife through the stories that Jones would hear over the next few days as a picture of Lanett began to emerge. She was regularly seen with hickeys on her neck. She liked to stand in Catawba Road outside her cousin's house, wave men down in passing cars, bum a cigarette, and strike up a conversation. She'd also been having simultaneous relations with at least two men, and there were others around the periphery. Some of her friends said they'd never seen her with any white friends in the time they'd known her.

When Jones finished with White's immediate family, he and Claypool went back to their hotel to get some sleep. They got up the next morning and had breakfast, but they didn't feel the need to rush.

"Most of these people aren't up and moving until 10 or 11 A.M.," Jones said.

Charlotte's neighborhood was in one of the city's older residential areas, inhabited primarily by low-income Latino families, where peddlers sold ice cream, snow cones, and fried corn munchies from three-wheeled carts, riding up and down the streets and honking their horns. In late 2007, chain-link fence or other barriers surrounded the small perimeter of most every house or multiunit dwelling. Some had plastic flamingos in the front yards, others abandoned cars. The aroma of home-cooked Mexican food filled the air along these residential streets, but along the boulevard, the air hung with a turpentinelike odor mixed with exhaust fumes from the nearby Highway 10.

The view from Charlotte's run-down building was a vacant dirt lot, scattered with industrial trailers and trucks. Her triplex was only a block from Valley Boulevard, a noisy throughway lined with car dealerships, strip malls, liquor stores, and auto repair shops. Cars with shiny silver hubcaps proudly cruised the strip, sharing their loud music and booming bass with their fellow motorists. Many billboards and business signs were written in Spanish.

Lanett and Charlotte frequented a liquor store around the corner. A couple of miles down the boulevard from

Charlotte's place were several truck stops—the Fontana Truck Stop, Three Sisters Truck Stop, and Truck Town. Hookers were known to frequent these and other well-traveled businesses like them, hoping to make some money by "dating" truck drivers who were looking for a little action to spice up those long hours alone.

It's unclear how Lanett ended up at one of these places, which were too far away, really, to walk to in high heels. According to Wayne, who said he picked her up on a frontage road near a truck stop on Cherry Street, she was upset and had been drinking the night she got into his big rig.

The two detectives gradually pieced together what happened in the days before Lanett disappeared on Sunday, September 20.

Early in the day, Lanett and Charlotte smoked some crank at their friend Michelle's house, returning to Catawba Road in the afternoon.

Lanett pushed her baby in the stroller to the corner liquor store, sometime between 5:15 and 6:00 P.M., to call her friend Mario. She came back with a bottle of Cisco, a cheap sweet, flavored wine similar to Ripple that has a 20 percent alcohol content.

Lanett's cousin Sharon told the detectives that Lanett stayed outside talking to a big guy in a white pickup truck while Charlotte took a nap. He was a white guy, six feet tall, 180 pounds, with graying hair, a thick mustache, and tattooed arms. Jones later learned that the guy was fifty-two-year-old Ralph Edward Bishop III, who admitted using a quarter-gram of crank a day and could not account for his whereabouts later that night. Jones added him to the list of suspects.

Charlotte woke up to see Lanett putting on a

black-and-brown dress, which she wore for her second trip to the liquor store around 7:30 P.M., returning with another bottle of Cisco.

Mario showed up about 9:00 P.M. Lanett went outside and gave him a hug, then sat in his lap, kissing him in the front yard.

Sharon, who had gone to lie down, woke up around ten o'clock because Lanett had turned on the hall light to change her clothes again. This time she put on a pair of tight faded jeans, a blue midriff tank top under a long-sleeved brownish plaid shirt, and a pair of black-and-white high-heeled sandals.

Lanett was sniffling as if she'd been crying, but she wouldn't tell Sharon what was wrong.

One of Lanett's children woke up and wanted some milk, but they were out, so she said she would walk to the liquor store—for the third time that night—and get some. This was the last time Sharon saw her cousin.

At some point after Lanett left, Charlotte was awakened by Lanett's baby crying. Mario told her that Lanett had gone to pick up her check at Baker's, then was supposed to meet someone at the liquor store to "make some money." The Baker's manager later looked at a photo of Lanett and said he'd never seen her before.

Mario woke Sharon around 11:00 P.M. to tell her he was worried that Lanett had not come home yet. Around 1:00 or 2:00 A.M., he walked around the block to see if he could find her. He spent the rest of the night on the couch, waiting for her.

Ignacio, another of Lanett's boyfriends and the father of her baby David, showed up the next morning. When he learned that Lanett hadn't come home, he waited around all day with Mario, hoping she'd show up.

Finally, around 5:00 P.M., they both went to the liquor store to see if anyone knew where she was, but no one had seen her since 9:30 the night before. At that point, Ignacio took his son to his grandmother's house.

On September 29, the detectives paid a visit to the liquor store, where Jones asked owner Sean Massis if they could watch the video surveillance tape. But upon checking the dates on the tape, they realized September 20 had already been recorded over.

So, next, Jones and Claypool went to the house of Bob Olson, the clerk who was working the night Lanett disappeared. Bob was a skinny sixty-year-old guy with dark hair and big-framed glasses. He said Lanett had come to the store three times that night and made three phone calls. On her last trip at 9:30 P.M., she said she'd be back at 11:00 P.M. to talk to him. Bob said she didn't show up, so he and Julie, the stock clerk, left at 11:07 P.M.

Jones found it suspicious that a twenty-five-year-old woman would be meeting up with this guy, who was more than twice her age, at that late hour.

"I didn't think at the time he was being totally honest," Jones recalled later, saying he added Bob to his mental list of suspects.

After that, the detectives interviewed Ignacio, who said he'd last seen Lanett on Saturday morning, September 19, after spending a few days with her at her cousin's place. That Sunday, he'd gone with his family to his sister's house in Victorville and didn't get back until late.

During a subsequent interview with Lanett's cousin Sharon Bailey, the detectives gained some new insight about why Lanett went to the liquor store so often.

First, Sharon said, there was no phone at Charlotte's, so they often used the pay phone at the store. Second, they shopped there for items other than alcohol. And third, as it turned out, Lanett had a little deal worked out with Bob the night clerk. Jones's instincts had been right.

On Saturday, the day before Lanett disappeared, she had gone to the liquor store twice. The first time, around 5:30 P.M., she made a remark to Sharon about coming back with $30, saying, "I'm just going to let him [Bob] touch me." She returned with the money in hand.

Sharon said Lanett made another trip at 9:30 P.M., saying she was supposed to go back around 11:30 to meet Bob and another guy for drinks and make $70 more. But she came back saying the "date" had been postponed until Sunday night.

When Lanett didn't come back on Sunday, her mother and cousins felt something was wrong; it wasn't like Lanett to leave her babies for that long. Yet, when Michelle suggested that Charlotte file a missing persons report, Charlotte said no, because Lanett had done this in the past. Still, she told Michelle that this time she thought Lanett was dead.

A few weeks later, Jones and Claypool made another trip south to San Bernardino County to conduct further interviews. Jones had learned that Theo Flores's real name was Darío Llamas Flores, so he brought a six-pack of photos, including Theo's, to show around.

After tracking down twenty-four-year-old Theo at his mother's house in Ontario, they stopped by to ask him some questions. Theo said he'd last seen Lanett around the first of September, and since his car had broken down, he couldn't have dumped her body in northern California.

His mother, speaking to the detectives in Spanish while her other son translated, confirmed Theo's story. She said she'd learned of Lanett's death from Debra

White and was upset by the news because she'd cared for the young woman.

On October 21, Claypool and Jones learned that Lanett had yet another ex-boyfriend with a temper. One of her friends said she could only remember his first name—Domingo—but she was sure he drove a red Mustang. She gave them a physical description and said he used to beat up on Lanett; it didn't seem to take much to set him off.

"The list of suspects—it was just huge," Jones said later. But, he added, "we had very minimal physical evidence, so we were just trying to get what we could."

In a matter of weeks, however, he would realize that none of these suspects was the guy he'd been looking for.

CHAPTER 13

PATRICIA ANNE TAMEZ

Detective Frank Gonzales was watching TV at his house in Rancho Cucamonga on Friday night, October 23, 1998, when his phone rang around ten o'clock.

It was his sergeant, Mike Lenihan.

"Hey, Gonzo, we've got a female floater in the California Aqueduct in Hesperia," Lenihan said. "I'll see you there within the hour."

The consummate professional, Gonzales, who was the lead on his team of four homicide detectives, put on his dark Oscar de la Renta suit and headed out the door. He kept a pair of overalls in the car in case he had to crawl through mud, but the evidence techs usually did most of the dirty work.

He didn't know it yet, but Tina Gibbs's body had been dumped by the same man a month earlier in the same aqueduct—385 miles to the north.

* * *

Gonzales pulled up to the pumping station on Amargosa Road, just west of Interstate 15, around 11:20 P.M. He walked through an opening in the chain-link fence and took a look around at the landscape. The aqueduct was surrounded by miles of flat desert, covered with chaparral.

Once the rest of his team arrived, they set up lights to illuminate the area so they could take photos and search for tire tracks, shoe prints, or any other evidence the killer might have left behind.

Gonzales walked along the narrow asphalt road that paralleled the canal, then headed down the dirt and gravel embankment toward the water, where he could see the victim's nude body floating underneath the pumping station. Two guards walking the aqueduct had found her there, caught up in one of the gates.

Because she was naked, Gonzales figured that she'd been killed during a sexual assault.

As he got closer, he saw something that shocked him, even after working at least two hundred homicides and observing more than a hundred autopsies over the past eight years: her chest had a yellow circular indentation where her left breast used to be.

That's when he knew that her death had been not just personal, but violent as well. He had a bad feeling that a man was roaming the region, assaulting and cutting up women. If so, this would be his first serial-killer case.

The sheriff's dive team suited up and got into the chilly water to retrieve her body. They tied a rope to one of her legs to make sure they didn't lose her to the current, floated her over to the east side of the aqueduct, and pulled her up in a metal basket. Then, fighting the current, they dived down to the bottom of the canal, looking for other evidence. They found none.

Now able to examine her more closely, Gonzales saw

a scar on her stomach and ligature marks on her wrists and ankles, which indicated that she'd been bound. The marks were about a half-inch wide, almost like a strap or dent in the skin, and were a different color than the surrounding area.

Before they placed her in a body bag—two, actually; one inside the other—Steve Foster, a coroner's investigator, took her fingerprints, which Detective Mike Gilliam entered into the California ID system later that night.

They got a hit within hours: twenty-nine-year-old Patricia Anne Tamez, five feet seven inches tall, 135 pounds, brown hair and eyes, and of Mexican descent. Based on her arrest record, she'd had quite a troubled past.

Patricia Tamez was born in McAllen, Texas, on April 25, 1969, to Rudolfo and Anna Tamez. She spent her first two years in the Rio Grande Valley before her parents divorced and Rudolfo took her to Santa Barbara. The two of them moved south to Ventura, then up to Berkeley, where she went to high school.

Patricia was a normal child who enjoyed doing normal things—playing with dolls, riding her bike, building sand castles, getting a tan, and riding the roller coaster at Magic Mountain. She kept several rabbits and a parakeet as pets, giving the bird a funeral after it died. She was an average student, but she could meet an intellectual challenge if she set her mind to it, such as memorizing the Greek alphabet. She also enjoyed playing chess, even though she wasn't very good at it.

Rudolfo would always remember the day when four-year-old Patricia couldn't wait for her father to get home so she could tell him she'd thrown all her baby bottles away. She was a big girl now and could drink from a glass.

Rudolfo remarried when Patricia was about eight, and

had two children with his new wife. Patricia got along well with her new siblings, holding her baby sister as they drove back from Santa Barbara so the toddler could see out the window. Rudolfo had promised that they could stop and get something at McDonald's if the little girl could spot one along the way.

As Patricia got older, she really liked to cook, especially tortillas with spicy El Pato tomato sauce, loaded with cheese. She also had a weakness for fast food—a Super Taco from Taco Bell or a Big Mac from McDonald's.

This was the start of her downfall, really, because she began thinking she was fat. She took diet pills to lose weight, then moved on to other drugs. Six months before she died, she admitted she'd used heroin, LSD, and PCP, and was addicted to meth, cocaine, and alcohol.

In 1988, Patricia was nineteen when she got married to a man whose last name was Prine.

In July 1990, Patricia was arrested in Lake County, in northern California, for possessing drugs and hypodermic needles. Rudolfo bailed her out of jail and said she took the fall for her addict husband because she had no criminal record. Patricia was sent to a diversion program, filed for divorce, and then joined her father in Hesperia, which is in southern California's high desert near Victorville, in 1992.

Rudolfo was encouraged when Patricia enrolled at a community college in Victorville and did very well. Hoping to become an X-ray technician, she applied to a vocational program, but she was rejected because she hadn't taken human anatomy. Instead of enrolling in an anatomy class and reapplying, she took the setback to heart. She felt unlucky, that nothing ever went right for her.

By January 1, 1993, she'd quit school and was in trouble again. The twenty-three-year-old had hooked up with another man heavily involved with drugs, but this time they were caught with more than a couple of needles.

Two sheriff's deputies arrested Patricia and eighteen-year-old James Listerman after seeing a drug scale and a mirror with a white powdery residue on the backseat of her 1976 Cadillac sedan. The car was parked at the Hesperia Motor Lodge in front of room two, where the couple had been staying.

A search of the car turned up a gun, meth pipes, numerous boxes containing the necessary chemicals and equipment for a portable meth lab, and more than ten pounds of the drug in various stages of cooking.

During an interview by Narcotics Detective G. Milani that night, Patricia said she'd returned to the motel to check out. She said she'd recently bought the Cadillac from a friend, Michael Murphy, for her boyfriend, James, but when he couldn't pay her for the car, they decided to sell it for $250 to a guy they knew.

Patricia said she usually stayed with her parents in Hesperia, but since she'd met James a month ago, they'd been living from motel to motel. She said she just used meth, claiming to know nothing about James's drug dealings or the meth-cooking paraphernalia.

Asked if she got her speed from James, she said, "Yes. No. I don't know. I can't say anything or I'll be dead. They'll kill me."

Milani told her that he knew the car was registered to her, and if she'd been hanging out with James for the past month, she had to be lying.

"It's the other guy's stuff!" Patricia said, explaining that James had picked up the items in the car from a friend at Carl's Jr. about half an hour before they returned to the motel.

Milani said he still didn't believe her.

"I'll come clean with you and tell you the truth," she replied, "but I want my attorney here, because I've told the truth to the cops before and they've used it against me to f*** me over."

James was arrested and charged with felony possession of pseudoephedrine (the main ingredient of meth) with the intent to manufacture meth. He was also charged with a count of selling or transporting meth, another felony. Patricia was charged with possession for sale of meth.

This incident was not enough to deter Patricia. Ten weeks later, she was at it again, and this time she was literally caught with her pants down.

Alerted by a confidential informant, two Ontario police officers responded to a call of possible narcotic activity in room 220 of the Days Inn. Officers J. Holloman and Franklyn went first to the front office, where they were told the room was rented to Michael Murphy and a woman named Patricia, whose Cadillac was parked in the lot.

The officers knocked at the second-floor room and Patricia answered. Seeing she had no pants on, Franklyn told her to get dressed.

She left the door slightly ajar, so they immediately recognized the chemical smell of meth cooking and the potentially lethal situation. Many people are injured or killed every year in explosions that can occur anywhere meth makers can plug in a hot plate: garages, warehouses, apartments, and cheap motel rooms.

Now dressed, Patricia said she would talk to them outside, but the officers weren't taking any chances. They pushed past her to find a man asleep in bed. He turned out to be none other than James Listerman, aka James Norton.

Franklyn approached the bathroom door, noticing

that it was closed with the light on. The toxic fumes were growing stronger with each step.

Inside, Franklyn found a glass vial floating in the bathtub, a hot plate behind the bathroom door, and a glass beacon and flask, filled with clear liquid, behind the toilet. The officers also found a propane tank with a heating element. Once the cooked mix cools and dries, it turns into crystals, thus the name crystal meth.

Patricia and James were both arrested for possession with intent to manufacture meth. Rudolfo got her an attorney, who plea-bargained the charges down on the two motel incidents. She was sentenced to 190 days in jail, but she was released on her own recognizance on the promise that she go to rehab.

At the time, she told her probation officer that she'd been using drugs since the age of thirteen and was $30,000 in debt.

She entered an inpatient rehab facility on May 26, 1993, and although she could've stayed a full year, she left after two months, just long enough to satisfy the court.

Her sentence was suspended in July and she got three years' probation, which was revoked after she tested positive for meth seven times in early 1994.

Although she was ordered to go to jail for a year, it appears she escaped incarceration and got sent to rehab again. Court records show that the now pregnant Patricia successfully completed a fifteen-hour parenting program from the Chaffey Adult School in Substance Abuse in Ontario on May 18, 1994.

Rudolfo found renewed hope in 1995, when Patricia gave birth to a baby girl. She seemed to be doing better, living in Barstow in low-income housing with the baby's father. Rudolfo thought she was a good mother.

But when the baby was eighteen months old, Patricia had a psychotic break, most likely caused by meth use, which can bring on schizophreniclike symptoms, such as hallucinations and delusional thinking.

Patricia called the police, claiming that someone had broken into her house and moved a knife on the counter. They picked her up on a "5150"—the term for when police deem someone is a danger to himself or others—and put the baby into protective custody. Rudolfo took Patricia's daughter home with him, where Patricia would often visit her.

Patricia spent sixty days at the MFI Recovery Center in Riverside that year, but again, it didn't stick.

Rudolfo was distressed that the drugs were increasingly affecting her mind. When she was sober, she was capable of having an intelligent discussion, but when she was high, she rambled and became irrational.

Rudolfo saw her less and less as she drifted in and out of his house, often choosing to stay with friends instead.

He felt he had tried everything: tough love, begging, getting angry, and sometimes just talking to Patricia for hours, urging her to do something with her life. But looking back later, he realized he'd always focused on the moral values of addiction; he'd been ignorant of the physiological aspects of the disease—the changes in brain chemistry that are brought on by methamphetamine.

Patricia used to tell him that she wasn't like other addicts she'd met in rehab, who'd had horrible childhood experiences that pushed them into drugs. To Rudolfo, that just proved addiction can devastate any family.

"You know, Dad, I don't ever want you to blame yourself for any bad decisions I might've made," she told him. "You're the best father any daughter could have ever wanted."

"We'll fight this demon," he replied. "We'll beat it."

* * *

In October 1996, Patricia was arrested for attempted grand theft of items worth $400 to $1,000 at St. Mary's Hospital in Apple Valley. Patricia was confronted by hospital staff after being seen pulling a linen cart through a corridor. After a brief struggle with security, she was handcuffed and detained.

She had stopped reporting to her probation officer in mid-June. However, there was no record of any charges being filed in the hospital incident.

Patricia's mental state was clearly disintegrating and the system was failing her.

On January 20, 1997, she was arrested in Victorville for commercial burglary, went to jail until February 7, and was arrested again on March 6, this time for sending a false bomb, stalking, and making terrorist threats at the army armory in Victorville.

She'd first gone to the armory in January, telling recruiter Jerry Astudillo that she was interested in signing up, but she was asked to leave after she started acting irrationally.

She subsequently pinned an envelope, addressed to her from Tony Rogers, to an armory bulletin board. She sent letters there as well, also addressed to Tony Rogers, which spoke of "secret government conspiracies" and wanting someone to "take out" a list of people. She also left threatening messages on Astudillo's answering machine.

(Tony Rogers, who was in prison when she was killed, later proved to be her last-known boyfriend, and likely her daughter's father. The District Attorney's Child Support Division filed a complaint against Patricia in May 1997 for repayment of public assistance the county had paid within the past three years for her child, Toni Rogers, born July 15, 1995.)

Things came to a head when a suitcase, bearing the same name and return address as the letters, was left on the armory doorstep the morning of March 6. Given Patricia's previous behavior, the employees alerted the sheriff's department that they had a potential bomb.

Patricia came back, retrieved her suitcase, and headed for the bus stop, where she was arrested and refused to speak to the officers. The bomb squad showed up and, after carefully opening the case, found it contained only an assortment of Bibles and other books.

Patricia was released on her own recognizance until sentencing.

In June, when she was arrested for petty theft from a retail store, someone finally noticed that Patricia's mental state was erratic at best, and the court ordered her to be psychologically evaluated before her prosecution went any further.

The report summarizing her August 7 assessment by forensic psychologist Robert L. Suiter is the only source of Patricia's version of reality in her court records.

Curiously, her negative perspective and some of her life experiences—not the least of which was that she'd been given Haldol while hospitalized for psychiatric problems—were in some ways remarkably similar to Wayne's.

She said she left high school after finishing the eleventh grade, completing her degree in 1995 through adult education. She said her marriage ended when her husband was charged with "throwing people off cliffs in carpets," but she refused to elaborate.

After her divorce, she said, she spent two years attending classes at two community colleges, but she didn't earn a degree. She said she "floated around," lived with a man and had his baby, who was now living with her mother. Her only job was a six-month stint at a college library. Most of the time, the report said, "She survived financially by begging. She stated she is at times homeless and, in certain instances, she 'sleeps in a sleeping bag under a bush.'"

She said she mostly took drugs at parties, but she had a history of consuming four mixed drinks a day. However, she denied having any alcohol since February 1997, when she said, she was voluntarily admitted to a psychiatric hospital for three days "to treat an alcohol problem."

The psychologist noted that she showed up fifteen minutes late to the interview, looking unkempt and disheveled. She had trouble filling out a fairly simple intake form, and she demonstrated "overt paranoia and delusional thought processes." He said she also didn't seem to understand the court system, or the roles of the prosecutor and her own attorney.

He diagnosed her with a nonspecific psychotic disorder with schizoid traits, found her incompetent "to assist with her own defense in a rational manner," and recommended that she be sent to Patton State Hospital in San Bernardino "for a period of observation and treatment." She was admitted to Patton on November 21.

Ninety percent of the population of California's five state hospitals is made up of forensic patients—ranging from people deemed mentally incompetent to stand trial to those who are found not guilty of crimes by reason of insanity.

After undergoing inpatient treatment at Patton for about six weeks, she was deemed competent to face the charges against her.

At the time, she was on four prescribed medications: BuSpar and Klonopin (also known as clonazepam), both of which are antianxiety drugs; Risperdal, an antipsychotic drug used to treat schizophrenia, bipolar, and other personality disorders; and trazodone, a sedative and antidepressant used to treat withdrawal from cocaine and other stimulants.

"It is critical that Ms. Tamez continue taking the prescribed medication while in custody in order to ensure continued competency," her doctors wrote upon her release from Patton.

Through another plea agreement in February 1998, Patricia pleaded guilty to making felony terrorist threats. But, yet again, she was placed on probation for three years in exchange for rehab and no jail time.

In a meeting with her probation officer on April 6, Patricia admitted that she'd left the suitcase at the armory a year earlier, but she denied any attempt to make it look like a bomb. She said she'd been suffering from severe hallucinations at the time, caused by her drug use.

"I don't think that I threatened him [Astudillo] at all," Patricia said. "I don't really remember what I said . . . but I must've done something because I was convicted."

Patricia told the officer that she'd attempted to check herself into a hospital with the suitcase, but the doctors refused to admit her, so she left the case at the armory.

When she came back for it the next day, the place was closed due to a bomb threat. She said she returned later to find that the police had blown up her suitcase. Patricia later said she'd believed that "the police were using computers and VCRs to do illegal things with people's minds." Based on her mental instability, it is unclear what actually happened that day.

"Ms. Tamez feels that she is in dire need of rehabilitation as well as psychological treatment," her probation officer wrote. "She is currently scheduled to enter a sober living rehabilitation program and hopes to be a resident of that program for approximately eight months."

"I just want to turn my life around," Patricia told the officer. "I know it's never too late. I want to work on my recovery, get a place of my own, and become a good citizen."

The officer noted that Patricia already had 409 days of "custody credit," and recommended that her probation be reinstated, underscoring that further violations could result in state prison time.

A few days after that meeting, Patricia was turned away from the Gibson House for Women in San Bernardino for being under the influence.

Unfortunately for Patricia, she earned the mercy of the court once again. In 2007, no court records for Patricia could be located after her April 17 court appearance, when she was placed back on three years' probation and released on her own recognizance.

However, after being rejected from the sober-living program, her case fell through the cracks of the system and she went back to life on the streets.

"You know, you get to the point where, when you've got this type of addiction . . . , you have nothing left to sell, you sell your body," Rudolfo said later. "It was the addiction that, you know, that put her there."

Rudolfo would always remember the last time he saw Patricia.

He had gone to a friend's house to use the Internet at 3:00 P.M. on a Saturday. Patricia was there, so Rudolfo used the opportunity to tell her once more, "Life is short. Don't waste it. Do something with your life."

Patricia seemed rational, lucid, and clear that day.

"I want you to have this, Dad," she said, handing him a red ribbon that said: "Drugs Destroy Dreams."

When she was about to leave, he offered to take her

for a hamburger, but he ended up having to stay and deal with a computer problem.

"Okay, *mi hija*, take care," Rudolfo said. (*Mi hija* means "my daughter" in Spanish.) He said it several times, wishing that he could offer her something more in the way of concrete advice, but this was the best he could do.

By the time he realized the full extent of his daughter's problem, it was too late. And despite her kind words, he still blamed himself for failing to do more research into addiction sooner.

"I guess I could've tied her down for two years to the bed, and then I would've ended up in deep trouble," Rudolfo said later.

Larry Halverson, a conductor for the Burlington Northern and Santa Fe Railroad, spent afternoons doing paperwork in his office, across the street from the southeast corner of 6th and D Streets in Victorville, where Patricia worked three to five days a week.

He would see her out of his picture window, standing provocatively with a couple of other "ladies of the evening." Soliciting dates by curling suggestively around the stop sign's pole, she would get into cars with men and return a while later to "advertise again."

Patricia would often come into Halverson's office to ask for food, water, or cigarettes, which he would sometimes give her.

On October 22, between 1:00 and 2:00 P.M., he saw a black eighteen-wheeler with white writing on the driver's side pull up to the corner and block his view of Patricia. As the truck was making a right-hand turn to head east on Highway 18, which is also called D Street, he saw her close the door and pull her jacket in through the window.

That was the last he ever saw of her.

He later told authorities that the driver was a white man in his midthirties with dark hair and several days' growth of beard.

The next night, Patricia was found dead in the aqueduct, about eight miles south of Victorville.

After staying up all night working Patricia's case, Gonzales went to talk to Michael Murphy, the contact she'd listed during her last arrest. Gonzales had no idea if he was a relative or a friend.

When Gonzales talked to Michael on the morning of October 24, he didn't tell him that Patricia was dead, only that she was missing.

Michael, an X-ray technician at Barstow Community Hospital, told Gonzales that he'd met Patricia when they were both attending Victor Valley College in 1992. He said they'd never had a sexual relationship and were just friends. He knew she was involved in drugs and prostitution, and he'd made several attempts over the years to help her get clean. He'd also given her money for food or a motel room and let her stay the night at his house occasionally. He said he hadn't seen her since he'd let her sleep in his car and dropped her off at her friend Spivey White's house before he'd gone to work a few nights ago.

Michael asked whether Gonzales had talked to Patricia's father. Gonzales said no, so Michael gave him Rudolfo's address. Michael also gave him Spivey's address and said Patricia used to frequent the Green Spot Motel, a well-known prostitute hangout near 7th and D Streets in the old part of Victorville.

Spivey wasn't a wealth of information. He said he'd known Patricia for four or five years and let her stay the night every once in a while because he felt sorry for her. When he last saw her at 8:00 A.M. on October 22, she'd been wearing white sweatpants, a burgundy sweater, a big white T-shirt, and black-and-white tennis shoes.

Spivey, a mechanic in his fifties, said Patricia was a little mentally off.

"He didn't really like her spending the night with him, but . . . the nights in the high desert can be very, very cold," Gonzales said later. "He felt that Patricia was taking things from his house, because sometimes things would come up missing. The items had no value, but, basically, he didn't trust her."

Later that morning, Gonzales and Detective Jeff Staggs went to Rudolfo's house in Hesperia to do the notification.

First, Gonzales asked Rudolfo if he was Patricia's father.

"Yes, I am."

"Can I see some ID?" Gonzales asked, just to make sure.

At first, Rudolfo thought they were there to tell him that Patricia had been arrested again, but it slowly dawned on him that police don't show up at your house for that purpose. It had to be something worse. But everything seemed to be happening in slow motion.

"When was the last time you saw Patricia?" Gonzales asked.

"It was a week ago," Rudolfo replied.

"Well, there is no easy way to say this, so I'm just going to say it," Gonzales said. "She's deceased."

As the detectives told him what had happened to Patricia, including the fact that her breast had been removed, Rudolfo felt as if he'd slipped out of his own body. He could almost see himself from above, his heart being ripped out of his chest. The pain was so great that he couldn't cry until the detectives were about to leave.

From that day on, Rudolfo was haunted by the thought that she might have been alive when she was placed in the aqueduct.

After the notification, Gonzales went back to the aqueduct to take another look around, returning the following day to do an expanded search with the sheriff's search-and-rescue team.

Because the area was wide open and in plain view of cars passing by on Amargosa Road, Gonzales figured that she had been dumped somewhere upstream and had floated down. Tracing the aqueduct west a few miles, he found a likely spot: a dirt turnout next to a bridge where the canal crossed Interstate 395, about a mile from Interstate 15.

Over the next few weeks, Detectives Gonzales, Staggs, and Rod Fulcher conducted interviews in the Victorville neighborhood where Patricia had worked, hoping someone might have seen something. Halverson, the railroad conductor, was the closest they came.

Gonzales talked to a woman named Sandra Lambert, who had called the sheriff's office after learning that Patricia had died.

Sandra, who was staying with her husband at the Green Spot Motel while they remodeled the place, said she'd last seen Patricia there around 3:00 P.M. on October 23. A week earlier, Patricia had told her that a black trucker beat her up because he thought she'd tried to take his wallet at a truck stop in Barstow.

Staggs interviewed another woman at the Green Spot who knew Patricia well. Carla Ponte said she saw Patricia on either October 22 or 23, when Patricia was having lunch at the St. Joan of Arc Church on C Street, which provided meals to the homeless. She said she also saw Patricia later that afternoon, walking by the railroad tracks near her usual corner. Carla said she last saw Patricia get into a silver pickup truck, which drove eastbound on Highway 18 toward Apple Valley.

On October 28, Dr. Steven Trenkle, a pathologist and a deputy medical examiner for San Bernardino County, conducted the autopsy on Patricia's body.

He took swabs for a sex kit and noted that she had hemorrhaging in the whites of her eyes and pinpoint hemorrhages on her face and upper lip, both indications that she was strangled.

She had pale marks around the wrists and ankles, as if she'd been bound. But after cutting under the skin, he saw that only the right ankle showed any hemorrhaging, which meant that the other bindings were likely tied while her heart was barely beating, if at all.

Trenkle also noted a six-by-six-inch hole in the deepest layer of fat over the chest wall muscle where her left breast had been cut away, apparently using a sawing motion with a fairly sharp instrument. He couldn't determine whether she was alive or dead when the breast was removed because that area has very little blood flow, and if there had been any bleeding, it would have washed away while she was in the water. A second pathologist, Dr. Yeager, examined the breast later and decided it had most likely been severed postmortem.

The right side of her nose was scraped and she had some small areas of hemorrhaging on her scalp, where she could have been injured or simply bumped her head. But she also had brain swelling, which occurs when the brain is deprived of oxygen, blood, or glucose, and is another indication of strangulation.

The most significant injury indicating strangulation was in the neck. There was no fracture, but Trenkle did see bleeding on the right side around the thyroid cartilage, where the Adam's apple protects the vocal cords.

Trenkle didn't always do this during an autopsy, but in this case, he cut open her back. There, he discovered a significant amount of bleeding in the center of her spine—and her back was broken. He determined that the injury occurred while she was still alive—although she could have been unconscious—rendering her paralyzed from the midchest down. This would have prevented her not only from breathing deeply, but also from struggling to escape.

He waited almost two months for the results to come back from the toxicology tests and microscopic examination of tissues before declaring the official cause of death to be strangulation, most likely by the killer's hands, not by a ligature. He also stated that the victim was dead before she was placed into the water.

The toxicology screening showed that Patricia's liver was inflamed, which is often seen in people who have taken prescription drugs or abused street drugs. But curiously, given Patricia's history, the tests detected no trace of any drugs, illicit or prescription, in her blood. If she was still using meth, she hadn't had any in several days.

PART III

CHAPTER 14

"YOU WON'T LOVE ME ANYMORE"

Wayne continued to make late-night calls to his mother until shortly before he turned himself in. He seemed dejected, and Brigitte feared he might commit suicide, so she tried to talk him out of it.

"There is no need to talk about suicide because this—whatever it is—it can be worked out," she told Wayne. "But you have to stop feeling sorry for yourself."

When that didn't work, she tried a different tack. "Look, Wayne, if you really want to commit suicide, nobody's going to be able to stop you, so let's not talk about it."

Brigitte said she tried discussing Wayne's psychological state with Rodney, who, coincidentally, had been talking to Brigitte's mother, Vera, about the same subject. He, too, thought Wayne had been acting weird lately.

But Brigitte said Rodney's only response to her queries was "Well, you know Wayne."

During Wayne's final call to his mother, he said he was going to hide in the woods, where no one would find him.

"Wayne, what is it that you're trying to run from?" she asked.

"Well, you're probably going to read about it in the paper," he said.

Up to that point, Brigitte had thought he was exaggerating his problems. He'd always been so emotional.

"Tell me what it is you did."

"No, Mom, because you won't love me."

"I will love you, Wayne, but tell me. Maybe we can work it out."

"I can't tell you, Mom. You won't love me anymore."

"I might not like what you've done, Wayne, and I might even be angry at you, but I will love you," she said. "That's not going to change."

But Wayne wouldn't budge.

Brigitte finally said, "Look, Wayne, if you've really done something serious, you can't run. Then you go see an attorney and you go to the police and you face what you've done."

Wayne seemed to agree with her on that point, so she continued on. "Even if you don't have money for an attorney, you know you'll get one if you need one. We'll work it out. Just call me. I'm going . . . back to India soon. Let's call each other again before I go and let me know what's happening."

"Okay, Mom."

Wayne had been frequenting a Christian bookstore in a McKinleyville strip mall, north of Arcata, where he prayed with owner Ballard Anderson "Andy" Lowery. Lowery also took Wayne to a Bible study group for men.

Wayne told Lowery that he'd done some things that didn't bother him much, so he didn't think he had a conscience.

"You're just going to have to get it together and figure out what's going on," Lowery told him, saying that God was trying to get Wayne's attention and lead him that way. "But you have a conscience, or you wouldn't be talking to me."

Wayne seemed confused and unsure how to deal with missing his son and the problems he was having with his ex-wife.

Wayne bought cassette tapes of the Bible and said he would play them on the road, but Lowery wondered if Wayne was only buying these items to appease him for the time they spent talking.

In late October 1998, Wayne went to the Bayshore Mall to buy a wallet at Ross.

At the checkout stand, clerk Candy Hogan noticed that Wayne smelled like smoke and alcohol, as if he'd been in a bar. He was wearing a green plaid jacket and jeans, and his hair was combed, but he looked like he hadn't shaved that day.

"Remember that face," he said as he showed her his photo ID. "That is the face of a serial killer."

"That's not funny," Hogan said. "That's not true." (When she later reported the incident to Detective Freeman, she couldn't remember whether Wayne called himself a serial killer or a murderer.)

"Well, you never know," he said.

Hogan told him he wouldn't be confessing such things to her if he'd really done them.

"Stranger things have happened," he said, laughing.

Hogan said Wayne had mentioned something about

liking to kill women. At the time, she'd thought he was trying to pick her up, which made his remarks seem even more loony. His comments took her by surprise, partly because he seemed happy, but also because he'd seemed so honest and straightforward. She'd never heard anything like that from a customer before.

She didn't think anything more of their exchange until she learned from the news that he was actually telling the truth.

On November 2, Wayne walked from his campsite down to the Ocean Grove Lodge in Trinidad, where he spent the afternoon drinking and playing pool with bartender Marco Ibarra.

"I was pretty excited because I beat him twice and he is a great pool player," Ibarra told the *Eureka Times-Standard* a few days later.

Wayne showed up around noon, ordered his first drink, asked for quarters to buy a newspaper, and read the police briefs. Then, as he and Ibarra shot several games of pool, Wayne drank four rum and Cokes, two Budweisers, and two coffees with Baileys Irish Cream.

"[He] told me that he wanted to get drunk and blow his brains out," Ibarra told the *San Francisco Chronicle*. "When he spoke, he swallowed a lot, like he had a broken heart. He told me his wife had split with his kid to Las Vegas and he hadn't seen [the child] since."

At one point, Wayne said he needed to call his brother on the pay phone outside. When he was done, he came back inside and ate two giant Polish hot dogs.

"It can't be that bad," one of the patrons told him. "Things will look better tomorrow."

Wayne often hung out in this bar, his truck parked

outside as he drank alongside the fishermen and other regulars.

"Usually, he'd have on a cowboy hat and boots," one of them told the *Times Standard*. "I really thought he was one of us."

CHAPTER 15

SURRENDER

Eureka is known for having one of California's best-preserved Victorian commercial districts. The seaport city grew up around Humboldt Bay more than 150 years ago, when miners, fishermen, and loggers, drawn by the redwood forests, made their living there.

Today, Eureka is home to government workers and people in the lumber, fishing, service, and tourism industries. People ranging from judges to lawyers, prostitutes and transients, can be seen walking the downtown area near the county courthouse, a five-story concrete building of grays, tans, and browns that takes up an entire city block and houses the sheriff's department and the jail.

Versions of the events that transpired in the sheriff's lobby on the evening of November 3, 1998, vary dramatically—depending on who is telling the story.

Rodney's recollection conflicts significantly with the memories of the two law enforcement officers—Deputy Michael Gainey and Sergeant Michael Thomas—who joined them, one at a time, after the Ford brothers had been waiting about twenty minutes. This discrepancy was not revealed until Rodney was interviewed for this book in October 2007.

As Rodney recalls what happened:

Gainey was the first to come out and talk to them. Wayne repeated his mantra for the deputy, saying he had hurt some people.

"What do you mean *hurt* people?" Gainey asked Rodney.

"I don't know, ask him," Rodney said

Wayne started rambling, and not making sense again. He looked at Rodney and asked, "Do you think I need an attorney?"

"Yes," Rodney said.

"What do you need an attorney for?" Gainey asked Wayne. "You're not even under arrest. We've got no reason to hold you. You can't just come in here and say you've hurt some people. We need to know what you did."

"I hurt some people real bad," Wayne said. "I know you won't believe me, so I'll just show you."

Wayne went to reach into one of his jacket's front pockets and started to retrieve its contents when Gainey exclaimed, "Stop! What are you doing?"

"I'm just going to pull it out," Wayne said, slowly revealing a plastic bag with some yellow fatty tissue that Rodney thought looked like a piece of raw chicken.

"What's that?" Gainey asked.

As the deputy reached out to touch it, Wayne turned the bag around so Gainey could get a better view. As soon as the nipple became visible, Gainey and Rodney realized what the bag contained.

Gainey immediately put his hand on his pistol. "Don't move," he shouted at Wayne, and again at Rodney.

"I'm not going anywhere," Rodney said. "I'm just sitting here."

Gainey made a beeline for the wall phone. "I need somebody else out here right away," he told the receptionist.

"Did you know what he had in his pocket?" Gainey asked Rodney, who was just as surprised as the deputy.

Sergeant Thomas came out a minute later, wearing latex gloves, and took the bag from Wayne.

"Should I get an attorney?" Wayne asked his brother again.

"You definitely need an attorney," Rodney said.

"I want an attorney," Wayne told the officers, who handcuffed him and started walking him to the jail next door.

"Where are you taking him?" Rodney asked.

The officers said they were moving Wayne somewhere safe, where he couldn't hurt anyone, until they could figure out what was going on.

Another officer took Rodney to the lieutenant's office.

Contrary to Gainey and Thomas's testimony, Freeman's investigative report confirmed Rodney's recollection that Wayne "pulled [the breast] out of his jacket pocket and handed it to Deputy Gainey and Sgt. Thomas."

Rodney wouldn't learn until a year later that the breast did not belong to Wayne's first victim, but his fourth. There were some things he just didn't want to know, so he hadn't read the newspaper or watched the TV news to find out.

A decade later, Rodney was still wondering what happened to the surveillance tape from the camera he saw in the sheriff's lobby, which he believed captured Wayne's repeated requests for an attorney.

If there was such a tape, Rodney said, it was "probably conveniently lost. . . . They didn't want to look stupid or like Barney Fife."

* * *

Detective Juan Freeman said that as far as he knows, that camera was only for observation purposes. If there had been a videotape, he said, he would have entered it as evidence.

Freeman acknowledged that "Mr. Ford asked for an attorney a whole bunch of times" in the lobby. However, he said, a suspect has to be in custody and under interrogation for that request to be valid.

"When Mr. Ford was asking for a lawyer [in the lobby], there was no interrogation taking place," he said, explaining that questions about booking information, such as name and address, don't meet the legal standard.

Freeman said Wayne invoked his right to an attorney during their first interview, so they stopped talking, but Wayne waived that right numerous times after talking to his brother.

"My belief is that Rodney is the hero of the case because he did the right thing [by bringing him in]," Freeman said.

Freeman, who was the detective on call for the weekend, was eating dinner and watching the news with his wife, Lynn, when he got the call from Sergeant Thomas around 6:30 P.M.

Freeman suggested they arrest Wayne on suspicion of mayhem so they could hold him until Freeman could get to the station.

The detective threw on his work clothes, and after arriving at the office around 7:00 P.M., Gainey and Thomas briefed him in more depth about what had transpired in the lobby.

Freeman asked to examine the notorious plastic bag;

then he had Thomas arrange for the DOJ crime lab in Eureka to collect the evidence and preserve it properly for trial. After speaking briefly with Rodney, Freeman went to talk to Wayne.

Freeman's interview with Wayne, which began at 7:47 P.M., lasted less than ten minutes.

"What Rod told me was that you had some things that you wanted to get off your chest, and he told me that you probably wouldn't have come in if he didn't bring you," Freeman said.

Freeman asked Wayne some basic questions about where he lived and kept his belongings so that Freeman could write up search warrant affidavits.

Wayne explained that he lived in the trailer park in Arcata, but spent little time there.

"I mean, I live there, but I never go there, 'cause I'm on the road," he said.

Getting right to the point, Freeman said, "It's obviously a female's breast, and you had that in your pocket. Your brother said that you said that that was just the tip of the iceberg, and you . . . didn't want to hurt anybody else. Is that right? You're nodding your head, yes?"

After mumbling his answer twice, Wayne finally spoke loud enough for the tape recorder to pick it up: "Yes."

"Okay. And the other thing that we need to clear up is that you did mention something about an attorney?"

"I need an attorney," Wayne said. "My brother said I need an attorney."

"Your brother said you need an attorney?"

"Yes."

Freeman explained that that meant he couldn't ask Wayne any more questions.

"I mean, obviously, there's a woman out there missing a breast. Or maybe more? . . . We don't know what else you might have done. You know, what other families you

may have hurt. And if you . . . need an attorney, there is
no way you're going to be able to clear your conscience,
so, I mean, that's okay. That's your right. But if you need
to get something off your chest and clear your conscience and maybe try to help some families and some
people that you've hurt, then you need to decide that
you don't want an attorney and you want to talk to me,
but that's strictly up to you. . . . I'm certainly not going
to try and twist your arm. . . . If you still feel like you need
an attorney, that will stop everything right now and
[we'll] just go from there. So it's up to you, Wayne."

"I need an attorney."

With that, Freeman told Gainey to walk Wayne back to
the jail and book him for mayhem; then he went back
to interview Rodney about the events leading up to their
arrival at the sheriff's department.

Meanwhile, Wayne went through the booking process
in another part of the jail.

After talking with Rodney, Freeman called Jim Dawson,
the chief investigator for the district attorney, to get some
help preparing search warrants for Wayne's campsite,
trailer, and motel room.

As Correctional Officer Anne Goldsmith filled out
Wayne's intake form, she asked if he had taken any drugs
or been drinking that day.

Wayne shook his head. "I just don't want to hurt anybody," he said.

A white-haired officer, Sergeant Larry Wolfe, came in
wearing latex gloves to assist Goldsmith and introduced
himself to Wayne as Larry.

"Have you ever thought of suicide?" Goldsmith asked.

"Yes," Wayne said.

"Are you, like, having suicidal thoughts right now?"

"No, you guys are going to kill me."

"We're not going to kill you."

"Yes," Wayne said, nodding.

"No, I don't like to kill people. I've never killed anyone.
I don't even kill animals. I can't even squash a spider. . . .
You're not feeling suicidal right now?" Goldsmith an-
swered.

"No."

Goldsmith asked when he last felt suicidal and Wayne
paused, as if he were having trouble answering.

"When my . . ."

"It's okay," Wolfe said reassuringly.

"I'm sorry," Goldsmith said, patting Wayne on the
shoulder.

"It's okay," Wolfe said again.

Wayne, who had started crying, choked out, "M-m . . .
when my wife, when my wife took my baby from me."

"Oh, how long ago was that?" Goldsmith asked.

"Two, two, three years ago."

Their conversation, which was interrupted by a voice
over the loudspeaker, became disjointed. Wayne had a
tendency to be a low-talker and mumble, so some of his
responses couldn't be heard on the videotape and also
didn't make their way into the transcript.

"I haven't been thinking good for a long time and it's
getting worse," Wayne said, trying to explain his slow
responses in what would be a constant refrain over the
next few days.

"Mr. Ford, excuse me," Goldsmith said to Wayne, who
seemed distracted. "Do you know where you are right
now?"

"It's where I should be."

"Where is that? What is this place, do you know?"

"This is your jail."

Wolfe started patting down Wayne, warning that he was going to take off Wayne's knitted cap.

"What's your first name?" Wolfe asked.

"I go by Adam," Wayne said.

Because Wayne was wearing a camouflage jacket, Wolfe asked if he was in the military. Wayne replied that he had been in the marines.

As Wolfe helped Wayne take off his street clothes, the deputies discussed that he needed to go into a padded cell when they were finished. Meanwhile, Wolfe kept trying to keep Wayne calm.

"I'm glad I was here to meet you, you seem like a nice guy," Wolfe said. "Just relax. Just relax."

The sergeant had Wayne sit on the floor, where he leaned against the wall with his knees bent as he slowly and deliberately took off his socks and boots. Wayne looked dazed, as if it were difficult to complete even this simple task.

Asked again about drug use or medical problems, Wayne said, "Just my head."

Wayne said he'd tried seeking psychiatric help at a local clinic a year or two earlier, but "it didn't do any good."

"What was it for?" Goldsmith asked. "Did you have a specific diagnosis or anything that you remember?"

"I was losing my . . . my ability to concentrate. I used to be pretty smart, but . . . I'm not anymore and I think I wanted them to give me something for depression because I heard they have medications. 'Cause I just have to get undepressed. Clear my head up."

But, Wayne said, they told him at the clinic that he didn't need any antidepressants.

Throughout the process, Wolfe was gentle and respectful with Wayne. When he started to cry again, Wolfe kneeled down and comforted him.

"It's okay, Wayne."

"I hurt people. I didn't really want to, but I hurt people. That's why you guys are just going to keep me. God's the only, the only thing left," he said, nodding. "I am ready to die. I'm not going to kill myself."

"Good. There's no need for you to die," Wolfe said, his gloved hand resting on Wayne's knee. "Nobody's asking for your life."

"Sometimes things are right and sometimes the same things are wrong," Wayne said cryptically. "And sometimes they're right again, and I can't figure it out."

"Sometimes life is very complicated."

"But my brother helped me."

"That's what family is for."

"He's a good brother. I'm okay."

"Do you have an attorney?"

"No, no, I need, my brother said I shouldn't say anything without one."

"Right," Wolfe said.

Deputy Gainey, who had come in with another sergeant, explained that some people were going to talk to Wayne, but it was up to him to decide how much he wanted to say without an attorney present.

"Obviously, they don't have access to a mainstream attorney right now," Gainey said. "But what they'll do is advise you of your rights, and . . . if I were you . . . you can take the advice of your brother and just say you want an attorney present before you even talk to anyone."

Wolfe then had Wayne strip down to the buff before he put on a jail-issued orange jumpsuit.

"Adam, I spoke with the other officer that was over in the lobby with us. And he's with your brother now, and he wanted me to tell you that your brother said he loved you."

Now dressed in his jail garb, Wayne walked down a

hallway with Gainey and into a secure cell by himself. Wayne asked for a Bible.

After talking to Freeman, Rodney asked to speak to Wayne, so the deputies let them talk in the visiting room, where they were separated by Plexiglas. Their conversation was taped by a hidden recorder.

"They were kind of mad I told you to get an attorney, but I had no idea how bad this was," Rodney said. "I thought maybe you just beat somebody up or broke somebody's arms or something. Shoot . . . the detectives told me that, unfortunately, at this point, because you do want an attorney, there's nothing they can do, and that they're, they're charging you with—I can't remember what it was—malicious mischief or something. Because you said, you know, you cut off, had a woman's tit. I know you don't want to get out."

"I don't belong out, and this is weird," Wayne said. "This is nuts."

"I don't know anything about what an attorney's going to tell you . . . but if you want to . . . make it right with God, and make it right with yourself . . . ," Rodney said, trailing off. "They don't even know if you're telling the truth or not. . . , They said that that breast is really, doesn't mean anything, because they don't know where you got it. . . . It doesn't prove anything."

"What do you think I should do?" Wayne asked. "Do you think I should just wait for an attorney?"

"I'm going to go back down and . . . tell them to come back and talk to you again. But you need to let them know if there's somebody that needs help."

"I need help."

"I know you need help."

They talked a bit more about what the police were

going to do next; then Wayne said, "I don't know. I think I'll just keep your advice. . . . The attorneys know what to say, but I can't, I can't keep things in order."

Rodney asked if there was someone out there who was hurt and needed help—meaning a woman, one of Wayne's victims.

"No. It's too late."

"So that's, ah, that's a done deal."

"Yeah, I didn't mean to," Wayne said.

"I know. I just want you to know I love you. Okay? . . . Hang in there."

"Yeah. I belong here."

"Well . . ."

"I do. Because I can't stop. You know, what's going on in my head, I couldn't stop. I love you."

"I love you, too."

"I know this is hard for you. . . . What the most important thing is—I stay here, you know?"

"Yeah. Well . . . the best thing to do is when they do get you an attorney is listen to him and cooperate as much as you can, you know. So that they can . . . figure things out."

"They got mad at you?" Wayne asked.

"Well, it's okay."

"But I heard 'em, when they shut the door, they said, 'It's his f***ing brother.'"

"I had no idea of—of how bad this was. I mean, I thought you just, you know, maybe beat somebody up or something. That's why I said you should get an attorney."

"Well, I just didn't think you should know. . . . I didn't think you really wanted to know. I know that you're going to find out, but, well, I wanted to spend some time with you."

Rodney started getting ready to leave, saying he was tired and needed to get some rest.

"Just don't do anything stupid," he said.

"I've had more than a lifetime's quota of stupid things, I know that," Wayne said. "It's really kind of funny, because I can't always . . . determine what I should do and what I shouldn't do. Whether it's right or whether it's wrong. Whether it's good or whether it's bad. And even when I make up my mind, I can't keep it made up, okay. I think that this is permanent here. Home."

"If . . . you . . . believe in God . . . ," Rodney said.

"I believe in God," Wayne said.

" . . . and believe in, in letting him help you. . . ."

"It's up to him. I sure don't know what to do."

"If you want to stay in here, I mean, if you don't want to be let out, you're going to have to help him to help you."

"You mean they're going to try to let me out of here?" Wayne said, astonished.

"Well, they don't have anything."

"It wasn't *mine*," Wayne said, apparently referring to the breast in his pocket.

"I know, I know," Rodney said. "Just read the Bible and do what you think is best."

"That's what I'm going to do. I'm going to talk to an attorney. If they let me out—I'll just come back in, because something's . . . got to stay still. And I don't want my baby to be an orphan. You know, he's lost his father."

The two of them debated the issue a bit longer.

"You told me today that . . . you've been a coward, right?" Rodney asked.

"Yeah," Wayne replied.

"Don't be one anymore."

"You don't think I should wait for an attorney?"

"I just think that there's other people out there that are probably hurting because they don't know. You know what I mean?" Rodney asked, referring to the victims' families.

"Yeah."

"And it would be like me losing one of my daughters

and not knowing. . . . I mean, an attorney legally is going to get you the help you need. But still, right now, on your own, you should help them so that they can help the rest of the people . . . because that's what . . . God would want you to do."

"Okay," Wayne said. "You want me to do that, I'll do that."

"So, if I go down there and tell them to come back and talk to you, I mean for them to take you seriously, I mean, you're going to have to tell them some things that they can—"

"Okay."

"Wouldn't you want to know?" Rodney asked.

CHAPTER 16

"I HAD TO MAKE HER SMALL"

After Rodney told Freeman that Wayne was ready to talk to him again, the detective brought Wayne to one of the jailhouse interview rooms that was essentially a ten-foot-square echo chamber, made out of cinder block, with a round table and several chairs in the middle. He also brought Gainey and a small portable tape recorder with him.

Based on the tenor of this interview and those that followed in the next couple of days with detectives from the three other counties involved, Wayne appeared to be of two conflicting minds. On the one hand, he wanted to get an attorney to protect himself legally, because he did not feel confident enough to do so on his own. But at the same time, he seemed to want to say enough to satisfy his brother and the detectives, and his reported desire to do the right thing by God, regardless of the circumstances. He seemed to know up front, no matter what he said, that he was going to be punished and that life as he knew it had ended.

What remains unclear is Wayne's understanding of his rights under the law, and whether he was simply too confused—or mentally unstable—to decide when to stop talking without an attorney present, because once he got started, he just kept going.

Years later, Joe Canty, Wayne's defense attorney, would argue, citing an opinion by a psychologist retained by Wayne's first attorney, that "the defendant's mental state was significantly impaired" at the time of the interviews. Canty noted that Wayne was being held in a "safety cell," where he was, essentially, on suicide watch.

Deborah Davis, a psychology professor from the University of Nevada in Reno, and an expert in police interrogation tactics, testified at a hearing in 2003 that after reading transcripts of these sessions, she determined that Wayne was tired, confused, and coerced by investigators.

"Everything he said was consistent with him not being able to think clearly," she said.

But the investigators and prosecutors—with whom the court would subsequently agree—maintained that Wayne understood enough to waive his right to an attorney during the initial interviews.

It was 9:12 P.M. when Freeman started their second interview.

Wayne was so soft-spoken at times that Freeman could barely hear him. Other times his words disintegrated into tears and became inaudible. As a result, the transcriber often couldn't make out what Wayne said on the tape, which left gaps in his statements.

When asked about a topic he didn't want to discuss,

such as the specifics of how he murdered these women, he'd look down and avoid Freeman's gaze, his affect depressed and his voice flat. He became more animated, however, when he talked about details unrelated to the women's deaths.

"I wouldn't say he felt remorse, but I do think he felt bad," Freeman recalled later.

Freeman tried to keep Wayne talking by maintaining an air of compassion, understanding, and sympathy.

"I was called by jail staff and they told me that you had decided that you wanted to talk to me," Freeman said. "Is that right?"

"My brother told me I should talk to you," Wayne said.

Freeman read Wayne his Miranda rights—his right to remain silent and his right to an attorney—and Wayne said that he understood them.

"Okay," Freeman said. "And do you still want to talk about what happened?"

"Yeah."

"So the question is . . . who does that breast belong to that you brought in here?"

Wayne said he didn't know, mumbling something about the 395 and 15 freeways and the California Aqueduct. "That's where the rest of her is."

Wayne explained that there was a truck stop close to the area where he put her body, near Adelanto or Victorville or Hesperia, in southern California. He said he didn't know her name, but she was a prostitute. As he was trying to remember more about her, he blurted out something else that grabbed Freeman's attention.

"There was a girl in the slough."

"In Eureka? That was you?" Freeman asked. "That was the one that was found a year ago."

Freeman left the room with Gainey for a second and came back with a California map, so Wayne could help them locate exactly where he'd dumped the woman with the missing breast.

"But you just told me that there was a girl in the slough, correct? Is, is that right, Wayne?"

"Yes."

"That was you that killed that girl?"

Wayne mumbled something.

"It's okay," Freeman said.

"I didn't mean to."

"You didn't mean to? . . . Was it an accident?"

"Sort of."

Wayne said he didn't know who the first woman was, only that he had picked her up on Broadway in Eureka, and that she had some sort of nickname he couldn't remember. He couldn't recall exactly where she was from, but he said it was out of state.

"I hope this helps," Wayne said.

With a little more coaxing, Wayne said she was white, weighed about 150 pounds, and was about five feet six inches tall.

Freeman explained that he knew this would be difficult for Wayne, but it was very important that he describe what he did to the woman he put in the slough so that Freeman could verify that Wayne didn't just read about her in the newspaper.

"Whoever killed her did some things to her that only I know about and the person knows about," Freeman said. "So you mind telling me?"

"I had to make her small so she would fit better."

"Okay."

"I cut her head off. I cut her breasts off. Her arms, her legs. I tried opening things up."

"You tried to open her up? Okay, and how did you do that?"

Wayne said he cut her down the middle with a razor

blade, then cut off her arms, legs, and head with a knife, which was now at his campsite in Trinidad. He said he stored the thighs in his freezer until recently, when he buried them at the foot of a stump about thirty feet from his tent and covered the hole with leaves.

Freeman asked if the arm found on Clam Beach several months later was from the same person.

"I think so. The funny thing is . . . it washed off the island there. And I don't know who else is doing what else around here, you know," Wayne said, suggesting there might be another killer at work in the area.

"Hasn't she come up as somebody missing?" Wayne asked.

Freeman said he'd looked at thousands of missing persons reports over the past year. "Actually, the 'Torso Girl' was my case. I've been working on it ever since she was found."

"What, are you a homicide detective?" Wayne asked.

"Yes, I am. I thank you and I thank God . . . because it's really been bothering me for a year. My wife and I have both been praying every night that this case gets solved. And we both knew that it would be nothing great that I did, it would be that whoever . . ."

"God did it," Wayne said, interrupting.

"God would send the responsible party. And he did, and I—I thank him for that, 'cause I think that's his work."

"It is," Wayne said. "I hope you can identify her."

Wayne added that she was about twenty-five years old, had a tattooed band of roses around her ankle, and seemed like she was on drugs. "I really think her brain was fried."

Wayne also said she looked like the Eureka teenage girl who had gone missing around the same time.

"It's not Karen Mitchell?" Freeman asked.

Wayne said no, but they had common features. He said

he also wasn't responsible for the death of the Samoan girl who'd been in the news recently.

"I was wondering, you know, what's going on. . . . I'm obviously losing my marbles, but thinking I'm not alone here," he said, referring again to another killer.

"I need to know how this girl died," Freeman said. "There were some other things done to her that—that you haven't told me about, right?"

Wayne blurted out another non sequitur, admitting that he had been arrested for killing a dog about five years earlier. He claimed that it was an accident, but even though he told a police officer that he'd shot the animal in self-defense, his report stated that Wayne "killed him because I wanted to."

Freeman tried to reassure him that he wouldn't and couldn't put words in Wayne's mouth, not with a tape recorder running.

"I want to help her, okay?" Wayne said.

"You're helping."

"I want to help you find out who that girl is. . . . It's extremely important to me. . . . I know where her head is, but I don't know if it's still there."

"Where?" Freeman asked. "Where is that?"

Wayne explained that he burned her clothes in the incinerator at the Readimix cement plant, where he used to work in Arcata, then put her head, lower legs, and arms in a nearby sandbar along the Mad River.

"I buried them in, buried and pushed and put them in the sand . . . and then the rains came."

"If the arm washed away, the head might've washed away, too, don't you think?" Freeman asked.

Wayne said he didn't know, but he had placed a foot-square piece of cement on top of her body parts, which he thought should still be there.

Freeman said the best way to identify the girl would be

to find her teeth and then track down her family through dental records.

"Would you want to take a trip out there and show us?"

"If you want me to," Wayne said.

Freeman asked if there were any more body parts in Wayne's trailer. He also asked a number of other questions, but couldn't get a straight answer out of Wayne, whose sentences were growing increasingly incoherent.

"Except for, I didn't know how to get rid of, you know," Wayne said. "After it happened, I panicked. In the trailer, I panicked, and I think I was already getting real messed up more than I am right now."

Clearly, something bad had happened in that trailer and Freeman wanted the details. But Wayne seemed incapable or unwilling to be more specific.

When Freeman asked Wayne again whether he would show investigators where he put the body parts in the river, Wayne responded with his own question.

"You willing to have an attorney along?" he asked.

"Anytime you want an attorney, we—we'll stop," Freeman said.

"Can't we just get the attorney and do all this, too?"

"No."

"Why?"

"Well, because what will happen is the attorney will tell you not to talk to me anymore," Freeman said, chuckling. "That's what attorneys do. As soon as you retain an attorney, the first thing the attorney tells you is, 'Don't talk to the deputy sheriffs or the investigators or the police.'"

"Well, I suppose if I was trying to weasel out of doing something that I did wrong somehow, that . . . ," Wayne said, mumbling something.

"Get an attorney?" Freeman asked.

"Yes. But I'm not trying to weasel out on anything. I

turned myself in. But I don't think very good, and I take my advice from my brother."

Freeman told him that as soon as Wayne mentioned the word "attorney," that Freeman had to be very careful, "because we have to make sure that if you want an attorney that—that we stop and get you one. So you have to be able to convince us that you really want help."

"I wanna help, but I can't fix anything," Wayne said. "What really screwed my head up, I know is, a, to cause the pain inside. It's not something to me physically, I don't know what it is, but it's got me in, it's got me crippled inside. It's taken some kind of physical damage on me. Holding things in too long."

Wayne cried, saying he understood that he'd caused pain to the women's families, too. "Every day they hurt. Because of me, they're suffering. So the less suffering, the quicker they know."

Wayne said he might have kept the breast in his truck refrigerator for a week or two, but he couldn't keep track of time very well.

Freeman had been waiting for the right moment to ask about the other victims he suspected were still out there. "You're probably expecting this—is there anyone else?"

"Yeah," Wayne said.

"How many would you say?"

"Two."

"Two others? And do you remember where these people . . ."

Wayne said he was trying to recall where he'd picked up the woman he'd put in the aqueduct, but he was having trouble. It was somewhere near an air force base, near where he'd made a pickup at a cement plant.

Freeman tried again to get Wayne to focus. "You feel like talking about the—the two others that you mentioned?"

"Ah, no, I can't."

"Can't think of it?"

"I don't know what I'm doing. My brain's not working right."

Wayne said he'd never done drugs, except some marijuana as a teenager. The pot made his mind come and go, sort of like what was happening to him now, only different. Sometimes, he said, he could concentrate and "sometimes I wander out to lunch." This had become a problem in his truck driving job, because there were times he couldn't even fill out the logbook, where he was supposed to record the miles he drove, along with his drop-offs and pickups.

"I used to be able to calculate in my head. Two- and four-digit numbers and problems. I never used a calculator in my whole life. Now I have to use a calculator just to do my log. Just really simple, simple stuff."

"Yeah, your brother told me, you had a really highly technical job with the service and everything," Freeman said.

"Was the best thing I ever did."

Freeman asked if one event had triggered things, perhaps something traumatic.

Initially, Wayne said there were two events—getting kicked out of the marines and his divorce. But then he said he actually had no idea.

"I couldn't play no more," he said, crying. "I had to fake like I was happy. Got so people didn't even want to be around me. I stopped sleeping right. . . . I didn't eat right. Started drinking at a prostitute bar . . . and darkness. Every time I'd see a little baby, it just ties me up in knots, and they're everywhere. . . . I love little babies. . . . They'll kill you with an enzyme."

"Sometimes, yeah," Freeman said, as if he understood. "So, before that, did you ever kill anybody, or was it after that, that this started?"

Wayne repeated that he didn't mean to, that he "tried to revive them."

"Some didn't die," he said.

Freeman asked if he meant that they got away.

"I let them go," Wayne said, crying harder now. "I didn't want to kill anybody. I just feel certain, certain things— I don't know what they are. Certain things, you know, it just makes me freeze up. I just want everything to stop."

"'Cause you strangle them?" Freeman asked.

"No," Wayne said.

"So you'd suffocate them?"

Freeman kept trying to get Wayne to discuss how he'd killed these women, but Wayne was either incapable or unwilling to be more specific.

"I know . . . I'm a killer. . . . [When I was young, if] I stepped on a bug, I'd cry, when somebody told somebody to go, I'd cry. . . . I felt bad. I was too sensitive. I was always sensitive like that."

Freeman asked if Wayne was too tired to keep talking.

"Yeah, I'm tired," Wayne said. "I can't be crying and shit."

Wayne said he didn't think he could say anything more to help, but Freeman figured he'd try one more time to learn more about the other two women. Wayne said he thought he'd picked one up in northern California and another in southern California, but he couldn't remember more than that without getting some sleep.

The taped portion of this interview with Freeman lasted a little more than an hour, but Freeman said they spoke for another twenty-five minutes or so after the tape ran out. He decided against stopping to get another tape because he didn't want to lose the momentum. It was lucky he didn't—lucky for the investigation, anyway—because Wayne showed him on the map where he'd picked up the three women and dumped their bodies.

Freeman told Wayne that he'd been looking at a suspect in Washington who was a necrophiliac. (The actual term, according to *Merriam-Webster's Medical Dictionary*, is "necrophile.")

"What's a necrophiliac?" Wayne asked.

"He has his fun after the girls are dead," Freeman explained.

Wayne said he could identify with that. "He's a sick man," he said.

Freeman found it curious that Wayne made a big deal of the fact that the "Torso Girl" was his first victim. But at the time, he didn't take anything Wayne said at face value.

"Nothing is ever as it appears to be or as it's told to you," Freeman said later.

However, he said, "I suppose all serial killers have to have a first one."

Freeman walked Wayne back to the jail and booked him for murder, telling the guards to keep an eye on him, because he seemed depressed. Freeman was concerned that Wayne might become self-destructive.

The detective believed that Wayne—and others like him—cut up and did other bizarre things to their victims' bodies so as to objectify them.

"They don't want to think about the victim as a human being," he said.

Typically, he said, their motivations were sexual, but they also liked to keep trophies or souvenirs of their crimes.

Wayne said he'd buried Jane Doe's body parts to get rid of the evidence that he'd killed her, but Freeman didn't believe him.

"I think it was sexual, definitely," he said.

Darryl Long, a psychiatric technician assigned to the jail, was called back to work from home that night to meet with Wayne, who was housed in a cell, five feet square, in the booking area. His job was to evaluate whether Wayne was suicidal and should be placed in a safety cell.

Long and the other officers who had talked to Wayne that night were concerned about his roller-coaster emotional state. He'd be fine one minute, then break down into tears the next. He seemed to have problems gathering and articulating his thoughts, and he kept making suicidal references.

Wayne held up a Bible and said something like, "You know, I've committed every sin in here except killing myself." He also said he deserved to be dead.

Long decided to move Wayne to a padded cell in the medical unit, and put him on suicide watch. The cell was five feet square, with a hole in the floor to use as a toilet. It had no bed or sheets, just a wraparound blanket. Wayne stayed there for two nights, and was prescribed Haldol and Ativan to calm him down, and Cogentin to counteract the Haldol's side effects.

Meanwhile, Freeman sent two deputies to secure Wayne's campsite so that he, Dawson, and an evidence technician could comb through it in the morning and retrieve the pair of thighs belonging to his Jane Doe.

When Gainey wrote up his report that night, he stated that Wayne was being held for 187 PC (murder) and 205 PC (mayhem), with a "possible 187 PC from out of the area also."

Referring to the breast in Wayne's pocket, he wrote, "Unknown female victim—to be identified."

CHAPTER 17

"PUNISH ME"

Around 9:00 A.M. on November 4, Detective Juan Freeman sent out a teletype to every police agency in the western states, describing Wayne and the women he'd confessed to killing:

"We have subject in custody for homicide. He has confessed to three other homicides of females. The most recent victim within the last two weeks came from Lucerne Valley. One female from Las Vegas. Both of them white. The third female, a Mexican or Indian, came from the Ontario, CA area. Dump sites: he believes he dumped one body near a truck stop in the Adelanto area of San Bernardino County, unknown when. He believes he dumped the Mexican or Indian female in or near an irrigation ditch near Lodi off of Highway 12, near either I-5 or Highway 99. He believes the Las Vegas female was put in the northern part of the California Aqueduct, unknown time. Subject: Ford, Wayne Adam, goes by Adam. WMA 6'2", 200, Haz, Bro, DOB/120361. Truck Driver."

The transmission was meant to be confidential—i.e., not media fodder—but Freeman later heard that an officer in nearby Redding, who was dating a reporter, relayed that information to his girlfriend, and that was that.

Later that morning, Freeman joined the team that was processing Wayne's campsite, where the ground was soggy and damp from the seasonal rain. By the time they'd finished, the investigators had collected a vast array of items from in and around the tent—176, all told.

The interior of the two-person domed tent was strewn with clothing and accessories, either contained in black plastic bags or spilling out of them. Next to the sleeping bag and air mattress was a large plastic ice chest that held several knives, including a thirteen-inch serrated hunting knife, a steak knife, and Scott Hayes's hunting knife. Inside a dark blue backpack they found a book titled *Blessings,* some women's shorts, a rosary, and a comb. In a small cooler they found a crucifix and a purple box of audiotapes labeled: Holy Bible, King James version.

They also found a rifle; a hard-core porno magazine; some Bic lighters; black shoe polish; a leather purse; blue-green and red-and-black ropes; Camel cigarettes; cans of tuna, beef stew and chili; garlic salt; a jar of decaf coffee; a wool face mask; a canister of 17 percent pepper spray; a pair of diving fins; camp gloves; mosquito netting; a pair of binoculars; $14.21 in coins; a black belt with a Marine Corps buckle; a guitar in a case; and some tools.

Outside, they found a hatchet, which criminalist Toby Baxter from the state DOJ lab in Eureka took with him to examine for traces of blood. Later, they sent the hatchet and knives, a hacksaw found at Wayne's trailer, and some of Jane Doe's bone pieces to the Los Angeles

County Department of Coroner to determine whether these implements had been used to cut her up.

They also found several blue tarps, a plastic bucket containing water, a sponge, and a dinner plate, and several more porno magazines, wet from the rain.

However, the thighs were nowhere to be found.

The same day, the sheriff's department issued a news release announcing that Wayne Adam Ford, a thirty-six-year-old Arcata man, had been arrested. Still attempting to keep the specific details under wraps and out of the media, the release stated:

"On Tuesday evening November 3, 1998, a subject came to our office in Eureka, asking to speak with officers concerning his possible criminal activities. The subject subsequently provided our officers with information concerning the human torso case. Based upon information attained from the subject, and some physical evidence discovered that helps to corroborate his story, the subject was arrested and booked on a charge of murder."

Nonetheless, news of the breast in Wayne's pocket soon spread.

A series of detectives, trying to solve similar murders in their areas, responded to Freeman's teletype in the coming days.

"Everyone is taking a look at him because his method of killing matches so many cases," Kern County sheriff's Sergeant Glenn Johnson in Bakersfield told the *Associated Press,* an international wire service also known as the AP.

Investigators from Vallejo, where a prostitute had been stabbed in November 1995, were among those who visited Eureka. About three weeks before he turned himself in, Wayne had been cited for driving his truck through a red-light area in Vallejo that was not an authorized truck route.

He also looked like a candidate for the death of a woman whose body was found in the aqueduct in Palmdale, in Los Angeles County, in August 1997.

Defense attorneys got in the act, too. Mark Topel, who represented convicted wife-killer Lawrence Angelel, claimed that Wayne, not his client, was responsible for murdering and beheading Lawrence's late wife, Lonna, whose truck was found at a truck stop in Eureka the day after she disappeared in December 1995.

But none of these women's deaths was ever attributed to Wayne.

Years later, Freeman said he suspected there were "lots of unresolved victims" Wayne never disclosed to authorities. He'd sensed that Wayne felt it was okay to admit he'd killed hookers, but not nice girls from nice families.

Following up on the missing thighs, Freeman and Dawson interviewed Wayne again around 2:00 P.M. on November 4, this time in an empty office in the detective bureau.

The acoustics were much better there, and given Wayne's tendency to drop his voice, Freeman figured the room would improve the tape's sound quality.

During the fifty-five-minute interview, Wayne seemed more rested and a bit more upbeat than he had the night before. Wayne tried to explain why he didn't make sense sometimes. It wasn't that he was lying, he said, he just couldn't remember things very well.

"If something that I say doesn't sound right, I'm not telling it to you untruthfully as I recall," Wayne said.

"Well, you know, last night I knew you were doing the best you could to remember everything and tell me," Freeman said, hoping to get him to go deeper.

"I figure I'm probably going to die," Wayne said, "which is what I want, but I'm not going to kill myself."

"Well, that's good!"

"I told them that, but they . . . don't want to believe it," Wayne said, referring to the jail officials.

"So you . . . want the system to do its job and—"

"Punish me."

"Yeah, okay."

Detective Freeman reminded Wayne that he'd advised him of his constitutional rights the night before and asked if he wanted to keep talking. "You remember that? Does that still—is that still true as far as you're concerned? You still want to cooperate and . . ."

"Yes."

". . . help us. Okay. Good enough, Jim?" Freeman asked Dawson to make sure his bases were covered. Dawson said he'd better read Wayne his rights one more time, so Freeman did so, and Wayne agreed to keep talking.

As they went over details of his first victim again, Wayne said she was on the chunky side. "She'd be fat if she was any heavier. . . . She had kind of . . . a chubby look to her face."

He also said he was in a car when he picked her up, not his big rig. He thought it was on October 14 or 15 of 1997.

Freeman tried again to get details of how Wayne actually killed her. "Do you remember what happened after you picked her up?"

"I don't know," Wayne said.

"You don't want to talk about it?"

"That part."

"Okay."

"What if I just tell you she wasn't a prostitute?" Wayne said, apparently hoping that would suffice.

But Freeman wanted more, so he got Wayne to repeat that he had killed her—albeit accidentally. He asked if she was dead when Wayne cut off her head and limbs.

"Yes," Wayne said simply.

Freeman explained that he had to ask these questions because it was the only way to find out what happened, but he understood how hard it was for Wayne to talk about it.

"I hate to put you through this, but I just have to. Okay?"

"No, you don't."

"Hmm?"

"It's kind of you to say that, though."

Freeman said he needed more details to make his case stronger, and he asked again what Wayne did to the victim. But Wayne wouldn't budge.

Freeman was able to learn, however, a more exact location of where Wayne had dumped the torso—near the Ryan Slough Bridge on Myrtle Avenue before it turned into Old Arcata Road.

"That's when I was going to turn myself in," Wayne said.

"Okay. And what . . . changed your mind?"

"How they treated me over at the mental-health place."

Freeman asked if they treated him poorly.

"The first guy I talked to was fine, but the next guy, he was just—he had someplace else to be. It was just his attitude was . . ."

"Who cares?"

"Yeah . . . turning yourself in is not an easy thing to do."

"True. Very, very true," Freeman replied.

"Wouldn't take a great deal to change your mind."

After discussing Wayne's work history in the Eureka area, Freeman moved on to what he really wanted to know.

"So you think the bears might have got the thighs that you had up there at your camp?" he asked.

Wayne said they might have. "Did you look in the wrong place?"

Freeman asked Wayne again if he would be willing to show investigators where he'd put them. Wayne said he was concerned about getting his clothes wet, so Freeman promised to get him some dry ones when they were finished.

"So you're the ones who . . . [are] going to put me in the hot seat?" Wayne asked.

"No."

"That's where I belong, isn't it?"

"I'm only glad you chose to turn yourself in," Dawson said, trying to forge his own relationship with Wayne. "We all belong in the hot seat. We've all done things wrong."

At this point, Dawson took over the questioning, starting with the basics: where Wayne was born, went to school, his time in the Marine Corps, and his previous relationships.

Wayne described his quick rise and fall in the marines.

"How did you do that?" Dawson said, laughing.

"Divorced . . . it's a long story."

Wayne said he didn't know when the depression started, but it began affecting his life to where he couldn't fight or control it, and so he got kicked out of the military.

As he talked about his most recent marriage and his son, Max, he made a cryptic allusion to what his friend Scott thought was a suicide attempt while Wayne sat in his garage with his El Camino running.

"I was in some weird . . . I can't describe how it was," Wayne said. ". . . I thought it was an exhaust leak or something."

He said he felt kind of light-headed in the El Camino,

almost as if he weren't really there. Then, after he left Scott's, he picked up the hitchhiker in Eureka that night.

He said she told him she wanted to go to Clam Beach and that she was causing problems for her family. "She was pretty down on herself."

"Did she do anything to you, or say anything to you to get you upset?" Dawson asked.

Wayne mumbled something.

"What did she say?" Dawson asked.

Apparently upset by this question, Wayne started crying. "If I could, I don't, okay, I don't, I don't want to talk about that, okay!"

"I know you don't," Dawson said.

"I can't."

"Okay."

Still crying, Wayne said he wanted to help them identify her, but he was having trouble signing his own "death warrant."

"It's hard. I'm fighting the fact that I know, that I, I deserve probably to die for what I've done and there's this guy right here that's going to do the best to put me there. . . . I know that I'm risking a lot by doing what I'm doing without an attorney. . . . I know talking to you is legally a very dangerous thing."

"It's the right thing. That's what we're talking about here."

"It is the right thing and I want to do the right thing . . . but my brain doesn't work. I have a bunch of conflicts going on now. Two years ago, no problem. . . . Whatever broke, broke. Whatever snapped, snapped."

Dawson asked if Wayne had been taking any drugs at the time.

"No, I wish to hell I could have an excuse like that."

Dawson asked if Wayne had ever had any problems

with alcohol, and Wayne said, "I could never develop a problem. I drank and drank and drank, but—"

The tension in the room was broken for a moment as Dawson and Freeman both laughed.

Asked what the hitchhiker had been wearing, Wayne started mumbling again.

"Try to work with me on this, okay?" Dawson asked.

"Believe me, the day that you guys kill me, I hope, that that makes them feel better," Wayne said, referring to the families to whom the investigators kept referring.

"It isn't going to make anybody feel better."

Wayne said he still had her backpack in the tent, but there was no identification in it.

"I remember tennis shoes. Small size," Wayne said. "Her clothes were those pants that . . . I don't know what you would call them, they looked like clown pants to me."

"Jogging pants?" Freeman asked.

"Yeah, you know, like kinda baggy ones. . . . They were just a wild pattern. . . . They were bluish-green in color."

He said she was wearing layers, with a sports bra underneath a couple of other shirts, and a jacket. She was carrying a "John Wayne" can opener and a plastic bag, which he thought had drugs in it. She also had very large breasts.

He couldn't remember where she was from, but he thought it was somewhere like Arizona or Colorado.

"Where did you take her?"

"Do I have to?"

Freeman wanted Wayne to describe how and where he'd actually cut her up, reminding Wayne that he'd already admitted to putting "parts and pieces of her in different places." But Wayne wouldn't elaborate.

"Would it be safe to say that, that was Clam Beach? Where she died?"

"I don't know."

When Freeman asked if Wayne had taken her to his trailer, Wayne still wouldn't give them a straight answer.

"Don't do this to me anymore," he said, crying again.

"Okay, I'm sorry. Okay," Dawson said.

"I know I deserve it, but it's not going to help me think."

"I understand that your whole . . . attitude is that you want to try to remember these things," Freeman said. "And that's why, if we force it on you, it's going to cause you to not be able to remember. So we don't want to force anything on you."

"I want to do the right thing," Wayne said. "I hate to say this, because it's almost blasphemous for me to use God's name, because of who I am. But I want to do what's right by God."

"Well, so far you are," Freeman said, thinking that he really wanted to hammer on Wayne, but at the same time he didn't want him to shut down. "I'm a religious guy. So is Jim, actually. . . . We feel like you are doing the right thing. Maybe we should stop talking and take a ride. What you think? That sound good?"

Nearly a decade later, Wayne revealed a few more details about Jane Doe to the producers of a documentary, who posted this audio clip of Wayne's comments on their Web site (roomzerothemovie.com):

"She was probably . . . early twenties. . . . She's Caucasian, probably five-five, five-six, weighed anywhere from 140, 150 pounds. She was top-heavy. I believe she had brown eyes. She had a real plump face, almost—I hate to even use the word—but piggish-looking, with big cheeks. She had a backpack and a sleeping bag. She wore a multicolored knit cap over her brown hair . . . just below the ears. . . . She said that her sister loved her, when I asked her about people who cared about her. She was having trouble with her par-

Wayne and his older brother Rodney tussled around growing up, but they were always very close. They're shown here in Cotati, California in 1964. (Courtesy of the Ford family/By John McCutchen)

Wayne and Rodney, shown here in 1966, traveled around the United States and to Japan as their father moved to different assignments in the Army. (Courtesy of the Ford family)

Wayne's 1979 graduation photo from Marine Corps boot camp at Camp Pendleton in San Diego County.
(Courtesy of the Ford family)

Wayne, shown here in 1984, liked to ride his motorcycle fast and got into two accidents after suffering a head injury in 1980.
(Courtesy of the Ford family)

Wayne spent the day on November 2, 1998, playing pool and drinking in the bar at the Ocean Grove Lodge in Trinidad, waiting for his brother to arrive. *(Courtesy of Ron Fleshman)*

Wayne called Rodney from this pay phone next to Room Zero at the motel, where they stayed the night before Wayne turned himself in. *(Courtesy of Ron Fleshman)*

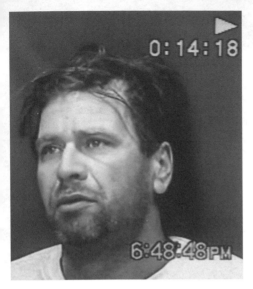

This is a frame from Wayne's booking video, filmed within an hour of his arrival at the sheriff's station in Eureka on November 3, 1998. *(Courtesy of the Humboldt County Sheriff's Department/ By Caitlin Rother)*

Wayne's booking photo. *(Courtesy of the Humboldt County Sheriff's Department/By John McCutchen)*

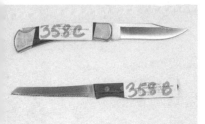

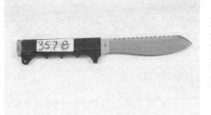

These items were collected as evidence from Wayne's tent.
*(Courtesy of the Humboldt County Sheriff's Department/
By John McCutchen)*

Wayne was driving this long-haul truck when he picked up his victims. *(Courtesy of the Humboldt County Sheriff's Department)*

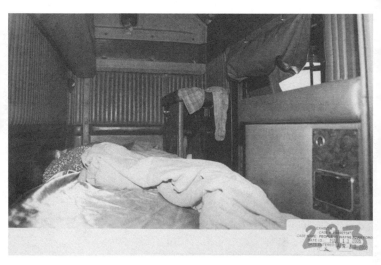

Wayne raped and strangled his victims in the sleeper of his truck.
*(Courtesy of the Humboldt County Sheriff's Department/
By John McCutchen)*

When he wasn't driving his truck, Wayne lived in this trailer in Arcata. *(Courtesy of the Humboldt County Sheriff's Department)*

Wayne kept this coffee can, filled with a substance rendered from baking his first victim's breasts, under his trailer's kitchen sink. *(Courtesy of the Humboldt County Sheriff's Department/By John McCutchen)*

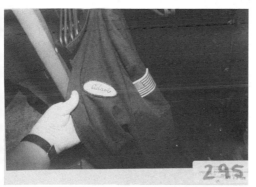

Wayne went by his middle name, Adam. *(Courtesy of the Humboldt County Sheriff's Department/By John McCutchen)*

The torso of Wayne's first victim was found here, in Ryan Slough in Eureka, in October 1997. *(Courtesy of the Humboldt County Sheriff's Department/By John McCutchen)*

Wayne lost his job at this cement and gravel plant before he got a job at Edeline Trucking. He buried some of his first victim's body parts in the Mad River behind the plant. *(Courtesy of the Humboldt County Sheriff's Department/By John McCutchen)*

Juan Freeman, now a retired sergeant from the Humboldt County Sheriff's Department, worked on the case of Wayne's first victim for a year before Wayne showed up at the sheriff's station in Eureka. *(By Brenda Godsey)*

Gary Rhoades, now a sergeant for the Kern County Sheriff's Department, worked on Tina Gibbs's case and spoke with her parents. *(Courtesy of the Kern County Sheriff's Department)*

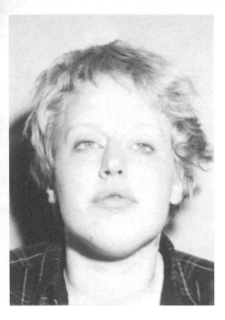

Tina Gibbs was working as a prostitute when Wayne picked her up in Las Vegas. He dumped her body in the California Aqueduct near Buttonwillow in Kern County, where it was found June 2, 1998. *(Courtesy of the Las Vegas Metropolitan Police Department)*

Rachel Holt, aka Sonoma County Doe, was the only one of Wayne's surviving victims to testify about her experiences in the black truck. *(By Ron Forbush/ John McCutchen)*

During his interview with detectives, Wayne said he picked up
Lanett White while she was walking along a road near this truck
stop in Fontana, which was a couple of miles from her house.
(By Caitlin Rother)

Patricia Tamez's body was found caught in this gate of the
California Aqueduct, which is near Hesperia in San Bernardino
County, on October 23, 1998. *(By Caitlin Rother)*

Mike Jones and Joe Herrera, now sergeants with the San Joaquin County Sheriff's Department, interviewed Wayne about the death of Lanett White. *(Courtesy of Vonda Kay Jones; San Joaquin Sheriff's Department)*

Frank Gonzales, now a lieutenant with the San Bernardino County Sheriff's Department, interviewed Wayne about the death of his last known victim, Patricia Tamez. *(Courtesy of Denise Cattern)*

David Mazurek, now a judge in San Bernardino County, prosecuted Wayne at trial in 2006, winning a conviction and a death sentence for the District Attorney's Office. *(By Caitlin Rother)*

San Bernardino County Superior Court Judge Michael Smith presided over Wayne's court proceedings, concluding with his sentencing on March 16, 2007. *(By John McCutchen)*

Wayne sits during his sentencing hearing with Joe Canty, his primary attorney from the Public Defender's Office. *(By John McCutchen)*

Steven Mapes, now a judge in San Bernardino County, helped Canty defend Wayne at his trial in 2006. *(By Caitlin Rother)*

Investigator Ron Forbush interviewed dozens of witnesses for Wayne's defense.
(By John McCutchen)

Victoria Redstall, an actress and former spokesmodel for a breast enhancement herbal supplement, met and befriended Wayne in jail after she decided to do a documentary on a serial killer.
(By John McCutchen)

Wayne breaks down during his sentencing hearing, after which he was sent to Death Row at San Quentin Prison.
(By John McCutchen)

Bill White Sr., Lanett's father, in the hallway outside the courtroom, surrounded by family and members of the media, on the day of Wayne's sentencing. *(By John McCutchen)*

Rodney Ford, shown here in October 2007, works as a construction superintendent and still stays in touch with his brother. *(By Caitlin Rother)*

ents, evidently, but she said her sister loved her. . . . Her
pubic hair went all the way up to her belly button, and all
the way across her torso, something I've never seen before.
Maybe it's more common than I know, but this is just something that struck me as unusual, so maybe it will help somebody, like her sister. In that backpack, she only had a
couple of things. She had . . . a Baggie with . . . something
that might have been heroin. She had a rosary bead cross,
one of those little plastic ones. . . . She didn't have any ID.
She didn't have any money. She didn't have any jewelry.
She was just very ill-equipped to be out in the middle of
nowhere. So I don't think she was out for very long."

After the interview with Freeman and Dawson, the
investigators drove Wayne to the campsite in Trinidad;
he genuinely seemed to want to help find her remains.

Redwood trees, two hundred and three hundred feet
tall, commanded both sides of Highway 101. To the west
of the Seawood Drive exit was Patrick's Point Drive, a
windy frontage road, lined with RV parks and beautiful
homes overlooking the ocean, which led to Patrick's
Point State Park. Wayne had set up camp in the wilder-
ness about one hundred feet east of the highway, where
there were no amenities such as electrical hookups, running water, or restrooms.

Freeman and Dawson walked beside Wayne up a short
trail, less than one hundred feet long, to the tent where
he'd been living for the past week. The area was dense with
mature "second-growth" redwood trees, which get their
names because redwoods keep growing even after they are
chopped down and are often found next to stumps.

The team of investigators was still at work there, collect-
ing and cataloging evidence. Knowing that they hadn't been

able to find the spot where he buried the thighs, Wayne pointed to two tall trees with high aboveground roots.

"It's under that stump, under some leaves," Wayne said.

Deputy Randy Held moved the leaves aside with his gloved hand and dug under the roots, exposing two white fleshy objects.

Wayne said they should keep digging because he'd also buried what was left of the victim's breasts. Dawson asked if Wayne had cut the girl up at his trailer, and Wayne said yes, in his bathtub. He said he'd baked her breasts in the oven and poured the melted fat into a coffee can, which he kept under the kitchen sink.

Freeman asked Held to radio dispatch and have them send someone from the coroner's office to take over the digging and to collect the remains.

Deputy Coroners Charlie Van Buskirk and Roy Horton, and pathologist Mark Super, soon arrived and did the honors, noting that the thighs were cold to the touch—too cold for having been buried in that dirt hole for long. They also seemed fresh and surprisingly pliable, given that they were separated from the torso more than a year ago.

In the same hole, they found two white plastic garbage bags, covered with a lumpy, sticky substance in neon rainbow colors that looked like cake frosting, along with three small pieces of what looked like human tissue, the largest being about four inches in diameter.

When they examined the body parts at the morgue the next day, they were hard and had a smoky odor mixed with a stale freezer smell.

From there, Freeman and Dawson drove Wayne to the Mad River, which was about twenty minutes away. Wayne led them to the gravel area on the riverbank, where he said he'd buried the head and other limbs. But there was no trace of them.

It had been more than a year since then, a year of storms and rain, not unlike most in Humboldt County. Freeman figured that nature had long since removed the remains from the sandbar and sent them west to the ocean, where the tides may have carried them north to Clam Beach or places unknown.

On the trip back to Eureka, they stopped to get Wayne a Whopper and an iced tea at Burger King, then took him back to jail.

Freeman knew it could become an issue whether Wayne had been properly advised of his Miranda rights enough to subsequently waive them, so he wanted to resolve the question sooner rather than later. There was no question in Freeman's mind, but he wanted to create a record that would hold up in court, so he called Rodney Ford on a recorded line.

"Remember last night, after I saw your brother for the first time, and he indicated he wanted an attorney and stuff? And then I interviewed you and we got through the whole thing of how you ended up at our department?" Freeman said.

"Right," Rodney said.

"And then I mentioned that I couldn't talk to him anymore because he told me that you had suggested he should get an attorney?"

"Yeah, that's correct."

"Right, and then a short time later, the way I recall it, is that you sort of approached me in the office and asked me if I wanted you to go talk to him," Freeman said.

"Basically, I told you that I wanted to talk to him because I wanted him to do the right thing," Rodney said.

"And if there was anybody that needed help, they needed to be helped, and at that point, I wanted to talk to my brother to try and convince him to do the right thing."

Freeman wanted Rodney to confirm on tape that the detective hadn't tried to strong-arm Rodney into persuading Wayne to be interviewed without an attorney.

"You did not ask me, you did not coerce," Rodney said. "I did this on my own free will."

"Okay, that's good and then . . . So you visited with Adam . . . correct?"

"Yeah, that's correct," Rodney said.

"Okay, and then later on, you were sitting in my lieutenant's office in the sheriff's department and I was called in there, and then you told me I should go talk to him?"

"Yes, that's correct."

"Very good. I just wanted to get all that settled and on the record and on tape because . . . actually our conversation was one of the more important things that's gone on with this case," Freeman said.

CHAPTER 18

"Babies"

On the afternoon of November 4, Detectives Frank Gonzales and Jeff Staggs and their sergeant, Mike Lenihan, jumped into a San Bernardino County Sheriff Department's plane and headed for Humboldt.

They arrived in Eureka at 6:35 P.M., a little shaken up, after weathering a frighteningly bumpy ride and being knocked around by rain and thunderstorms. The visibility was so bad that the pilot had to fly using only instruments; they almost got diverted to another airport.

Although several media trucks were parked outside the typically quiet courthouse, no reporters approached the detectives as they walked inside.

Detectives Mike Jones and Joe Herrera, who had driven up from San Joaquin County, were meeting with Freeman when Gonzalez and Staggs got there around 7:45 P.M. Knowing that Wayne would be arraigned within forty-eight hours, they all wanted to talk to him before he went to court, or "lawyered up."

"I remember you, you brought a torso down to our office about a year ago," Herrera said to Freeman.

"Oh, yes, I remember you, too," said Freeman as they reminisced about the joke shoulder patch he had given Herrera, featuring a skeleton standing with a cane, labeled "Humboldt County Coroner's Office."

"I still have that," Herrera said.

The detectives sat around a table as Freeman told them that Wayne was being cooperative; he liked to be called "Adam."

Even though they were from three different jurisdictions, working three different cases, they all wanted the same thing—to keep Wayne talking.

"Once he says the word 'lawyer,' then none of us can talk to him," Gonzales said.

Herrera told his counterparts from San Bernardino that he and Jones should go first. "Here's the bottom line— if Adam decides not to speak to us, then we really don't have a case," Herrera said. "Even if he invokes his right to remain silent or asks for an attorney, you still have a case because of the DNA."

"Well, you're right," Lenihan said. "Why don't you guys go ahead."

Jones and Herrera sat down with Wayne at 9:00 P.M., first making sure he was aware of his Miranda rights and that he still wanted to talk to them.

Jones took the lead, saying they wanted to ask him about a woman found in the Lodi area. Wayne mostly replied with abrupt responses and sentence fragments, rubbing his head as he tried to remember details. There were many long pauses as the detectives waited for him to answer.

Throughout the interview, Jones believed Wayne was being "somewhat deceptive," telling the truth, but not the whole truth. He and Herrera tried to stay away from calling Wayne a murderer straight out. Being that direct with someone like Wayne would likely shut him down, so the detectives took a more gentle, compassionate approach.

"Do you know who we're talking about?" Jones asked.

"Yes," Wayne said.

Herrera told Wayne that if he was just guessing or couldn't remember, he should say so.

Wayne said his mind didn't "work real good," yet he seemed to remember very specific details about Lanett White, with little or no problem. That is, until they got to the sexual activities that led to her death.

Wayne recognized her from a photo that Jones showed him, and asked if she was a prostitute. Herrera said she might be, but that the important thing was how Wayne knew her.

"I remember her tattoos," Wayne said, saying one read, "*mi madre* something" on one side of her chest, and on the other side was a blue one written in blue capital and cursive letters.

Wayne said he met her off Highway 10 in southern California "close to a truck stop."

"You know who she is?" Wayne asked.

But the detectives weren't ready to go there yet. First they wanted to make sure he was talking about their victim. They were throwing out the names of cities and counties when Wayne blurted out the name of a street.

"Cherry Lane."

"Okay, Cherry Lane. Do you know what town that's in? . . . Is that associated with this girl?"

"Think so. Where did she live?" Wayne asked.

"She lives in that area. . . . There's a Cherry Lane in the town of Fontana. It's near the town of Ontario."

Wayne said he thought that sounded right because he remembered leaving a truck stop on Cherry Street in Ontario, called Three Sisters, when he saw her walking up and down a street as he was turning left to go over the 10 freeway. He was hoping to get something to eat on the other side of the bridge. He stopped and asked her where to go, and she got into the truck with him.

He said she was wearing a beige or tan vest with some matching pants and tennis shoes, and was carrying a black purse.

"Seems like she was dressed nice," Wayne said.

"So, when you stopped and talked to her, what did you guys talk about?" Jones asked.

"Babies," Wayne said softly.

"Huh?" Jones asked. "I couldn't hear you."

"'Babies'? Is that what you said?" Herrera asked.

"My baby," Wayne said, explaining that his son was about to turn three.

Wayne said it was about nine or ten o'clock when they met, but they stayed on the road talking for a long time.

"I don't know these things for sure," he said.

Jones said he understood that Wayne had been with a lot of women and that they might run together. "Is that what's happening?"

"Yes."

Jones said he would try to help Wayne remember details if he ran into a wall.

Wayne said she told him she had a three-year-old and a baby son. Her sister had six kids, but he didn't remember her name or her sister's.

"Does the name Lanett or Nettie ring a bell to you?"

"No," Wayne said. "She didn't tell me that, if that's what it is."

Wayne said he could tell that she'd been drinking

before they met up; she seemed upset and told him it was because of her kids. "Too much stress," he said.

"When you guys were in the cab, okay, did you continue to talk, or did you do something else?" Jones asked.

"Something else."

"Okay, what did you do?"

"Got intimate."

"By 'intimate' you mean you had sex?"

Wayne continued to respond with one-word affirmative answers as Jones asked if they'd had sexual intercourse and oral sex. But when Jones asked for more specifics, Wayne changed the subject.

"She said she wasn't a hooker," Wayne replied, adding that he started kissing her because "she looked nice." He said she took off her clothes, then he took off his and they gave each other oral sex at the same time.

As Jones asked for more details, Wayne acknowledged that he put his mouth on her breasts, but he wasn't sure if he had ejaculated or not.

"You don't remember if you had an orgasm or not?"

"I've had a lot of them," Wayne replied.

Wayne said he didn't remember how long they had sex, only that he was on top and didn't wear a condom. He thought he'd probably had anal sex with her, but he said it could have been with a different woman.

"Did she ask you for anything in exchange for sex?" Jones asked.

Wayne paused and then said, yes, but he couldn't remember whether it was $30 or $60.

Given that Wayne had just said she wasn't a prostitute, Jones asked for clarification. Wayne replied that he'd actually asked her if she wanted money, not the other way around.

"So after you guys had finished having sex, what happened then?" Jones asked.

"Same point I got with the other one. I think I hurt her, but I'm not sure how or why."

Jones said he wanted to hear more about this and help Wayne understand how this happened. He asked whether perhaps Wayne had been overzealous and whether, when he had sex with women, he got aggressive sometimes.

"Sometimes things just don't, don't make sense," Wayne said.

"What things don't make sense?" Jones asked.

"I remember giving her mouth-to-mouth resuscitation," Wayne said, adding that they were both fully clothed by then.

This sequence of events didn't make much sense to Jones, but as he tried to get Wayne to clarify his statement, Wayne said his memories often got confused. Before he could say what he remembered, he said, some other memory came into his head that didn't make sense.

"I thought I remembered she dressed herself, then I remember I dressed her," Wayne said.

Then, he said, he couldn't remember whether they'd even had sexual intercourse. Jones reminded him that he had already said that he was on top.

"What were your hands doing while you were having sex with her?" Jones asked.

"Up by her head," Wayne said.

"You think your hands may have been around her neck?"

"Might of."

"Could your hands have been around her neck while you were having sex with her and something happened? And this is how she got hurt?"

"I think so," Wayne said softly.

"Is it that you don't remember how it happened, or it's just real difficult for you to talk about how that happened?"

"Not sure."

By this point, Wayne was shaking and nodding his head rather than responding verbally.

"But you think it's possible it could have happened that way. You're shaking your head yes. You think so? After she gets hurt, what did you do?"

"Try to make her breathe."

Jones asked Wayne to run through the steps he took to bring her back, so Wayne recited the steps of CPR, as if he were reading them from a book: "Clear the airway. Tilt her head back. Cover the mouth. Breathe in it. First start off with one quick breath. Watch her stomach. Five-part compressions. One breath. Watch the chest rise. Continue to do that."

Jones asked how long he did that, but Wayne said he had trouble with time.

"Was it about five minutes, ten minutes?" Jones asked.

"Long time."

"It seems like a real long time, especially when it doesn't seem like things are working," Jones said, using the compassion technique to the hilt.

"Wasn't."

"It wasn't working, was it?"

"No."

Jones said that must have been difficult for him, but he knew Wayne had tried his best. "What did you do then?"

"Went crazy," Wayne said.

Asked to elaborate, Wayne said he didn't remember. All he knew was that she was dead and he needed to secure her body, using the ties and ropes he kept in the truck, before he headed to Arizona to make a pickup.

He'd already been up all night and knew he'd be driving for the next twenty-four hours, so he stopped to get some coffee and a burrito to keep him going.

"Part of me says she got out of the truck and walked away," Wayne said.

"Is that because you wanted her to get out of the truck and walk away?" Jones asked.

"I do. I wished."

"But she didn't get out of the truck and walk away."

"She didn't . . . I don't know what happens. : . . That's why I came here. I don't know what's going on. . . . I end up with these problems. I know I cause them. I'm not sure exactly . . ."

"Exactly how," Jones finished for him.

"I know that I play rough sometimes."

Jones asked if Wayne had ever choked anybody when they were having sex, not meaning to hurt them, but because he wanted to increase the orgasm's intensity. "Is that what you mean when you say you play rough, or do you do a lot of other things?"

"I always try to get them off," Wayne said.

"How do you try to get them off?"

"Whatever they like the most."

Jones rattled off a series of common sex acts, encouraging Wayne to open up by saying he'd seen all kinds of things working in the sex crimes unit. Then he delved into the kinkier sex practices, where he knew Wayne liked to go.

"Some women, I've been told, like to be choked up when they're having sex. Okay? What did she like?" Jones asked, waiting for Wayne to answer. "Do you remember what she liked, Adam?"

"No. I think I hurt her."

When Jones tried to delve deeper, Wayne changed the subject again.

"She's beautiful," he said.

Prodded by Jones to refocus on the relevant details, Wayne explained how he propped her up, secured her with some rope, and wrapped her in a blue tarp that he bought at a truck stop in Kingman, Arizona, on his return to California. Then, he tied her to the top bunk in the sleeper—only she fell down.

"What you mean she fell?"

"She fell forward. I pulled and I pulled and I pulled and I couldn't get her back up. Fell in between the bunk and the front seat. And her foot was sticking out, behind the front seat," Wayne said, gesturing.

He said he noticed that her head was a darker color than the rest of her body, even using the correct technical term—"lividity"—to describe it. Initially, he said, she was on her back, but she turned upside down when she fell in between the seats, so that the top of her body was resting against the truck floor, which got very hot. When her body started leaking, he wiped up the fluid with paper towels and threw them out the window.

Before he got to the weight station at the Grapevine on Interstate 5, he pulled the curtain down to try to cover her up. After he pulled up to the scales, an officer got into the cab next to him, and Wayne was sure he would figure out what was behind that curtain. Wayne even hoped that he would.

"How long did you keep this girl in the cab with you?"

"Too long," Wayne said. "I should have taken her straight to a hospital."

Jones asked if he started noticing "something about her."

"Yes."

"What?"

"[It's] not very nice to talk about someone like that," Wayne said.

"She start to smell, real bad? . . . So, what you do with her?"

It was nighttime, Wayne said, when he put her in the water along State Route 12, somewhere around a Texaco truck stop off State Route 99, across the street from a grain silo. He put on a pair of leather gloves, pulled her out through the emergency exit, dragged her along the dirt, and put her into the ditch next to a big tree. He left the gloves and tarp in the ditch and threw her clothes out the truck window somewhere else—he didn't remember where.

Jones showed some of the crime scene photos, and Wayne confirmed that was the spot where he dumped her.

Herrera asked if Wayne saved anything of hers to remember her by (a common practice of serial killers so they can enjoy their crime all over again—and relive the sexual pleasure of it), but Wayne said no.

Herrera asked Wayne how he felt, being responsible for this woman's death.

"I'd feel better if you'd shoot me," Wayne said.

"In other words, you're not glad that this happened?"

"Right."

"Are you sorry this happened?"

"Sorry."

"Course you're sorry," Herrera said. "That's one of the reasons why you came into the sheriff's office here, to try to make things right. Or, why did you come in?"

"That's another decision that I have trouble with. I think it's for one reason and then I think it's for another. . . . It just keeps happening."

"You want it to stop?"

"Yeah, and if I can just get away from it. Don't want to see any babies. Because every time I see a baby, I just lose it. . . . I can be driving down the road and doing just fine . . . but then I see a baby."

"Or you begin to talk about it. I noticed every time you talk about it, you get upset, is that right?" Herrera asked.

"Yes."

"Is that what got you upset the day when you met this

girl, when she began talking about her babies? And you thought about your . . . baby?"

"Uh-huh."

Wayne explained that's why he called his brother, because he wasn't sure how he was going to stop otherwise. "I think that I would have went after my wife," Wayne said.

"You didn't want to do that?"

"No."

"That was a smart move."

Herrera asked if all the women Wayne had hurt had talked about babies, and Wayne nodded. Jones tried to get Wayne to be more specific about his motivation—what he was thinking when he hurt them, but he wouldn't answer.

"How long have you wanted to hurt your ex-wife?" Herrera asked.

"I don't know."

Wayne tried to deflect once again.

"My dad was into violence," he said. "And he wanted me to be, so I was for a long time. Then I decided I didn't want to be treated like that."

Herrera pulled him back to the women, asking if he'd ever considered taking Lanett home so that he could cut her up like the other women.

"No," Wayne said.

Herrera asked if Wayne got rough while the two of them were having sex and that made her stop breathing.

"I think I stopped her from breathing," Wayne said.

"And you do not remember how, or are you afraid to say it, or what is it?" Herrera asked.

"I don't clearly remember. Sometimes I just have to tell things stop. . . . Can't think, can't do anything. . . . Just want everything to stop."

Herrera asked if Wayne had learned about choke holds and carotid restraints while he was in the service. Wayne said no, it was at the Institute for Better Health, before he entered the marines. Herrera asked if he might have used a carotid restraint on this girl or any of the others.

Wayne sat silently, so Herrera asked again.

"I don't know," Wayne said. "There's a beginning and there's an ending. There's no middle."

Herrera asked him to explain.

"I remember being with her. I remember trying to make her breathe again. . . . Sometimes that's the hard part, seems all I can remember."

Wayne said that he was able to revive some women and let them go, the last one being a hooker from San Francisco.

Jones asked if he'd ever done the carotid move with any girlfriend or wife. Wayne said he'd tried it once with his second wife, tying a red robe belt around her neck so that she lost consciousness for a second.

"I wouldn't hurt her. She didn't want [to have sex], and it made me a little mad, so I guess I ended up getting rough with her in sex."

Jones asked if this was something she wanted or asked him to do.

"No. I did it. She didn't protest it."

"Did she seem to enjoy it?"

"At the time, she seemed to, but she later on said that she didn't."

Jones tried to walk Wayne through the pathways that his mind took with each of these women.

"Do you see your ex-wife's face when you're talking to these girls? Does it become that you're not talking to these girls, that you're talking to your ex-wife?"

"Yeah," Wayne said.

Jones asked Wayne to visualize what happened when these women talked about babies and he started thinking about how his wife took his son away from him.

Wayne said he wanted the women to stop talking. "Just freeze. Stop her."

"She's talking about her babies and she's making you think about your babies."

"Yeah. I don't want to think about my baby now," Wayne said.

Nonetheless, he proceeded to tell Jones about the time he spent the day with Max, when he took him to the toy store. He said Max didn't want him to leave the child care center, so he figured he would wait for his wife to come and get their son.

"She didn't show up," Wayne said. "Took Max in and all he could say was 'No, Daddy. No, Daddy. No, Daddy.' He's crying. . . . I didn't want to leave him, so I took him in there . . . laid there on the floor, told Max to go to sleep. I laid him on my chest . . . and he laid there for an hour or two, never moved a muscle. His eyes are wide open. He wasn't going to sleep, he wasn't saying nothing . . . didn't want me to leave. Just wanted to be content. Just wanted to be secure. I finally had to leave."

Wayne said he sat outside in his grandparents' car, upset that there was only one girl inside, taking care of ten little kids—but not really paying attention to them—and feeding them watered-down Kool-Aid and stale bread with peanut butter.

He said he hadn't gone back to see his son since that day.

"I can't. Because I wouldn't leave him. I'd take him," Wayne said, adding that he knew that wouldn't be right.

Herrera asked Wayne again if he was sorry the woman they'd been talking about earlier was dead.

"I didn't mean to kill her. I killed her—I didn't try to kill her. I don't want her dead now, I didn't want her dead then."

Herrera asked Wayne to explain what was involved in

a carotid restraint, and again, Wayne answered very technically, switching to his instructor's voice.

"It's where you cut off two—the two carotid arteries. Both sides of your neck supply blood to the brain. . . . You apply pressure . . . you'd use a hold, standing off to the right. You can use a rope or something."

Herrera asked how many women—Wayne had had sex with and then revived with CPR.

"Fifty," Wayne replied.

"When you saved them . . . what would happen after that?"

"They'd leave."

In his wrap-up questions, Jones asked Wayne again how many days he kept Lanett's body in his truck before dumping her.

"Two or three. Couldn't figure out what to do."

With that, they ended the interview. It was 11:55 P.M.

From the way Wayne was mumbling, Jones later said, he got the sense Wayne was "somewhat remorseful" and possibly even ashamed about what he'd done to these women—so much so that he couldn't bear to hear himself say it out loud.

"I honestly think he didn't want to keep doing it," Jones said.

Still, Jones said he didn't believe Wayne's excuse— that his actions were triggered by the women's talk of babies—nor did he believe that Wayne was mentally ill.

"He knew what he was doing at the time he did it," and knew it was wrong, Jones said.

Jones wondered if Wayne might have been hoping he'd get a sympathetic jury that felt prostitutes deserved to die because of their lifestyle. Or maybe he simply hoped that if he told the truth, he would go to a mental hospital instead of prison.

"I think there was a lot of acting on his part," Jones said. "He realized his life is over and he has to do everything he can to try to make the best of it."

Herrera agreed. He said Wayne seemed fine when he was remembering details that weren't criminal, describing how Wayne would hesitate, rub his head, and sit silently, overcome by "amnesia." Herrera figured that Wayne was ashamed and therefore reluctant to explain in detail how he'd killed these women.

"I felt at the time, during the interview, that he did remember, but he didn't want to go there," Herrera said later.

The detectives gave Wayne a break of less than ten minutes before handing him over to Gonzales and Staggs.

Gonzales was concerned that Wayne's defense attorney might later take issue with such a prolonged period of questioning, but he went ahead with a nearly two-and-a-half-hour interview to get what he could out of Wayne before stopping for the night.

"I wanted to establish a relationship with him from the outset with the hopes of reinterviewing him the next day," said Gonzales, who came well-equipped with eight 60-minute tapes for his handheld recorder.

As the interview proceeded, however, Gonzales grew increasingly concerned about "the fatigue factor." Wayne looked tired and frazzled, his hair a mess.

Apparently, Wayne was not used to seeing a sheriff's detective wearing a suit.

"You FBI?" he asked Gonzales before they got started.

"Oh, no," Gonzales replied. "I'm just from San Bernardino County."

The next thing Wayne asked was whether they would take off his handcuffs, which were fastened in front.

"I'm not a danger," Wayne said. "That's why I'm here. I don't want to be a danger. . . . If I was going to run, I wouldn't have turned myself in."

Wayne said he'd been increasingly losing his ability to think on the road over the past year. "I don't know why, just been getting worse and worse," he said. "That's why I came home."

Asked to talk about his trip through Victorville, Wayne said he was on his way to pick up his weirdest load ever— bags of concrete that he was supposed to drop off in Los Banos. When he got to the drop-off point, the warehouse was empty except for a brand-new forklift, which he was supposed to use to unload the bags, all by himself.

"We're not forklift operators, we're truck drivers," he explained. "It's like some shady deal. A lot of work."

Along the way, he said, he was driving through town on Highway 18 when he saw a woman standing next to a stop sign, across the street from a park, in the middle of town. He was still some distance away, so he slowed down, thinking she wanted to cross the street. But instead, she waved and flagged him over, lifting up her long white T-shirt to flash her panties at him.

He couldn't stop and pull his big, heavy truck over that suddenly, so he went around the block and came back, parking in front of a nearby building.

She got into his truck and gave him a price, but she didn't mention her name. Wayne noticed that she had "a funny nose," as if it had been broken once. He couldn't remember the fee she asked for, he said, because at the time he was too distracted with worry that his big truck was blocking traffic.

Gonzales showed him a photo of Patricia Tamez, and Wayne recognized her immediately.

"That's her," he said.

Wayne said they started driving toward Lucerne, but they stopped along the way. Before he would give any more details, Wayne wanted to know more about the woman. He wanted to know her name.

"Her name was Patricia, okay? She was from that area, and from the information that we have, just like you had mentioned to me earlier, that she was a prostitute."

"Seems like an oddball area to have a prostitute," Wayne said.

Gonzales went on to say that her family lived in the area as well.

"Tell them I'm sorry," Wayne said.

"I will do that," Gonzales said.

"Tell them I didn't mean to."

Wayne went on, explaining that he stopped the truck in a dirt lot next to a Circle K or 7-Eleven that was on the way to Los Banos so they could have sex in the truck.

Like the other detectives before him, Gonzales started asking Wayne for specifics, aiming to work his way up to whatever Wayne did to kill her.

"I remember we were having sex, and I was, I was talking to her."

"Okay."

Wayne asked for another cup of coffee. "I'm trying to pull this out of my head, but it's not coming," he said.

Gonzales said he understood that these were difficult things to talk about.

"It's more than that," Wayne countered.

"You know, you're probably right," Gonzales said.

"No, this is the same point that I can't, I don't exactly [know] what happens."

Gonzales asked if Wayne was blanking out on that part because it wasn't something good to remember.

"I try," Wayne said.

Gonzales said that was perfectly okay—people did that all the time—but he needed to go back to this woman's family and explain what happened to her.

"I was trying to revive her," Wayne said. "She wasn't breathing."

"Adam, what happened to her? How did she get to the point where you had to try to revive her?"

But just as in the previous interviews, Wayne wouldn't—or couldn't—go there, and no matter how many different times or different ways Gonzales would ask, Wayne would only say that he gave her CPR, but he couldn't bring her back.

"Was there a point in time that you knew that she was dead?" Gonzales asked.

"After I got too tired."

"Too tired of doing what?"

"Breathing, pressing."

Gonzales tried one more time to try to get Wayne to describe what made Patricia stop breathing.

"I did it. I made her not breathe."

"You made her not breathe."

"I must have. I was the only one there."

"I know we're at a bad spot now, okay. We're at a point . . . where it's not pleasant. But we got to get over that hump, Adam."

"My mind is not here."

"Okay. We'll go back to that."

"Having sex. Makes it feel better," Wayne said a few minutes later.

"If what . . ." Gonzales said, trying to coax Wayne into elaborating.

"If you cut off—"

"Cut off their airway," Gonzales offered.

"No, the blood. The carotid arteries."

Wayne said he did this while he gave women oral sex—

sometimes choking them with his hands and sometimes with a necktie, but he didn't remember doing that to this particular woman.

When he started giving her CPR, he recalled thinking that this had happened too many times, and that he wanted to take her to the hospital or to the police department.

"After you left the parking lot . . . where did you go?" Gonzales asked.

Wayne said he stopped somewhere along Highway 18.

"What did you do with Patricia?"

"I tried, tried again," Wayne said. "I knew it wasn't meant to die. I wanted to—I cried."

"Why did you cry, Adam?"

"'Cause I didn't want that to happen."

"Did you cry because you knew it was wrong, Adam?"

"Yeah. It shouldn't have happened."

Gonzales asked what he did next.

"Put her in the water," Wayne said.

He said he always saw the California Aqueduct while was driving his truck. So he picked a dirt area, where somebody had dug what looked like a grave, near a bridge over the aqueduct on Highway 395. Later, he threw her clothes out the window somewhere, maybe in the desert.

Gonzales asked Wayne if thought he might have injured Patricia by doing CPR too hard. Wayne said he knew that was possible to do, but he didn't think that occurred in this case, because he couldn't make hard compressions on his sleeper mattress.

"At any point in time, did she offend you? Did she hit you? Did she do anything like that?"

"No, I don't think so," Wayne said. "She was a nice person."

When Wayne turned himself in, Gonzales asked, "You had something with you, right?"

"It was hers," Wayne said.

"What was that?"

"Her breast."

As Gonzales walked Wayne through what happened after he stopped trying to revive her, Wayne told a very disjointed story that was nowhere near chronological.

He was in a hurry to pick up his load of cement bags, so he quickly tied her feet and hands with some rope, then lashed her entire body to the top bunk so that she wouldn't roll forward when he stopped.

After that, he went to the cement plant in Lucerne and loaded more than one hundred pounds of cement bags onto his flatbed. The whole time he was loading, no one at the plant knew he had a body in his truck. Wayne said he had a lot of trouble loading that day, and it took more than four hours—putting on bags and taking some of them off—to get the weight right.

"I told him 'I quit.' I told him, 'I'm not coming back here no more.' I was upset. I was mad. Things were just not going right. I was really . . . messed up—that's what it was," Wayne said.

After he picked the spot along the aqueduct, he laid a tarp on the ground, then pulled the body out of the emergency door so she was feetfirst and faceup. He cut some rope so he could drag the tarp over to the canal, then used a Kershsaw hunting knife with a sawtooth blade, eight or ten inches long, with a black handle, to cut off her left breast.

"Why did you do that?"

"I think I wanted to turn it in. . . . I don't know that I planned it."

He explained that he kept the knife in a pocket on the truck's passenger-side door when he wasn't planning to use it, and on the driver's side when he was. That day, it was on the passenger side.

He said he wanted to put her in the water, not to conceal her, but "so she wouldn't smell." He was afraid that he wouldn't be able to roll her body down the cement. He also thought he might fall in if he went down and tried to push her in, so he took the rope and tied it around one of her breasts, thinking she would roll like a yo-yo. But things didn't go as he'd imagined.

"I removed the breast when she didn't roll," he said.

Gonzales asked Wayne how she ended up with such severe back injuries. At first, Wayne said he had no idea, but then said it might've happened when he pulled her out of the truck.

Wayne said he didn't try to support her body and lay her on the ground, he just pulled and down she came. That's because he was in a hurry. There were lots of cars going by and his truck was in the way.

He managed to get her body close to the water, but then he had to figure out a way to get her into it.

"I know this isn't very respectful—I kicked her down into the water . . . not really kick, you know, pushed, pushed."

He got back in his truck and drove back up to the highway, from the 58 to the 5 to the 152, stopping at the truck stop in Four Corners, where he tried to sleep, but couldn't.

"Why do you think this happened?" Gonzales asked.

"Something wrong with me."

"What do you think that is, Adam?"

"I wish I knew. If I knew, it wouldn't be wrong with me."

Wayne said he went out into the woods in Trinidad because he didn't want to see or hear anything anymore, or to think about things that caused him pain, but he still couldn't stop thinking about his wife. So instead of going to get her, he called Rodney. He asked his brother if he should stay in the woods or turn himself in. His brother told him to do the latter.

"I don't want to see babies anymore," Wayne said. "I don't want to see any more women."

"Because this might happen again?"

"Yeah."

Gonzales asked Wayne if he had left any other victims in San Bernardino County. Wayne said he didn't know, but he would look at a picture.

It was getting close to 2:30 A.M., so Gonzales decided to stop the interview and let Wayne get some rest. They would pick up again in the morning.

When Wayne cried during the interview, Gonzales believed that they weren't tears of remorse for the victim, but rather an expression of sadness for how his acts were affecting his own life.

"I do think that Ford was driven by his ex-wife. Something to do with his son . . . he lost reality and turned to this. But did he have any deep sorrow for these victims? No, because they were prostitutes and they weren't important to him. They were the way to get back at his personal life."

CHAPTER 19

"HE ALWAYS KEPT HIS TRUCK CLEAN"

By the morning of November 5, reporters from all over California had descended on Humboldt County. The number of media had increased by at least fourfold, with more than a dozen satellite camera trucks encircling the square-block perimeter of the courthouse.

As Detective Frank Gonzales was leaving the station later that day, he and his sergeant had to walk through a gauntlet of reporters. Gonzales was toting a Styrofoam ice chest that contained Patricia Tamez's breast and one of six vials of blood that Toby Baxter from the DOJ lab had drawn from Wayne for DNA matching.

But the reporters were oblivious. None of them asked about the chest's contents.

"Mike," Gonzales whispered, "if they only knew what I was carrying, they'd be all over me."

"Well, bro," Lenihan whispered back, "don't say anything."

* * *

The AP ran a story that morning, updating the huge news story that cast a rare spotlight on the typically quiet coastal town of Eureka: "A trucker who walked into the Sheriff's Department here, pulled a severed breast out of his pocket and said he killed four women, was under investigation Thursday in as many as six slayings throughout California, authorities said."

As is often the case with early news reports that are hastily assembled and put out on the wire, some details turned out to be wrong. The AP report said the four known victims were female hitchhikers; it also said the breast in Wayne's pocket came from a victim other than Patricia Tamez.

Reporters spent the day scouring the area for people to interview: the bartender from the Ocean Grove Lodge, coroner's and sheriff's officials, forensic psychologists, and Wayne's boss, coworkers, and trailer park neighbors.

"The fact that he turned himself in makes this case highly unusual," psychologist John Podboy told the *Eureka Times-Standard*. "He wanted to be stopped, which is not the case with most serial killers."

Edeline dispatcher Mike Peters told the AP that he'd taken an immediate liking to Wayne. He'd brought him home to dinner, gone to bars with him, and had taken him on family trips and car races. He went so far as to say that if he'd had a sister, he would have set her up with Wayne "in a heartbeat."

Dennis Keehn, Wayne's boss, was equally baffled: "How the hell do you trust anybody who does his job that well and he turns out like this?" he told the AP. "If you went down Eureka or Arcata at night, you would see some characters that might make you wonder about packing a firearm, but this guy, you wouldn't worry about him.

"He was clean-cut. He always kept his truck clean. Now we know why," Keehn said. "All indications were he loved his job. Then look what he was. God Almighty."

People who had thought they had known Wayne expressed their surprise.

"He would come in and buy his beer and cigarettes and complain about how his back was feeling," store clerk Jeremy Fugate told the AP. "I would go out and have a cigarette with him and trade jokes."

Jeremy said he often wondered about the mental health of some of his customers, but he'd always thought Wayne was all right.

Around 9:30 that morning, Wayne met in his cell with psychologist Paul Berg, who had flown up from Oakland to conduct an evaluation for the Humboldt County District Attorney's Office. The hour-long taped conversation was later ruled inadmissible at trial because of Wayne's persistent requests for an attorney.

Berg presented a letter for Wayne to sign, explaining that he was not providing treatment, that their discussion would not be confidential, and that Wayne would be speaking to Berg voluntarily.

"I don't have an attorney yet," Wayne said.

"I know that, and that's the reason for giving you the letter," Berg said. "I would like to interview you and what I'm interested in mostly is your mental state."

"Oh, boy," Wayne said. "I still don't know why I don't have an attorney. I thought you would be my attorney."

As they went back and forth about the preliminaries, Wayne started crying, as he did four or five times during the interview. He seemed to be in a fog.

"You promised I could see an attorney and I haven't seen one yet," Wayne said.

Berg assured Wayne that he would get an attorney, probably when he got arraigned. Wayne seemed confused and didn't really understand why Berg was there, so Berg went over everything again. With that, Wayne agreed to sign the letter and speak with Berg.

Wayne said he had trouble moving thoughts from his mind to his mouth. "It's there for just a second, and the harder I try to think, it's like I can't, it's gone. . . . I used to be smart."

Wayne said he started noticing this when he was living with his father in Napa. "I asked him if, um, if you lose your marbles, do you realize it?"

"What did he say?"

"I don't know what he said. I just told him that I felt I was losing mine."

Wayne said he didn't continue treatment after going to the clinic in Eureka because his problem had gone away.

After telling Berg that the crimes began after his wife left him and took his baby, Wayne started weeping and said he didn't want to talk about it anymore. He said he used to have problems with anger, but he'd since gotten over that.

Asked how he managed that, Wayne said, "Just stopped. And just—held things in more. Just, you know, just let things go."

Wayne described his head injury from 1980, but said he didn't remember having any problem thinking after that, nor had he ever heard voices or had visions or hallucinations.

"Strange ideas?" Berg asked.

"I can't make up my mind."

As they discussed Wayne's history with women, Wayne said, "People just don't see this, I guess . . . how dangerous they are. . . . They kill you from the inside. . . . They don't like it to be over, they like to keep hurting you. . . .

Once you get involved, you fall in love and all that, then it's over. . . . They really seem to get a kick out of that."

He said Wadad was the only woman he'd met who was good to him, unlike his first wife, a slut who had sex with other women in front of him.

"Good, strong Kuwaiti girl. Beautiful girl," he said of Wadad, adding that they broke up because she thought he'd cheated on her, when all he did was fondle a girl's breasts.

It soon became unclear which woman he was blaming from moment to moment as they all began to blur together into one common cause of his pain.

When Elizabeth left him, Wayne said, "she sucked my heart right through my penis. And everything else—wallet, money, baby, everything. . . . I was just, she used. . . . her female charms to take . . . everything I had. I don't think she had a heart. . . . I still love her."

At one point in the interview, Wayne appeared to be talking about Kelly, but he could have just as easily been talking about Wadad or Elizabeth.

"Did you ever hit her?"

"Yes, it was controlled because I didn't want to hurt her."

"Controlled, meaning not beating the shit out of her? Controlled means slapping her or something, hitting her once?"

"I used a belt on her."

"Didn't she fight back?"

"This was agreed upon."

"She liked it?"

"No."

"She agreed that you could punish her?"

"Right . . . because I told her how much it hurt me that she had hit me and—"

"This was payback and she agreed?"

"Right. No respect. I can't hit her hard because it would hurt her too much."

Moving on to why he was in jail, Wayne said, "I'm here because I should be. . . . I didn't mean to do it, but it's my fault. . . . I'm not a murderer. I wouldn't do that."

"But you did do it."

"I had to."

"Do you remember doing it?"

"No," Wayne said, crying. "I don't remember."

"You would see the results after."

"That's right."

"You remember dismembering the victims?"

"I remember trying to save them. All of them."

"How did you try to save them?"

"CPR," Wayne said.

"I only tore one of them up," he added, saying that he didn't like Berg's use of the word "cut" or "dismember."

Asked whether his first victim was already dead when he cut her up, Wayne said, "That's sick."

"What's sick?"

"Thinking she would be alive."

When Wayne said again that he wanted an attorney, Berg decided he should cut the interview short. He would've liked to spend many more hours talking to Wayne, but he felt that would be inappropriate.

That same morning, Freeman, a team of local investigators, and detectives from San Bernardino and San Joaquin Counties searched Wayne's thirty-two-foot silver Airstream at the trailer park in Arcata.

His blue Jeep, which was parked there, sported a red-white-and-blue Marine Corps sticker on its back bumper; a plastic sheriff's badge was pasted onto the front license plate.

When evidence tech Judy Taylor walked into the trailer, she thought someone had ransacked it. Wayne's belongings were so crammed into the small space it was hard to move around. The living room was to the right, with a circular couch and a large toolbox. The kitchen area was to the left, leading to a bunk bed, hallway, and bathroom.

While Taylor photographed and videotaped inside and outside the trailer, other investigators gathered up an odd collection of items, including a box of latex gloves, a hacksaw, a pair of pink women's panties, and a white plastic bag with a *Flying J* logo.

Taylor looked under the kitchen sink and found the Yuban coffee can, three-quarters full of a fatty substance, that Wayne had told Freeman about. The contents were semi-solid and a gold color, like butter or cooking grease.

In the freezer, they found the same fluorescent-colored substance, which looked like melted sherbet, that they'd seen on the white plastic bags they'd pulled from the hole with the thighs at the campsite.

Meanwhile, the detectives interviewed Wayne's neighbors. The woman who lived next door said she rarely saw him around. His curtains were always closed, he never seemed to have visitors and he stayed up until the wee hours. Others reported that he kept a row of ceramic ducks, all lined up, on the windowsill.

Park manager Frankie Yeakley said Wayne paid his rent on time or before it was due. She described him as very laid-back, easygoing, honest, and really trustworthy; he never seemed sad, angry, or depressed.

"He would tell stories about his family, but always seemed to be happy," Detective Mike Jones wrote in his case report. "She went on to describe him as somebody, who . . . she would have gone to have coffee [with] and would not have felt threatened."

Big news stories tend to attract people who want to be

part of the action. One neighbor, for example, told the *San Jose Mercury News* that she watched investigators remove a decaying human forearm from behind Wayne's trailer and a foot-long clump of women's hair from inside the trailer, as if it were a trophy. It's possible that she was so freaked out by learning that she'd lived next door to a serial killer that her imagination ran away with her, because nothing like that was ever reported or documented by authorities.

Another woman contacted police—and visited Wayne in jail—claiming that he had confided all sorts of horrors to her before surrendering. After talking with her for a while, however, Freeman realized that she had pulled details from the newspaper and was either seeking attention or just plain delusional. She later appeared on the *Leeza Gibbons* talk show, where she took credit for persuading Wayne to turn himself in.

After the initial search, the investigators transported the trailer to the sheriff's boatyard in Eureka, where they strung an evidence seal across the door, safeguarding it until the techs could come back and take a more intensive look.

The next afternoon, Taylor, her colleague John Parrish, and two DOJ criminalists, Toby Baxter and Kay Belschner, came back to follow up. Baxter and Belschner were looking for cutting or sawing tools that Wayne might have used to cut up Jane Doe, and any furniture, clothing, or paraphernalia that might have blood on it.

Because Wayne said he cut her up in the bathtub, they sprayed the bathroom with luminol, a substance used to find blood that the naked eye can't see. (The blood actually takes on a fluorescent glow when the lights are turned off. But bleach, copper, and brass will also cause a reaction.) As expected, they discovered traces of blood in the toilet, around the ring of the bathtub drain, and in the sink. They got a reaction from the wood floor, but it faded quickly, so they figured the luminol was reacting to something else. They wondered if perhaps the floor had been covered with carpet that had since been removed.

"There was blood all over the place in there," Freeman said later. "The place lit up like the Fourth of July."

Taylor and the other techs returned two more times to collect fingerprints and other evidence.

Among the items they took was the book *Seven Promises of the Promise Keeper,* which, according to Amazon.com, details several men's stories and insights on how they "deepened their Christian walk." Other items included some rusty kitchen knives, half a bottle of cologne, a small wooden rack, containing a mustache comb and wax, and a yellow rubber duck bath toy.

At 12:30 P.M. on November 5, Wayne met with San Bernardino detectives Gonzales and Lenihan for a brief interview to see if Wayne would admit to any other victims—dead or alive—or to information that would make him a suspect in any of their unsolved cases. They were also hoping he would reveal new details about how he killed the known victims.

Wayne gave them little else, but he did reveal a new victim—a Mexican prostitute he had picked up in Anaheim, then left tied up, alive, near the 71 and 91 freeways.

Kern County Detectives John Fidler and Ron Taylor sat down for their first interview with Wayne just after one o'clock.

As soon as Wayne identified Tina Gibbs as the woman he'd met on Tropicana Boulevard in Las Vegas, he asked if he could take a cigarette break.

"I've got to talk to you about my baby, and I don't want to do that," he said.

When they came back, Wayne said he and Tina left Las Vegas because she liked the truck and agreed to go for a ride with him. He described the route he took to Salinas, California, where he was going to drop off a shipment, but he said he couldn't remember whether he'd dropped her in the aqueduct before or after he went to Salinas.

The interview was very similar to the previous ones in that he said he couldn't remember details to why Tina had fallen unconscious. All he said he could remember was trying to revive her with CPR, then dumping her in the aqueduct at Interstate 5 and State Route 46.

"She was in the truck with me for too long" because she "started to smell," Wayne said.

"So she could have been in the truck with you for a couple of days?"

"Longer," Wayne said.

Asked if he'd had sex with Tina after she was dead, Wayne said, "I think so."

The detectives kept trying to try to jog his memory, and eventually some new facts emerged.

Wayne said he could picture her when he first saw her; she was wearing shorts. He said they went to a truck stop in Las Vegas, where she stopped breathing. (In a different interview, he said he had sex with her in his truck at the King 8 Motel on Tropicana Boulevard and a couple more times on his way to Salinas.)

When the detectives asked for details about the rough sex, Wayne said again that he was confused.

"There's been a lot of them," he said.

"How many?" Fidler asked. "More than four or more than five?"

"There's been a whole bunch."

Asked if there were more women he'd picked up on the route to Las Vegas, Wayne said, "Not hurt."

He explained that he'd picked up some women at truck

stops—including three at Bruce's, near Bakersfield on Highway 58—who got out of the truck and walked away.

He said he'd left one of them tied up loosely enough that she could free herself on some grass next to a closed Texaco station near the 46 and the 5, but off the road so no one would find her right away.

He also said he'd picked up women at the Tulare rest area, and in Fresno, Anaheim, Ontario, and Santa Rosa.

"Lots of places," he said.

Wayne said he remembered picking up a woman at Bruce's and leaving her tied up on a truck turnout, just off the 58 freeway in Tehachapi. He didn't remember her name, only that she was twenty-nine, had dark hair and a thin build, and had left her expensive watch in the truck under the mat.

"You just put her out to the side or something?" Fidler asked.

"Yeah, she rolled a little farther than I wanted her to."

The detectives showed him more photos of missing women, but Wayne said he didn't recognize any of them.

"Did you have a certain kind of girl you usually picked up?" Fidler asked.

"She had to be attractive to me."

"You ever pick any black girls?"

"No."

"What about Mexican girls?" Taylor asked.

"A couple of times, but one of them I left on the 71."

"When you left her, was she breathing?" Taylor asked.

"She was fine."

Wayne said he tied the women's hands and feet separately, then tied them together, behind their bodies.

"How many of those girls you think you left like that?" Fidler asked.

"Ten."

"Why would you tie them up?" Fidler asked.

"'Cause everything just went wrong."

"You didn't want them to tell on you, or something? What do you mean, 'everything went wrong'?"

"I scared them and I didn't want to."

Fidler asked how he knew they were scared. "They would cry, or something," Wayne said.

Fidler said he wondered why none of these women ever reported this. Wayne pointed out that the woman from Santa Rosa did—referring to Rachel Holt—because the incident was in the newspaper a week later. He heard some of the guys joking at the truck stop that one of their trucks matched the description.

"They weren't joking about mine, because mine didn't fit the description anymore," Wayne said. "It had a different trailer when I picked her up."

He said he'd had rough sex with the one from Santa Rosa, tied a tie around her throat. She stopped breathing, but he "got her started."

"How was that?"

"She screamed."

Asked whether he'd tied up the girl from Las Vegas, Wayne said he didn't know. "This is sickening, isn't it?"

Fidler said he just wanted to make sure there were only the four who quit breathing.

"Four. Sometimes I think . . ."

"More?"

"Yeah."

"Could be more—if some—some that you tied up and left alongside the road, and nobody found them."

"I know," Wayne said.

Asked when all of this started, Wayne said it was after he saw Max in October 1997.

"That's when things just changed. That's when . . . it started, when the first girl. It, I couldn't get her started breathing. . . . I stopped remembering things."

Wayne said that was one of the four women he'd told them about.

"But I want to know if I'm responsible for some other ones," he said, offering to look at more photos, ropes, or ties to see if they were his.

After the interview, Taylor said Wayne was not the kind of man he'd expected to meet.

"He was a pretty decent guy when we talked to him. He was apologetic as to what he had done," Taylor told the AP. "He was pretty open. He gave us information on our homicide that only he would have known."

Detectives Joe Herrera and Mike Jones from San Joaquin County had another shot at Wayne a couple of hours later.

Herrera asked if Wayne had used any instrument to hit these women.

"I used a belt," Wayne finally said. He said he preferred using a tie, because he didn't want to hurt the woman, and a tie didn't chafe the skin.

"It doesn't leave marks?" Herrera asked.

"It doesn't hurt her."

Herrera asked if he got more aggressive when he grew sexually aroused.

"I don't remember being really aggressive. If the girl likes it, then I do it. She doesn't like it, then I don't do it. She likes it, I like it. If she doesn't like it, I don't like it."

"That's why you do this, because you think they may like it and they tell you or show you that they like it, so you do more, is that right?"

"Right. Sometimes . . . I think that they'll change their mind and they'll start crying and I don't want anybody to be scared."

Jones asked if it made Wayne feel like these women were

having a more intense orgasm when he reached his hand up to their neck as he was performing oral sex on them.

"They are," Wayne said.

"Can you describe what their body does when they're doing this?"

Wayne did not respond, so Jones offered, "Their body shakes?"

"Yeah," Wayne said.

"Trembles?"

"Yeah."

"What happens to their eyes?"

"Usually, I can't see their eyes. They just get real intense and then they're relieved."

"What happens when they're relieved? Is that when they go unconscious?"

"Sometimes. . . . That's happened, yes."

"Did that happen with these girls that you couldn't bring back?"

"I don't know."

"It happened with the girls that you brought back?"

"Yes . . . it doesn't make any sense, does it?"

"No, it makes sense."

At the end of the interview, Wayne tried one last time to tell the detectives that he really didn't mean to kill anyone.

"I picked up a lot of girls," he said. "I didn't plan on hurting anybody."

Wayne was scheduled to be arraigned that afternoon in Judge W. Bruce Watson's courtroom.

Watson told Kevin Robinson, an attorney with the alternate counsel's office, that Wayne was indigent and could not afford a private attorney, so he would need a public defender to represent him. Watson appointed Robinson.

Deputy District Attorney Worth Dikeman told the

judge that Wayne wasn't "immediately available" and
asked to push the arraignment back a day.

Watson agreed and set the hearing for 10:00 A.M. the
following day.

However, when Robinson went to visit Wayne at the jail
the next morning, he was surprised and frustrated to
hear the same thing he'd heard in court the day before—
that Wayne was "not available."

Robinson returned to his office and typed up a letter to
Chief Deputy Ben Doan, commander of the jail, letting
him know that he had been denied access to his client.

"I want Mr. Ford to know that he has counsel seeking
to meet with him," Robinson wrote, copying Judge
Watson and Dikeman on the letter. "I would request
access to Mr. Ford and direct that all contact with Mr.
Ford not authorized by me cease."

Robinson later learned that Wayne had been "unavail-
able" that morning because he was being interviewed—
for the fourth consecutive day without an attorney—this
time by Eureka police detective Dave Parris and Frank
Jager, the Humboldt County coroner.

Wayne, who broke down in tears several times during
the three-hour interview, took a polygraph examination
after revealing some interesting perceptions about himself.

"Most of the time . . . I've been alone," he said. "Until recently, I didn't realize that the way I felt wasn't normal . . .
because I thought that being alone was normal. . . . There's
something not tangible but valuable about being around
other people."

Wayne said he usually had one really good friend at a
time, but while he was in the Marine Corps and was
singing karaoke, he felt as if too many people liked him.

"There's people that—that wanted to be around me

and I didn't . . . like them. They wanted something, but I didn't know what they wanted. But now I know they didn't want anything. They knew more than I knew."

About his son, Max, he said, "I can't tell you why he needs me. He does. I don't know what it is. But he's going to grow up just like me. . . . Whatever it is that my baby needs, he's not getting it.

"I'll be dead before he's an adult," Wayne said. "If he doesn't ever know me, it's best."

They moved on to other topics, such as Wayne's vehicles and jobs, but Parris was most interested in determining whether Wayne was responsible for the disappearance of Karen Mitchell, the missing Eureka teenager.

"Do you think it's possible that you picked up Karen and you're not quite remembering it?" Parris asked.

"I would have said no," Wayne said. "But there's things I don't remember."

Wayne said the hitchhiker he'd picked up was different from the others because she wasn't a prostitute. Nonetheless, she still wanted to have sex with him.

"I don't think she really wanted sex with me—just wanted sex, I guess," he said, adding that it was also possible that she wanted something else—like love or a relationship or just not to be alone.

Wayne said he stopped to get cigarettes at the market in Eureka, and as he was getting into his car, she asked which way he was heading. He told her he was going north to Arcata and she asked if he could take her to Clam Beach.

Wayne agreed that she looked similar in the face to Karen Mitchell, only heavier. Wayne said he figured that the investigators could tell whether they were one and the same girl from "the parts that were recovered."

"Well, we don't know that yet," Parris said. "Although, obviously, we don't have her head, as . . . you're aware."

Parris said Karen Mitchell wasn't a transient or a runaway. "She was very dependable. Something interrupted her—her path that day."

Wayne said the girl he met "was like I am now—not . . . not mentally cohesive, I guess you can call it. But not clear, not focused."

He said he'd met a lot of women with that kind of disorder. "They're not all there. That's what it is. It's just that they're not present."

Wayne asked if they could take a break and get some coffee, because he was really tired. "How long do you think it'll take to put me to death?" he asked.

"Well, that's not a decision that we're in a position to make," Parris said.

Jager said they were trying to get information to give closure to the families involved.

"Will my attorney know more?" Wayne asked.

"Yes," Parris said.

"Then how come I haven't talked to him yet?"

"You'll be going to arraignment this morning . . . probably in about two hours. And then you can ask those questions of him."

Before taking the polygraph test, Wayne said it seemed that if somebody wanted to lie, they could do so by controlling their breathing.

"I'm going to know . . . if you're doing that," Jager said. "I hope you're not going to try and do that with the test. You have no reason to, if you're telling us the truth, do you?"

"No, absolutely not," Wayne said.

After the interview, Jager, who had worked in law enforcement in Humboldt since 1971, told the *San Jose Mercury News* that Wayne was different from most of the homicide suspects he'd interviewed.

"He struck me as being very remorseful and very ashamed of what he had done," he said.

Furthermore, Jager said, he thought Wayne was telling the truth.

A group led by Gary Philp, the chief deputy in charge of the jail, escorted Wayne to the courtroom for his arraignment later that day.

While they were waiting outside in the security hallway, Wayne told Philp about his trip to the river with Freeman and Dawson, saying he felt that the officers hadn't looked thoroughly enough for Jane Doe's head. Wayne asked Philp if he could make sure they went back and looked again.

"I told him that we would be going back to that location and doing as thorough a search as possible," Philp, who had become sheriff by the time Wayne's trial started, testified later.

Judge Watson's courtroom was packed with more than a dozen television cameras and dozens of reporters who came from all over the state to cover Wayne's arraignment on a single count of murder.

"Sir, do you understand the charge?" Watson asked Wayne.

"Yes."

"Do you have an attorney in the matter?"

"I keep asking for one."

"Would you like to speak to an attorney?"

"Yes, sir."

"Do you have money to hire an attorney? Money available?"

"I can't hire an attorney."

Robinson was officially appointed and introduced to his new client. Wayne entered a plea of not guilty. The judge set bail at $1 million and scheduled the preliminary hearing for November 16.

The media presence at the courthouse that morning created "the kind of spectacle seldom witnessed in Humboldt County," the *North Coast Journal* reported. "Questioned by media outside the courtroom, public defender Kevin Robinson appeared miffed when a microphone narrowly missed hitting him in the jaw."

At a hearing a few days later, Watson granted Robinson's request for a gag order preventing all attorneys, investigating police agencies, and court personnel from speaking to the media.

In addition, Watson directed all jail employees to disallow media interviews with Wayne. Anyone who violated this order, he decreed, "may be punished as a contempt."

Watson said he'd received a "significant number" of requests to film or photograph the preliminary hearing. After Robinson asked to limit the number of cameras to "one or none," Watson said media pooling seemed a good way to address the defense's request. (Pooling generally means that only one still camera and one TV camera are allowed in the courtroom, and then must feed their broadcast footage and still photos to all like outlets.)

That afternoon, the sheriff's department received a call from Bill O'Neill, a supervisor at Arcata Readimix, who wanted to report that one of his workers had found a bone, wrapped in pink plastic, lying on a pile of rocks on the riverbank.

In light of Wayne's arrest, O'Neill said he felt he should alert the authorities because Wayne used to go down to the riverbank after work and drink beer with his coworkers.

Chris Rodriguez, another Readimix worker, told

authorities that he'd also found a few small white bones while running a machine that washed and screened out impurities during the cement mixing, and had saved one of them in the equipment shack.

The items, along with another bone and part of a shoe that turned up on the riverbank, were collected and analyzed. However, the bones turned out to be of animal, not human, origins.

By Saturday, November 7, news of Wayne's confessions hit the papers in Las Vegas, where they were of local interest because Tina Gibbs had worked there, Wayne had been a driver for the North Las Vegas Cab Company, and Wayne's ex-wife and son still lived in the area.

"His patterns indicate he was a disorganized predator who didn't really plan out what he was going to do," Kern County sheriff's Sergeant Glenn Johnson told the *Las Vegas Review-Journal.* "He also didn't offer a reason as to why he kept the body."

Las Vegas police reviewed old homicide and missing persons cases for possible ties to Wayne, including a case involving a woman's torso that was found on a conveyor belt at a local recycling plant. However, they found no connections.

"Dismemberment homicides are extremely rare, but it doesn't appear the timeframe fits," Homicide Lieutenant Wayne Peterson told the *Review-Journal.*

As the news slowly spread south, people who had known Wayne in Orange County came forward to tell the media how stunned they were to learn that he was a serial killer.

"Everybody is talking about it; they're basically shocked," Mike Mattingly, an employee at Taka-O, the sushi bar in

Laguna Niguel where Wayne used to work, told the *Orange County Register.*

Trino Llamas, who worked at an auto repair shop with Wayne, and considered him a close friend, said his hand started shaking when he saw Wayne on television. Llamas's wife couldn't believe that Wayne had actually sat in their living room and had dinner with them.

"I never saw him blow his top," Llamas said. "He was very mellow."

Llamas noted, however, that Wayne used to get depressed pretty easily. He said Wayne used to tell him that he and his then-wife, Elizabeth, fought frequently.

"He still loved her," Llamas said. "The next day (after a fight), they'd be in each other's arms. It was one of those deals."

When Scott and Linda Hayes heard about Wayne's crimes, they were horrified to learn that Wayne had been in their house with their children—twice—after having committed murder, and yet they still had not been able to detect any change in his behavior.

In the beginning, Wayne's family came to visit him in jail, where the officials let his aunt Vickie give him regular haircuts.

The first month, his aunt Doris came nine times, his father Gene only once. His brother, his cousin Tori, his grandmother, and his uncle Jimmy all stopped by as well.

Wayne called his family members collect so many times that he ran up their phone bills. Gene finally had to tell Wayne to call only once a month.

The irony did not escape Wayne that Arcata Readimix, his former employer, had supplied the cement for the jail that was now his home.

"I'm in the jail I helped build," he told Rodney.

The media was all over the family that first year, and depending on who said what, family members turned against each other, split, and divided over what was said.

Some of Wayne's relatives recalled how he used to play his guitar and sing Garth Brooks's country songs for them. How they'd go to hear him sing karaoke in the local bars. He sung a mean Elvis tune, they said, even making tapes of himself, which he tried but was unable to sell.

They told the *San Jose Mercury News* that he seemed to have a split personality, because he always seemed so sweet, good-looking, and polite. Never cussing in front of women. Never loud or boisterous.

But the embarrassment of it all often kept them from giving their names to the newspaper. "We don't condone what he did. We're horrified by it," one relative told the *Mercury News*. "But there is a sadness here and that is someone seeking acceptance, love and wants love from his earliest stage to his latest stage."

Several days after Wayne turned himself in, a TV reporter came banging on Rodney's windows at 2:00 A.M., demanding an interview and scaring Rodney's wife and kids so much that he immediately moved the family to another location.

Meanwhile, Rodney felt tortured, asking himself the same questions over and over: *Could I have prevented some of this? Why did I do some of the things I did to my brother? What should I say in court? Do I want my brother to die?*

In early November, Freeman and another deputy made the five-hour trip to Gene's house in Napa with a pickup and car trailer to collect the El Camino. Wayne had bought the vehicle from his father, then gave it back when he didn't want it anymore.

After lifting fingerprints and spraying the interior with

luminol, the investigators determined that the vehicle was clean, except for some blood on the driver's side of the pickup bed. Two months later, Freeman released the truck back to Gene, after Wayne's defense attorney and the prosecutor said they had no further interest in it.

Freemen met with Officer Dave Parris again, and after reviewing statements from the Ford family, decided to try to locate the teal Toyota sedan that Valerie Rondi had mentioned. Some of Wayne's relatives recalled that the car had a bad, unexplainable odor after he'd used it over the Labor Day weekend in 1997.

The car had been repossessed and sold to new owners in Willow Creek, but they allowed the officers to search the car and process it for blood. There was a trace amount in the trunk, but the DNA didn't match any of Wayne's known victims.

"I concluded there was another victim and we don't know who it is," Freeman recalled later. "I think he was at this for quite a long time. I think he started as a serial rapist."

Meanwhile, as Wayne met with his attorney, Kevin Robinson, he still seemed preoccupied with identifying Jane Doe and locating her missing head and limbs. Robinson hired criminalist John Thornton to try to find them.

Robinson also arranged to see if Wayne could recognize any missing women in a book of photos. He didn't.

Thornton and Cisco Lassiter, an investigator with the alternate counsel's office, met with Wayne at the jail on December 1, 1998, to get a description of where he'd buried the body parts. Wayne drew them a map of what he described as "the boneyard," an area on the riverbank surrounded by high willows, where Readimix stored equipment and junk.

Wayne said he'd buried the head three feet deep, under a concrete slab, in the slushy sand next to the boneyard.

Within an hour, Thornton and Lassiter went to the site, but the current was raging so hard they were unable to get anywhere near it. They took pictures of the river to prove that the described area was underwater.

Thornton made a second trip, on September 28, 1999, when the river was significantly lower. This time, Thornton was able to poke around, but he was unable to locate the slab block or any body parts.

The New York Times Magazine ran a blurb on December 20, 1998, making light of Wayne's arrest, with the head-line, "Something About Wayne."

"Norman Bates is getting all the attention lately, but there's a case to be made for Wayne as the official name of scary guys," it read.

The article proceeded to list murderers, including John Wayne Gacy, Wayne Williams, Wayne Boden, and John Wayne Glover, as well as other "unsettling Waynes" in the news, such as John Wayne Bobbitt.

"Coincidence? Lorenda Bardell, president of the Vancouver-based Kabalarian Philosophy, a group that tries to analyze how names relate to personality, says Wayne 'creates very caustic moods which prevent harmony in close associations.'"

PART IV

CHAPTER 20

NEW CHARGES, NEW ATTORNEYS

On September 17, 1998—just days before Lanett White got into Wayne's truck—California Governor Pete Wilson signed the "Serial Killer—Single Trial" bill into law.

Authored by state Senator Richard Rainey, R–Walnut Creek, the measure allowed district attorneys in different counties to consolidate multiple charges of murders, committed in a similar fashion, into a single trial to be held in any of the respective jurisdictions.

"Serial killers who go on brutal killing rampages do so without consideration of county lines," Rainey, a former county sheriff, said before Wilson signed the bill. "The current system is not only a waste of time and money, but it causes unnecessary pain for victims and their loved ones."

Proponents, who'd spent the past decade lobbying for such a bill, argued that the law could have saved taxpayers half the $2.1 million cost of convicting "Freeway Killer" William Bonin in Orange and Los Angeles Counties, where he raped and strangled fourteen boys in the early 1980s. (Bonin was executed in 1996.) Richard Ramirez, the "Night Stalker," and David Carpenter, the "Trailside Killer," were also prosecuted in several counties, forcing some witnesses to testify six times.

Opponents, including defense attorney groups and the American Civil Liberties Union, countered that piling multiple cases into one would ratchet up the cost of transporting witnesses and putting them up in hotels far from home, but, more important, would result in unfair trials for defendants.

"Prosecutors should not be able to 'forum shop' to have a defendant tried for a murder committed in one county in another county where the prosecution believes it will be more likely to get a conviction or the death penalty," the California Attorneys for Criminal Justice argued.

Wayne was to be the first defendant to face prosecution under the new law, which went into effect January 1, 1999.

Three months later, the Humboldt County Grand Jury indicted Wayne on a single count of first-degree murder for Jane Doe's death. His trial was set for July.

Meanwhile, prosecutors from Humboldt, Kern, San Joaquin, and San Bernardino Counties were discussing behind the scenes how best to consolidate the four murders into one new case, possibly elsewhere.

When San Bernardino prosecutor David Whitney heard about the Ford case, he told his assistant, Diana Soren, that it would be groundbreaking if he could bring it to their office.

So that's exactly what he set out to do.

"He was jazzed about it," Soren recalled later. "He loved a challenge."

Because there is no public record of these conversations, it's unknown how, when, or why this choice was made, but Whitney had clearly been pursuing his goal for months.

"This just makes sense for the most expedient way to do it," Whitney told the Riverside *Press-Enterprise* in November 1998. "It is more efficient."

Two of the four victims were from San Bernardino County, which had a broader tax base and was far more conservative than Humboldt when it came to sentencing defendants to Death Row.

Of the more than 660 inmates sitting on the row in September 2007, thirty-six were from San Bernardino, a mountainous and desert region of freeways, dust, and heat that ranked sixth among the state's fifty-eight counties in handing down death sentences. Only two of those inmates were from Humboldt, widely known as the nation's "marijuana country," where locals say their relaxed, bucolic life is sheltered by a "redwood curtain" from the rest of the world.

Ultimately, the other DAs agreed to let Whitney take the case.

On June 29, 1999, Whitney filed a new set of charges in San Bernardino as required under the new Rainey law.

Unlike the original complaint in Humboldt, which carried a possible sentence of life in prison without parole, this one packed a potentially fatal punch: Wayne now faced four counts of first-degree murder and the special circumstance allegation of multiple murders, which made him eligible for the death penalty. (He wasn't charged with the rape of "Sonoma County Doe" because it didn't fall under the new law.)

Around this same time, Ron Forbush, an investigator contracted by the San Bernardino County Public

Defender's Office, traveled to Eureka to ask Wayne if he wanted a public defender to represent him on the new charges.

Soon after Wayne said yes, Deputy Public Defender Joe Canty stepped in as a battle of legal heavyweights began to take shape in San Bernardino.

After earning his law degree and taking classes toward a Ph.D. in legal philosophy at the University of California, Los Angeles, David Whitney started his legal career as a deputy public defender in Los Angeles County in 1972.

Two years later, he left the public sector to become a criminal defense attorney, first in L.A., then in San Bernardino County, where he switched sides and joined the DA's office as a senior deputy in 1986.

Over the years, Whitney earned a reputation as a formidable courtroom force. He took on the role of coordinator for death penalty and psychiatric issues in the DA's office, rising to become lead attorney in its Major Crimes Unit and a member of the Capital Litigation Committee for the California District Attorneys Association in 1995. He also taught law courses and testified as an expert witness in state and federal death cases.

Soren went to work as Whitney's litigation assistant years after he'd defended one of four teen gang members who had murdered her father in 1981.

"Of all the attorneys, he treated my mother and I with respect," she said later.

Whitney started his long days working at home and didn't care for publicity. He had a dry sense of humor and enjoyed making people laugh, but he could also be very serious. Although he wasn't theatrical in the courtroom, he could be folksy if he sensed that would appeal to a jury.

"Juries absolutely loved him," Soren said. "He knew

when to be lighthearted with them. He knew when he had to be tough. He never lost a case when I was there. It was amazing to watch him."

Joe Canty was formidable in his own right.

After earning a bachelor's degree in political science at the University of California, Riverside, Canty entered law school at UCLA. Following graduation, Canty served as an Army Judge Advocate General (JAG) officer and then as a reserve JAG officer until 1974, while he was working as a prosecutor in the San Bernardino County DA's Office.

He rose through the ranks and became chief deputy in 1974, prosecuting high-profile cases while also earning a reputation for helping the helpless. In the process, he met Forbush, then a sheriff's homicide detective, and formed what would become a decades-long friendship.

Canty was similar to Whitney in that he, too, switched sides after a stint in private practice. During his time as a criminal defense attorney, Canty developed cancer. After battling the disease into remission, he joined the public defender's office in 1990.

"He fought the fight and he prevailed," Forbush said later. "He always had residual medical issues because of that, but he beat it."

Forbush, who started with the sheriff's department as a correctional officer, left as a homicide lieutenant on a disability retirement in 1977, shortly after a traumatic fatal shooting during an arrest.

He tried real estate for a while, then became a private investigator. While working for the public defender's office, he was often paired up with Canty, who had since become lead attorney in the Public Defender's Capital Defense Unit.

It was only natural that Canty get the high-profile Ford case, and for Forbush to join him.

Canty strongly opposed the death penalty, feelings that stemmed from his deep Catholic faith. An altar boy growing up, he attended a Catholic high school and later became a Eucharistic minister. He was known as "Papa Joe" to his nine children.

"He felt life is sacred," said Forbush, who shared those feelings with Canty.

Meanwhile, Kevin Robinson, Wayne's Humboldt attorney, still had a trial date on the docket, so he arranged for his client to undergo some medical tests in San Francisco.

Freeman tagged along with Correctional Officer Don Vizgaudis on the June trip, in case Wayne made any spontaneous comments. Freeman and Wayne spent much of the drive playing "Can You Top This?" a game that involves identifying the brands and years of passing cars.

Wayne made two remarks during the trip that later found their way into court papers. The first he said to a paramedic: "If I had been given Paxil ten years ago, it would have saved a lot of people."

He uttered the second one on the way back to Eureka. They were approaching the Benicia Bridge on Interstate 680 when they saw a woman standing with her children at the side of the road next to a car with its hood up.

"It's too bad that we can't stop and help because we have a prisoner," Freeman said to Vizgaudis.

"If we stopped to help her," Wayne chimed in, "she could tell her grandchildren how one time she was helped by two nice cops and a serial killer."

* * *

After learning that Wayne was going to be transferred to a jail in San Bernardino County, Robinson tried to block the move.

"What the district attorney is apparently attempting to do is deprive me of access to my client while I prepare for trial, on some theory that he gets to charge the same case in as many different counties as he can find are connected in their commission, and whichever district attorney wishes to go to . . . bat first gets to choose," Robinson argued at a hearing before Humboldt County Superior Court Judge Bruce Watson.

Watson rejected the motion, so Robinson petitioned the First District Court of Appeal in San Francisco to intervene.

But the momentum had already begun.

Wayne was transferred.

It didn't take long for the media to find out that Wayne had arrived at the West Valley Detention Center in Rancho Cucamonga.

In October, Wayne gave what appears to be his first and last interview to a newspaper reporter. He told James Rainey, a *Los Angeles Times* staff writer, that he had not understood "all the elements of the crimes" when he spoke to detectives back in November, and his requests for an attorney were denied at least nine times.

Since then, he'd clearly learned about the legal factors constituting murder, saying he'd realized that he "did not commit four murders."

The *Times* story said he also claimed that Humboldt County authorities had "'broken the law' during his initial interrogation" and "coerced him into making incriminating statements."

Wayne had not only been on medication since his confessions, he also seemed to have been educated about a possible insanity or diminished-capacity defense, based on the head injury he suffered in 1980.

But he exaggerated the facts surrounding that incident, telling Rainey that he'd been in a coma for nine days. He attempted to prove his claim by pushing the dental bridge holding his two front teeth forward with his tongue and pointing to a scar on his upper lip.

"I'm not saying I should be set free. Maybe I should spend the rest of my life in a hospital," Wayne said. "This should have been treated medically from the very beginning."

Still, Wayne said he didn't expect to be let off the hook and was ready for whatever punishment came his way—whether it be time in a psychiatric hospital, "forty years in prison" or the death penalty.

"It's in God's hands," he said.

CHAPTER 21

PREPARING FOR TRIAL

Rather than show his hand to Canty at a preliminary hearing, Whitney took the case to a grand jury in San Bernardino County in July 2000. With an indictment in hand, he was hoping to proceed directly to trial.

However, he was stifled by one delay after another. By December, dozens of motions had been filed in the case, including an unsuccessful challenge to the legality of the Rainey law.

Canty was so tenacious that he became the butt of jokes that played on his name, as in "Can't he get the case to trial?"

But Canty didn't mind.

"We thought it was humorous," Forbush said.

Before a second attorney, Deputy Public Defender Steven Mapes, was assigned to the case, Canty and Forbush worked as a team to prepare for a trial that both sides expected to hinge on psychological testimony about Wayne's mental state.

Their first goal was to explore Wayne's social and medical history, which Forbush described as "Death Penalty 101," so they could provide the jury with mitigating circumstances for Wayne's crimes.

"The jury has to know these things so that they can make a competent decision on whether to take this person's life or not," Forbush explained.

Canty and Forbush each formed a bond with their client. Forbush did this by avoiding discussion of the gory details and focusing more on the outdoors or Jeeps. Canty had a good but different kind of relationship with Wayne, who often didn't want to listen to his advice. That said, Wayne did give in to Canty's better judgment about not taking the stand.

"There was a time he . . . may have wanted to testify, but on his lawyer's advice, he accepted that it wouldn't work out the way he thought it might have," Forbush said.

Wayne would later jeopardize that decision, however, by confiding in an attractive woman who visited him in jail during his trial and recorded many hours of phone conversations for a documentary on his case.

As Forbush and Canty spoke with Ford family members, the issue of Wayne's mother kept coming up. So, Forbush tracked her down in Dehradun, India, and traveled there to speak with her.

For him, the high point of the interview, which lasted about eight hours over two days, was her candidness about her shortcomings as a mother and how she focused more on the search for herself than she did on raising her two boys.

Forbush said he and Canty felt that Brigitte's admitted lack of affection toward Wayne while he was growing up, and his feeling that she abandoned him, proved very important to the case.

One of the defense team's challenges was to sift through the conflicting opinions of the psychological experts who had assessed Wayne. Canty and his team did not support the theories generated by the first team, which had been leaning toward a defense that Wayne's brain was physically or structurally damaged. The new team attributed Wayne's inability to remember how he'd killed these women to seizures or amnesia.

Canty and forensic psychologist Reid Meloy, whom he hired in March 2000 at $360 an hour, viewed Wayne's deficiencies on a more psychological and emotional level. Ultimately, Meloy would spend about one hundred hours over six years on the case.

Among the psychological tests that Meloy administered to Wayne was the Rorschach, which he saw as a good way to show that Wayne's thinking was not organized in a logical or sequential way.

The Rorschach consists of ten cards with inkblots on them. In Meloy's view, the power of the test in a forensic case is that defendants don't know how to fake their answers, so it tends to convey more about their personality and psychology than they are aware of. Because he had done research in this area, studying about four hundred antisocial children and adults, he was able to compare Wayne's responses to normal people and those with similar diagnoses. Meloy was so interested in the Rorschach that he cowrote two books about it.

Wayne's test answers were interesting, and many of them were, not surprisingly, quite sexual.

"What might this be?" Meloy said as he showed Wayne the first card.

282   *Caitlin Rother*

"A spill on one side of a mirror," Wayne said. "A bug that's been squashed, poor bastard. A vagina down there."

Meloy put the card facedown and handed him the second one.

"A face in there," Wayne said, pausing. "A butterfly. Overall, I don't like it. It looks bad. Like a vagina in a way."

After seeing female genitalia on four out of the first seven cards, Wayne asked, "Am I undersexed?"

Wayne described the ninth card, which was in color, as "a gross picture, like an autopsy picture."

Of the tenth and final card, he said, "Colorful. Some flowers. Spinal type of splaying open. I don't like it. A spinelike structure. And then a clitoris at the bottom."

Wayne wasn't stupid. In fact, his IQ was 117, putting him into the bright-normal range. Meloy believed that Wayne was not only paranoid, but he also got his fantasies mixed up with reality. (Paranoid people typically have higher than average IQs.) To him, Wayne's paranoia explained why he reacted so angrily and impulsively when women unwittingly said or did things that he viewed as provocative and malevolent.

Meanwhile, the wheels of justice continued to grind slowly along as Canty filed more motions.

In February 2002, he asked Superior Court Judge Michael Smith to throw out the indictment, contending that it violated state law and Wayne's statutory right to a grand jury that was "randomly selected from a representative cross section of the population eligible for jury service in this county." Canty filed another motion to throw out the indictment in October 2004; Smith denied both of them.

In late 2003, Smith heard Canty's motion to exclude all of Wayne's guilty statements—during the interviews with detectives and the prosecution's psychologist, and his two remarks on the San Francisco trip—because he did not have an attorney present.

Smith issued a detailed fifty-five-page ruling in early January 2004, suppressing some, but certainly not the bulk, of Wayne's statements. Smith ruled as inadmissible the portion of Wayne's first brief interview with Freeman after he said he needed an attorney. Smith also suppressed the Berg interview, the three interviews with detectives that Wayne did that same day, and the following day's interview with Jager and Parris, which included the polygraph examination.

Smith allowed the other interviews, however, ruling that Wayne understood he could have stopped talking at any time by asserting his right to an attorney.

Canty and Forbush believed that they should've won on the Miranda issues.

"I felt the sheriff's people—they handled it pretty straight up," Forbush said later. "I just think Juan [Freeman] wriggled a little bit. Juan knew what he needed to do and he made it work. I think Rodney was used by Freeman and duped, if you will. Wayne, of course, was pretty fragile when he was arrested. I mean, that's pretty obvious."

Wayne's trial was scheduled to begin on March 1, 2004, but it was not to be.

At a hearing in January, prosecutor David Whitney announced that he was retiring and that Deputy District Attorney Dave Mazurek was taking his place.

"Having the case for so many years, it was hard to leave it," Whitney told the *Press-Enterprise*.

Wayne agreed to waive his right to have a trial within six months of his next hearing in February to allow Mazurek to become familiar with the complex case.

* * *

As a teenager, Dave Mazurek was recruited to play quarterback for the Cornell University football team, but he had to return to California two years later after tearing his rotator cuff and coming down with mononucleosis.

He transferred to San Francisco State University, where he became managing editor of the *Golden Gater* and graduated with a journalism degree. He earned a law degree from the University of La Verne in Ontario, California, in 1993, then went into private practice in nearby Claremont, taking any case that would pay the rent.

After three years, he decided to pursue trial work, and despite his lack of criminal experience, he landed a job with the DA's office in San Bernardino in 1996.

Mazurek won his first two death penalty cases, in 2003 and 2004. He was already having a very busy year in 2004, expecting to do four murder trials, when he inherited the Ford case, his third death penalty case.

Mazurek already knew of it from reading about it in the newspaper and chatting with Whitney.

"I think everybody had heard of this case," Mazurek said later, recalling that Wayne was known as "the guy who walked in with a breast in his pocket."

"It was pretty shocking," he said. "It kind of had the Jack the Ripper quality—the dismemberment, the girls who were disadvantaged and vulnerable and at bad places in their lives, living the kind of lifestyle that put them in his path, and the brutality that he carried out . . . on [them]."

Mazurek first saw Wayne in court in 2004, dressed in a sport coat, looking somewhat subdued, his shoulders slumped. He looked older and smaller than Mazurek had expected, given how he'd physically dominated his victims.

"There's no such thing as somebody who looks like a killer," Mazurek said, hastily adding the exception of serial

killer Richard Ramirez. "You would have seen him [Wayne]
walk down the street and wouldn't have given him a second
thought."

It also surprised him that Wayne seemed to enjoy talking to people, regardless of which side they were on.
Wayne would start conversations with Mazurek about
what he had for lunch, for example, stopping only after
Canty leaned over and said, "Don't talk to him. He's not
your friend."

Then, to Mazurek, Canty would say, "Please don't talk
to him."

Mazurek didn't start digging into the case until January 2005. He walked into the DA's board room, which
was lined with walls of blue binders containing more
than twelve thousand pages—forty-eight binders full—
of discovery materials.

When Whitney had handed over the case, he gestured
at these binders, saying they contained everything
Mazurek needed to know.

"If you have any questions, call me," Whitney said, just
as a father would hand the car keys to his son and tell
him to have fun driving it.

Mazurek felt overwhelmed by the sheer volume of
paper. But once he got over the initial shock, he began
formulating ideas and talking to the various detectives
involved.

At first, he was struck by the fact that Wayne had
turned himself in. However, he later decided that
Rodney had essentially talked him into it.

"Had his brother not been involved, I don't think he
ever would have gone to the sheriff's station, and more
girls would have been murdered," he said.

He felt it would be a natural human reaction for a

juror to dismiss Wayne's peculiar behavior as crazy, so Mazurek set out to craft a counterargument so as to say, "No, he's very disturbed, a sick individual and a perverted individual, but he still is somebody who deserves to be accountable for what he did."

Sadly, Mazurek was already familiar with Patricia Tamez's history because he had seen her around the courthouse before she was killed.

The prosecutor didn't think Wayne met the standard for an insanity defense, because he "was far too aware of what was going on and he knew it was wrong." Wayne went to elaborate lengths to cover up his crimes and was able to hold a steady job.

Mazurek noticed there was so much finger-pointing between Wayne's mother and father that it was virtually impossible to know who was telling the truth. That said, he didn't blame either one of them for the way Wayne turned out.

"It's his choice and his decision. There are lots of kids who grow up in messed-up houses and don't go on to become serial killers," he said, noting that a local boy had parents who chained him to his bed and fed him dog food. "Rodney went through the same thing and he turned out all right."

Mazurek was going through a few personal issues of his own when he became immersed in the case. He and his wife had not been getting along while he was in back-to-back trials in 2004; the Ford case didn't help matters.

After they separated in early 2005, Mazurek moved to his parents' house in La Quinta, which more than tripled his commute to three hours a day. But he became so involved in trial preparation that he was happy to have that time to think. He'd listen to witness interviews on CD, anticipate what the defense would say on direct, and come up with his responses for cross-examination.

"When you're in trial, it just becomes what you eat, live, and breathe," he said.

By the time the trial started in 2006, Mazurek was in the throes of divorce and faced another complication as well. After applying to become a judge in late 2005, Mazurek was called in for interviews with the governor's office and the Judicial Nominating Evaluation Committee, both in the middle of the trial.

Steven Mapes, a deputy public defender who considered Canty a mentor in the Death Penalty Unit, eventually joined the defense team.

A graduate of Brigham Young University, Mapes spent a year at a Spanish-language weekly newspaper in Washington State before earning his law degree from Valparaiso University School of Law in Indiana. The son of a Los Angeles Police Department officer and a dispatcher, Mapes worked for three years as a criminal defense attorney on indigent cases with which the public defender's office had a conflict of interest, then joined that office in 1998.

The prosecution team was able to track down Rachel Holt, aka "Sonoma County Doe," as well as the prostitute known as "Orange County Doe." They found "OC Doe" homeless in Arizona, but decided she was too strung out on meth to be an effective witness.

Mazurek met a number of times with forensic psychiatrist Park Dietz, with whom Whitney had consulted. He also ordered every book that Reid Meloy had written, so he'd be prepared to cross-examine him about inconsistencies in his testimony.

"It wasn't a whodunit," Mazurek said. "It was what was

his psychological state at the time he was murdering these girls."

In Mazurek's view, Wayne did not feel remorse for the brutal acts he'd committed against these women, merely sorry for himself.

Early in his career, Mazurek was bothered by the gruesome details of his murder cases. But over time, he—like most prosecutors—became desensitized to such things.

That changed with the Ford case. Looking at the autopsy and crime scene photos of Wayne's victims brought back the same kind of queasy feeling. Ironic as it was for a prosecutor to avoid funerals and talk of death, dealing with those pictures meant Mazurek had to confront one of his greatest fears, which previously he'd been able to squash.

Sometimes, while he was trying to fall asleep, his mind conjured up visions of Wayne opening and closing his freezer, taking out the neon-colored sherbet and putting it back, next to the frozen limbs. Or of Wayne cooking Jane Doe's breasts in his trailer oven.

He was particularly haunted by the fact that Wayne had carried Lanett White's body—black and bloated— in his truck for days, then dumped her in an irrigation ditch so many miles from home.

"There was something about that that really bothered me," he recalled.

Mazurek didn't speak to any of Wayne's family members, but he did interview the victims' parents before trial. They all seemed to have the surreal expectation or hope that their child would walk through their door one day.

Lanett's mother, Debra, cried when they talked. Tina's mother, Mary, seemed completely devastated, speaking very softly and choking up in the middle of sentences. Patricia's father Rudolfo's voice cracked and wavered as his eyes welled up with tears.

"There's something about seeing an older gentleman break down and cry," Mazurek said. "He seemed almost defeated by the whole experience and very regretful for perhaps not being able to be successful in getting Patricia off drugs and back home."

None of them seemed to be able to come to grips with what had happened.

"The pain and the grief never go away," Mazurek said.

CHAPTER 22

PROSECUTION: SADISTIC, SEXUAL PREDATOR

Jury selection started on January 17, 2006, more than seven years after Wayne turned himself in.

After screening a pool of nine hundred potential jurors, Canty and Mapes had 275 of them fill out questionnaires, winnowing the pool down to eighty-five. From there, they were able to select the final panel of six men and six women, plus six alternates.

This was Darlena Murray's first case as a juror. The English teacher from San Gorgonio High School in San Bernardino had been called for jury service before, but was never chosen.

When she first saw Wayne, sitting quietly, looking well-dressed and nicely groomed at the defense table during jury selection, she thought he was one of the attorneys.

But by the time the trial started, the forty-seven-year-old instructor had learned otherwise.

She also soon realized that this case would stick with her for the rest of her life.

The guilt phase of the trial was expected to last four to six months. If the jury found Wayne guilty, a penalty trial, estimated to go for two to three weeks, would determine whether Wayne should receive a death sentence.

Canty told the San Bernardino *Sun* that his client was ready to have a jury decide his future. But, he said, "Nobody looks forward to facing capital murder charges."

As judges go, Michael Smith was likable, relaxed, and easygoing.

Born in Los Angeles, he grew up in Commerce and suburban Monterey Park. His father worked in quality control at North American Aviation; his mother was an insurance agent and owned a dress shop.

Smith earned a bachelor's degree in political science from California State University, Los Angeles, in just three years by taking heavy loads and no summer breaks. From there, he attended law school at the private University of San Diego, clerking at two law firms that specialized in personal injury cases.

Smith was hired as a prosecutor by the San Bernardino County DA's Office in 1974, while he was still waiting for his bar exam results.

He'd also applied to the DA's offices in San Diego, Santa Barbara, and Ventura Counties, hoping for a nice beach area. But "San Berdoo," as it's nicknamed, was the first to call and offer him a job. He started there as a clerk, then became a full-blown prosecutor once he passed the bar.

"I always wanted to do trial work," he said later.

His original intention was to be a prosecutor for three

or four years, then go into private practice. But something unexpected happened along the way—he and a group of young turks found that they enjoyed the DA's office so much that they just stayed on.

"Next thing you know, it was twelve years later," he said.

Smith had never intended to become a judge, either, but he began eyeing open seats on the bench in the early 1980s.

"It just seemed like a logical progression," he said, adding that he thought it would be nice to make legal rulings for a change, rather than be subject to them.

Smith ran for an open seat in 1986, edging out his opponent by 2 percent and only two thousand votes out of 150,000 cast.

He had presided over eight or nine death penalty cases when he got the Ford case, which seemed to him like four cases combined, given that it involved four counties and four sets of investigators.

"It was different [from other] cases because there were multiple victims over a relatively long period of time and that's unusual," he said. "And the fact that he turned himself in, which is a very unusual circumstance."

As the judge who handled the county's longest and most complex cases, this one was right up his alley.

The trial finally began on the afternoon of March 13 as the media crowded into Smith's courtroom in the Central Courthouse for opening statements.

Wayne wore a jacket and tie, his hair slicked back, and sported a mustache. He could've been mistaken for a cop.

The judge announced that he'd decided to prohibit the half-dozen media cameras present from taking pictures or video while court was in session. At the defense's request, Smith said, he also wouldn't allow conversations between Wayne and his attorneys to be photographed.

Even before the prosecution could start its statement, Canty's second chair, Deputy Public Defender Steven Mapes, made the first of many defense motions for a mistrial and asked the judge to strike the jury.

Mapes accused Mazurek of targeting and upsetting teachers in the jury pool during voir dire—"people of helping professions," who might be sympathetic to Wayne—such that "they volunteered themselves off the jury." This, Mapes argued, then saved Mazurek from using up peremptory challenges during the selection process.

The judge denied the motion. He said teachers didn't fit the standard Mapes cited, and besides, he should've made the motion earlier, during voir dire. (Not to mention that Murray had been seated on the jury.)

Canty then launched the first of many objections he would make to photographs and exhibits Mazurek planned to show the jury, arguing that they were inflammatory and prejudicial. In general, Smith allowed Mazurek to show most of the photographs he wanted, and although he did order the withdrawal of some of the more gruesome images, there were plenty left to leave a lasting impression on the jury.

As Mazurek delivered his twenty-five-minute opening, he roamed around the courtroom, gesturing and animated, laying the blame for these murders squarely on Wayne's shoulders.

"Wayne Adam Ford knows what he's done. Knows what he's done to four young women. He knows what he is. And through the course of the evidence in this trial, you will know what the defendant has done and what he is.

"The evidence will show that the defendant was

responsible for the rape, the torture, for his sexual gratification, and the deaths of four women in their twenties.
He then discarded their bodies, some dismembered,
some decomposing, in various counties throughout the
state of California. Discarded them all in bodies of water.
Left them with no identification, no means for their
loved ones knowing what ultimately happened to them."

From there, Mazurek proceeded to lay out the details
of each grisly crime, attempting to preemptively knock
down whatever sympathy the defense would try to build
for its client.

Starting with Jane Doe, Mazurek recounted parts of
Wayne's interview with Detective Juan Freeman in which
he said that she—like his other victims—died accidentally.

"The defendant never, never specifies what, exactly, the
accident was that happened with this girl. But he did talk
about why she ended up the way that she did. He said he
had to make her small, to get rid of her parts. And so what
he did was, in his bathtub of his trailer, he cut her up, using
a survival knife that he had at his camp, because he wanted
to dispose of the parts."

Mazurek set out to cast doubt on Wayne's sincerity and
truthfulness, telling the jury that they would notice a
large—and suspiciously telling—gap in Wayne's memory.

"The defendant will say he had sex with all of these
girls, and that they all died, possibly, somehow, during sex.
And what you'll hear and what you'll notice is that the defendant can describe in detail where he meets these girls
. . . and then he can describe, after they're dead, what happened to them, where he left them. . . . But he never can
describe, and claims he can't remember, how they died.
But it was possibly, possibly during rough sex . . . [when]
sometimes he likes to put his hands or a rope around
women's necks and choke them."

Mazurek told the jury that the evidence would show that none of these girls died accidentally.

"He bound these women, engaged in sex with them, killed them, all because he liked to do it."

Mazurek closed by using Wayne's own words in June 1999 against him: "'That lady could have told her grandchildren she was helped by two nice policemen and a serial killer.'

"Wayne Adam Ford is a serial killer," Mazurek said, "a serial killer who knew what he was doing, killed for personal satisfaction, killed for sexual pleasure. The evidence will show he is guilty of four counts of first-degree murder."

Canty's oratorical style was a study in contrast to the jovial Mazurek, both in his limited movement and his expression. Although Canty was a friendly guy outside the courtroom, he rarely smiled in court, his expression so serious it bordered on dour. It was almost as if he had taken the gravity of the case inside him. He was clearly a believer in the cause, so he was credible to the jurors, making eye contact with them when he wanted to press a point.

Canty's opening statement also lasted twenty-five minutes, during which he cast Wayne in a sympathetic light, while also attempting to remove the necessary precursors to prove first-degree murder. He painted Wayne as a mentally addled man who did not intend to kill these women and whose "encounters" with them were not premeditated. He reminded the jury that Wayne was on trial now because he had turned himself in, knowing he was giving up his freedom forever.

"Now, he wasn't being sought, there were no APBs, the police had no clue as to who committed any of these four crimes that you heard described by the prosecutor.

Nobody was focusing on him, nobody was trying to find Mr. Ford. He just walked in, and of his own volition, because he decided that the killing had to stop."

Canty, playing a careful semantic game so as not to place blame on Wayne for murder, told the jury that these actions were significant in determining Wayne's state of mind when "the four decedents' lives were taken.

"The important thing about Wayne Ford is that he, himself, recognized there was something wrong with him. He had that insight."

Canty told the jury they were "about to take a very long ride together," which, for some people, may have conjured up an unwelcome image of Wayne driving around for days with the bodies in his truck. Nonetheless, Canty asked the jurors to keep an open mind during this ride, until the defense could present its case some months down the road.

He started by showing the jury a photo of Wayne in the pumpkin patch with his two-year-old son, Max, in October 1997, just before Wayne picked up his first victim. He recounted how Wayne couldn't bear to leave his son crying in the child care center on his first birthday, so he stayed and comforted him. How he couldn't bear to go back to see Max because he couldn't trust himself not to steal the boy away. Canty then jumped to Wayne's state of mind right after turning himself in, noting that he was very depressed and often broke into tears, raising concerns he might commit suicide.

Continuing with the social history, Canty showed the jury photos of Wayne's parents, whom he characterized as neglectful.

"Suffice it to say, at this point, that Brigitte did not want her son Wayne, and was a cold, unfeeling woman who did not see the value of hugging or showing affection to another. Suffice it to say that Gene, Wayne's dad, was a career military officer in the army intelligence, was just gone a lot, and struck fear into Wayne's heart when he was home. Suffice it to say, at this point, that both parents had agendas other than raising Wayne. And after the divorce, when he was a young teen, he and his brother were left to fend for themselves."

Canty said he would present evidence that would also help the jury to understand Wayne's mental problems when the homicides occurred.

Although he primed the jury for the testimony of a psychological expert in the field of sexual murders, Canty explained that this was not an insanity case because Wayne knew right from wrong. That said, "The evidence will challenge you to attempt to understand the workings of Wayne's mind. Truly, a journey into the outer reaches of psychological knowledge and beyond. We openly agree that in some respects what you'll see and hear reflects the mind of a person who at some period of time was out on Mars."

"So let's take that ride," Canty said.

After calling Bob Pottberg, who found the torso and alerted authorities, and Charlie Van Buskirk, the deputy coroner who collected and transported the remains to San Joaquin County with Freeman, Mazurek called the pathologist who conducted the autopsy of Jane Doe.

Dr. Robert Lawrence described the state of the body and gave a detailed description of Wayne's surgical techniques.

"The breasts were removed, in what I would describe as a careful, skillful dissection," he said. "I'm not saying a doctor did it, but I'm saying that it was done in a way that was neat, thorough. The entire breasts were removed on both sides. They were exactly the same on both sides. . . .

There were no, what I would call, mistakes made as the breasts were removed. Really quite impressive."

Lawrence testified that he couldn't tell if the victim had been strangled because the upper part of the neck was missing.

"I would say, though, that the bruising pattern on the right rear of her shoulder could indicate that someone held her tightly with the left hand, while maybe possibly strangling her with the right hand. But there's no way I could tell that. I'm just saying that's one possibility."

"In this case, do you have an opinion, given all the items that were removed, how long it would take to do that, based on your experience?" Mazurek asked.

"I'd say at least a couple of hours. . . . If this was done outdoors, it would have to be somewhere very isolated, where a person felt secure enough to undertake such a chore. If it were done indoors, it would usually be done in a bathtub. . . . Again, very messy. The way the breasts were removed indicates the type of precision and care that would take time, instead of just slashing and cutting. And I would say that the same thing applies, to a lesser extent, to the removal of the head and the extremities. . . . I think for a non-pathologist, you know, amateur, to do this kind of work would take quite a while."

On the morning of March 16, Canty moved to exclude the presentation of Wayne's hacksaw, hatchet, and knives to the jury—then also tried to exclude the testimony of the criminalist who had analyzed and compared them to Jane Doe's remains—because there was no scientific evidence that they were *the* implements used to cut her up.

"These items should not be paraded in front of the jury," Canty said.

Judge Smith said there was nothing "inherently prejudicial" about the items, which were lawful to possess, and relevant to Mazurek's case.

Canty disagreed, saying they were prejudicial.

"Anybody could come in and say these things," he said.

When Canty also questioned the relevance of the criminalist's testimony, Smith said, "It goes to the manner in which the crimes were committed, the manner in which the bodies were disposed of, and that is circumstantial evidence of intent."

Smith overruled Canty's objection, allowing Los Angeles criminalist Steve Dowell to take the stand.

Dowell compared each of the tools to the cutting marks on the bones, but he could not identify any one tool that did the cutting because some of the implements had multiple features and uses for sawing, cutting, and chopping.

Referring to the marks on the vertebrae where the head was severed, Dowell said, "Any sharp object, including any of the knives that were submitted to me, could possibly produce those marks."

"The marks that are left are consistent with the tools that you examined?"

"Correct."

Mapes's cross-examination was short and sweet.

"So what you can tell us is that the tools that you examined may have been used [to produce the marks] . . . you examined, correct?"

"Yes."

"Or they may not have been used?"

"Correct."

After questioning the witnesses about the forensic evidence, Mazurek called the sheriff's dispatcher and sergeant who talked to Wayne in the station lobby when he turned himself in.

They finished up in court early that Friday, but the

weekend break turned out to be longer than Mazurek had planned for.

Canty called Mazurek the next day, saying, "We might have to take next week off. There's an issue with Wayne."

"Okay, just keep me posted," Mazurek said.

On Monday morning, Canty announced that Wayne had become so agitated with the prosecution's presentation of the evidence the previous week that he was falling apart mentally. The judge allowed Canty's request for a week's break to allow Wayne to see a doctor and change his medication, which screwed up the travel plans for the prosecution witnesses scheduled to testify that week.

When the trial reconvened the following Monday, March 27, 2006, Mazurek called Detective Juan Freeman to testify about some of the horrific acts to which Wayne had admitted.

Wayne, who looked clean-cut in a dark blue suit, glanced through the transcripts of his interviews with Freeman, which had also been distributed to the jury.

Mazurek had Freeman prepare the jury for Wayne to be so soft-spoken at times that it was often difficult to hear him on the tape. Mazurek then played the first interview.

Before playing the tape of Freeman's next interview, Mazurek asked, "Did he express any reservations to you about talking with you?"

"No, sir, he didn't."

Freeman described Wayne's emotional state as "still somewhat down," noting that "he did break down a bit here and there" when asked how the victims died. He later testified that Wayne's answers were "evasive and nonresponsive."

While they were at the campsite, Freeman said, Wayne was "being helpful" by directing the investigators to the hole where he had buried the victim's thighs. He also explained what he had done with her body parts, specifically to her breasts, after cutting her up at his trailer.

"He said that they had been—they had shriveled up to almost nothing because he had cooked them and rendered the fat off the breasts into a coffee can," Freeman said.

"He said that she was . . . physically bigger than he thought she'd be. . . . He said he was trying to flush her guts down the toilet."

"Did he ever tell you why?"

"I don't believe he did."

The judge called a recess until the next morning, when Mazurek asked Freeman a few more questions.

On cross-examination, Canty led Freeman through an exercise that created the impression the prosecution was hiding something from the jury. He pointed out that the transcript in the jury's hands was different from the one that had been previously prepared for the grand jury, then asked Freeman to make note in the dozen or so places where the notation of Wayne crying had been omitted.

Next, Canty let the prosecution witness make the defense's case. By having Freeman admit that he'd tried to appeal to Wayne's conscience during the interrogation, Canty, in effect, was able to show that even the detective thought Wayne had a conscience.

He also got Freeman to acknowledge that Wayne went quite willingly to the riverbank to help them locate Jane Doe's head.

"And he didn't resist that or say, 'Gee, I don't want to

do that'? He seemed anxious to help you find things. Would that be fair?"

"That would be fair to say," Freeman said, adding that it was also fair to say that Wayne seemed genuinely interested in trying to help identify his victim, another counterpoint to Freeman's earlier testimony that Wayne was unresponsive and evasive during the interviews.

Freeman acknowledged that he'd advised the correctional officers that Wayne was depressed and that he "thought it'd be a good idea if they kept an eye on him . . . [in case] he became self-destructive."

Canty asked Freeman, who had told the jury he had a psychology degree, if looking at the floor was another symptom of Wayne's depression.

"It can be," Freeman said, adding that, as Canty suggested, it could also be an indication of shame.

One day when Mazurek was questioning one of the coroners on the stand, some schoolchildren on a field trip filed into the courtroom and sat in the back row.

During the morning recess, Wayne was sitting at the counsel table, and the judge came down from the bench to chat with the kids and answer some of their questions.

"What kind of trial is this?" one of them asked.

"It's a murder case," Smith replied.

Eventually, the children wanted to know where the murderer was sitting, but the judge was reticent to answer.

Wayne, who was wearing his sport coat and tie, turned toward the kids, raised his hand, smiled, and waved.

On March 29, Dianne Vertes, the pathologist who did the autopsy on Lanett White, testified that the toxicology test of the victim's chest blood showed .09 percent ethanol, or alcohol, but noted that this level can increase after death. (California's legal limit for driving under the influence is .08 percent.)

Vertes said the blood also showed a level of .23 micrograms per milliliter of methamphetamine, or speed, which would not change upon death, but she noted that neither substance, nor a combination of the two, would have caused her death.

Mazurek asked Vertes to describe what the jury was seeing in a particular photo of Lanett's neck.

Vertes testified that the pattern of red marks above the very pale area was consistent with someone having pressed a chain against her skin with an object. Skin goes pale, she said, when blood has been drained from it.

Asked if the marks were consistent with someone strangling Lanett, with, say, a nylon braided rope, Vertes said yes.

On cross-examination, Mapes began what would be a series of questions aimed at raising the possibility that these women died as a result of their own drug habits, not by Wayne squeezing their necks to cut off blood to their brains.

Mapes asked if what Vertes saw in the autopsy could also be consistent with a carotid hold used during erotic asphyxia.

"Yes," she said.

"And not the strangulation by ligature, as Mr. Mazurek refers to it?"

"Yes. That's right."

Mapes moved on to the toxicology results and asked if people who use methamphetamine can develop arrhythmias, which are abnormal changes to the heart rhythm.

"Absolutely," Vertes said.

Because speed itself could cause such a change to the heart rhythm, Mapes asked if the chances of developing an arrhythmia were even greater for people engaged in erotic asphyxia while they were high on meth.

"There are so many factors involved in answering that question, that, I mean, it's, like, anything is possible," Vertes said. "I mean, I could give you another scenario, too, that's just as likely."

"Well, the fact is, we don't know what happened?" Mapes asked.

"We don't know what happened. And it's possible."

Mapes pointed out that the toxicology results showed no trace of amphetamine, which shows up in the blood after the body starts to metabolize the meth, so he concluded that Lanett was high when she died.

"So we only see the parent drug, which means it hadn't started to wear off?" Mapes asked.

"Yes."

Next, Mazurek called Mike Jones, the lead detective on Lanett's case. Jones testified that after interviewing Lanett's family and friends, he "basically ended up following some leads that turned out to go nowhere" until Wayne surrendered to authorities.

Mazurek passed out transcripts to the jury and played the tape of the two-and-a-half-hour interview by Jones and his partner, Joe Herrera, so the panel could hear Wayne's own words for itself. He would do the same thing before calling detectives from each of the other counties, playing their respective interview tapes and questioning them about Wayne's "amnesia" about the killings.

Under cross-examination by Canty, Jones acknowledged that he'd encountered cases involving sexual asphyxia and carotid holds during his time on sex detail.

Canty asked him to demonstrate the practice to the jury.

"It's actually two pressure points, and it's on the side of the neck at the carotid veins, which would be in this position about right here," Jones said, placing his fingers against his own neck.

Jones explained that the idea was to apply enough pressure to cut off blood and/or oxygen to the brain, both of which ultimately translate into a lack of oxygen and result in a partial or full state of unconsciousness.

"The reason again that you learned of this in your training . . . is that [it] in some manner increases the pleasures associated with the orgasmic event?" Canty asked, trying to make the practice seem less malevolent.

Jones acknowledged that it was called autoerotic asphyxia when a person attempted to do it to himself, and that some couples also engaged in the practice.

"Is it part of your training and experience that sometimes people engaging in this behavior can make a mistake and hold the pressure too long, deprive the other person of oxygen . . . thereby causing significant injury or death?" Canty asked.

Jones said yes. He'd never seen that in couples, but he said, "I'm sure it's possible."

On redirect by Mazurek, Jones said Wayne did not seem overly tired during the interview, nor did he seem to have problems understanding any questions or say he was too tired and ask to stop.

"People engage in erotic asphyxia sometimes for the pleasure of the person that's being restrained, is that correct?"

"That's correct."

"And sometimes it is for the pleasure of the person that's doing the restraining?"

"That is correct also."

Mazurek reiterated Canty's question about somebody making a mistake while engaging in this practice.

"Probably not likely that somebody would make four mistakes?" Mazurek asked.

"Probably not."

On Monday, April 10, Mazurek called Donna Brown, the pathologist who did the autopsy on Tina Gibbs, referring to whatever photos the judge had allowed after Canty's objections to virtually all of those Mazurek wanted to show.

As Brown described the bruises in Tina's neck, Mazurek asked her to demonstrate how someone would cause such injuries. She did so, and Judge Smith translated for the court reporter.

"For the record, you're indicating a hand around either the chin or throat area, where you're separating your thumb from the other fingers, the thumb being on one side of the neck and the rest of the fingers on the other side of the neck?"

"Yes," she said.

She then described the broken bones, saying the injuries were consistent with "manual strangulation with the hands. . . . Tina died because of asphyxia. She couldn't breathe because she was strangled."

Anticipating Mapes's question on cross that arrhythmias had caused Tina's death, Mazurek asked Brown if she'd explored any possible causes for a natural death.

"Yes," Brown said. "And she was pretty healthy."

On cross-examination, Mapes questioned Brown about the amounts of cocaine and alcohol found in Tina's blood, which were 3,070 nanograms per milliliter, and .12 percent, respectively. (Depending on the state, 50 to 300 nanograms per milliliter of cocaine is considered a positive test result.)

Brown noted that decomposition could have contributed to the alcohol level, despite her body being found in cold water.

As expected, Mapes did bring up the possibility of arrhythmia caused by the cocaine, complicated by the sexual asphyxiation, as Tina struggled for air. Pointing to an autopsy photo, Mapes then tried to get Brown to say that the marks on Tina's neck and face could have been caused by someone doing CPR.

"It's conceivable that that's possible?"

But Brown wouldn't go there. "I don't think it's very possible. You'd have to use two hands, one to hold the nose and the other to stabilize the jaw."

On redirect, Mazurek brought that point home, saying the bruising "to a reasonable degree of medical certainty, [was] not done while somebody was rendering CPR to her, correct?" Or for that matter, he added, the ligature marks around her neck.

"Correct," she said.

Asked how much pressure it would take to fracture someone's thyroid cartilage, she said, "It would be a large amount. Someone would have to do it, more likely, in the heat of anger or something like that, where their force would be applied more than" ordinary CPR.

With erotic asphyxiation, she said, people "pass out to the point where they just block main vessels. They don't break larynx and thyroid cartilages and hyoid bones."

Before the next witness, Canty and Mapes renewed their objection to the upcoming testimony of "Sonoma County Doe," aka Rachel Holt, in light of the testimony by the three previous pathologists about injuries to the victims that were completely different from Rachel's.

"There hasn't been any evidence on any of the victims

about premortem tying up," burns to the vagina, or bruising to the breast, Mapes said.

Canty noted that there were a number of other dissimilarities between the crimes, alleging that Jane Doe died at Clam Beach after Wayne drove her there in a private vehicle, and Tina Gibbs died in a motel in Las Vegas, not in Wayne's truck.

But none of this had come out at trial.

"Well, that's not what we have in evidence," Mazurek said.

Mazurek said the testimony would establish similarities in intent and motive, and underscore the crucial commonality that most, if not all, of Wayne's victims were strangled after getting into his truck and having sex in the sleeper.

"She can talk about his intent was clearly not to satisfy her sexually, but to satisfy himself sexually through the use of strangulation, ligatures around her neck, being rendered unconscious, being revived, being rendered unconscious, several times," he said. "How he engaged in . . . what I'm going to term sadistic acts. . . . [She] can testify this is what he clearly engaged in, were conscious choices, not accidents."

Judge Smith ruled that the pattern of injuries and sexual activity was consistent overall, making the testimony of "Sonoma County Doe" "highly relevant," certainly enough to outweigh any potential prejudicial impact.

Next up was Dr. Steven Trenkle, who conducted the autopsy on Patricia Tamez. Mazurek planned to use his testimony to paint Wayne as a monster who tortured and inflicted pain on his victims while they were still alive.

Trenkle testified that Patricia may not have been

conscious when her back was broken, but she was still breathing.

"Her heart was beating and blood was circulating," he said, adding that it was the type of injury you might see in an automobile accident, or when someone fell and landed on their back when it was acutely hyperextended or stretched backward, or when someone was struck with a hard blow, kicked with a boot, or kneed in the back. But, he said, it could not have been caused by someone doing CPR on a mattress in the back of a truck.

Referring to the step or ledge beneath the truck's passenger-side door, Mazurek asked, "What if they fell on that as they were pulled out of the cab?"

"Oh, that might do it, yes."

Trenkle explained that if a person's carotid and vertebral arteries were cut off at the neck, he would be unconscious within ten seconds.

"How long would you have to restrict blood flow to the brain for it to be fatal?"

"It would be generally in the area of five minutes. . . . Some people might be dead after three minutes, and others, after six or seven minutes, they might recover."

"But at three to five minutes, you've got to be choking somebody out for that period of time consistently to restrict the blood flow and cause death?"

"Yes."

Trenkle said he determined the cause of Patricia's death to be manual strangulation, meaning not by a rope or tie.

On cross-examination by Mapes, Trenkle said he determined that she was dead by the time her body was placed in the water.

Again, Mapes tried to raise the possibility that Patricia died as a result of erotic asphyxia, but this line of questioning did not go so well for the defense.

"I think the injuries to the neck could occur in a sexual

asphyxia scenario, sure," Trenkle said. But, he added, "What I know of sexual asphyxia doesn't include breaking someone's back."

Although no drugs were found in Patricia's blood, Mapes still tried to link her death to her past abuse. He noted that minuscule amounts would not have been detected by the toxicology tests and that a meth user can develop an enlarged heart, as Patricia had.

Trying to undo the damage caused by the image of Wayne squeezing these women's necks for five minutes straight, Mapes went down the same road of arrhythmia with Trenkle as he had with the other pathologists, suggesting that such heart problems could have contributed to the deaths during the erotic asphyxia.

But Mazurek cut through the potential distraction for the jury on redirect.

"There's no physical evidence of a heart arrhythmia?" he asked.

"No," Trenkle replied.

"Even assuming Miss Tamez had an arrhythmia under the defense's scenarios, it wouldn't have happened if she . . . wasn't being strangled, correct?"

"That's the way I interpreted his scenario."

"And, of course, Miss Tamez wouldn't have died at this time had she not been strangled, correct?"

"Correct, yes."

On Tuesday, April 11, Rachel Holt was sworn in as "Sonoma County Doe." Because she was the only living victim who would testify about her experience in Wayne's big black truck, her testimony was pivotal for the prosecution.

As allowed under the law for rape victims, she brought an unidentified person to sit with her at the witness stand.

Acknowledging that she was nervous, she testified that she was living in San Francisco and had continued to work as a prostitute since the incident with Wayne.

Mazurek walked her through the escalating events of that night, establishing the point where consensual sex turned to rape.

"Did you ever tell him no?"

"I probably did once or twice, but then after I realized it wouldn't even have been an option for me, I don't think I said anything more after that," she said, feeling Wayne's stare as she testified.

"What's going on now after he's tied you up and flipped you on your back? Is this part of the deal that you made, to engage with the defendant in this type of sex?"

"No."

When they got to questions about Wayne getting aroused as he punched and hit her between the legs with a belt buckle, Rachel asked if she could take a break. The judge called a ten-minute recess.

After they came back, Mazurek asked, "While you were on the floor, did you say anything or make any complaint to the defendant?"

"I couldn't too much, because he had me to where I couldn't. He had some kind of tie or something tied around my mouth. Like, I was kind of gagged."

Mazurek said he knew this was hard for her to think about. "Have you tried to put this out of your mind?"

"Oh, yeah."

She testified that she couldn't stop crying the whole time Wayne was strangling her, causing her to pass out, then reviving her.

"Was he saying anything to you while he was doing that?"

"All I can remember is that he just kept telling me to 'shut up, shut up. Don't look at me. Shut up or I'll kill you.' I couldn't help but cry. That's something you just can't stop. And that's all I remember."

Reiterating Wayne's defense, that "he put ties around women's necks to cut off the carotid arteries, to give them pleasure," Mazurek asked, "Did you feel like that's what he was doing with you?"

"Oh, no."

"Why not?"

"'Cause if I'm crying and it hurts, that's not pleasurable to me."

"And were you passing out?"

"Oh, yeah."

"Did he seem to be getting turned on by doing that to you?"

"It seemed like the whole time, mostly, he was still real frustrated . . . and really nervous."

Mazurek reminded her that she had told investigators that it seemed as if Wayne "was getting turned on" by strangling her during sex.

"When you pass out and black out so many times and you're scared, it's, like, it's hard to remember anything anytime later," she said.

"Was he being kind and gentle during the sex, or was he being a different person?"

"Oh, no, no, no."

"How was he being?"

"Rough and forceful and mean. . . . So, eventually, I just played lifeless, 'cause I didn't know what else to do."

Mazurek asked how long it took for Wayne to stop. Rachel said it seemed like it went on for five or six hours. She couldn't say for sure because she didn't have a watch and couldn't have looked at it even if she did.

"It seemed like forever. I thought it was never going to end."

Referring to the conversation they had about Wayne's

son and ex-wife after the rape, he asked, "So there was nothing, no—no conversation about that, that set him off to do the things that he did?"

"No."

After the lunch break, Canty launched into his cross-examination and immediately began his mission to impeach Rachel by raising inconsistencies in her statements to investigators, including the defense's own, Ron Forbush.

Rachel admitted she felt sympathy for Wayne as Canty reiterated her earlier testimony that he'd seemed very depressed when he apologized to her and displayed a remorseful expression she would never forget.

"Never. Never, ever, ever," she said, confirming her previous statement.

"And you said that he cried for fifteen minutes . . . and he had his head on your shoulder, correct?"

"Yes, sir."

"And you actually felt empathy, you felt sorry for him?"

"For a minute. At that time. But only for about a minute."

Canty returned to his focus on impeachment, listing her many arrests for prostitution.

"Twenty, thirty?" Canty asked.

"It's possible," she replied.

When Canty asked about her pimp, Mazurek objected and the judge sustained it on the grounds of relevancy.

Canty asked for a bench conference, explaining that Rachel had told his investigator that she got into the truck because she was desperate. Canty said he believed that she may have needed money to pay her pimp, which gave her a motive to exaggerate the night's events.

Mapes chimed in, saying, "Our theory is that she engaged in some S and M voluntarily, consensually, and it got out of hand. . . . She normally never gets into a big rig."

Smith ruled in favor of the defense, overruling Mazurek's objection.

Rachel went on to testify that her pimp was the first person she called from the pay phone when she got off the freeway in Cloverdale.

Canty returned to the subject of Rachel's arrests, asking her to confirm them, one by one. She admitted to pleading guilty to a misdemeanor after being charged with felony hit-and-run. She said she didn't remember being arrested for contributing to the delinquency of a minor and she denied being convicted for burglary, although she acknowledged she was arrested on the charge.

"How about possession of a stolen auto?" Canty asked.

"No."

"Back in West Virginia?"

"That was ten years ago. You expect me to remember that?"

Rachel began looking noticeably uncomfortable, fidgeting and shifting in her chair as she caught on to what Canty was doing. "What relevance does any of this have to do with right now in this case, anyway?" she asked.

So, Canty told her, bringing up a second rape report she made to police shortly after her encounter with Wayne.

"About a few months after your encounter with Mr. Ford, you reported another case, falsely, about being raped. Is that correct?"

"Falsely?"

"Yes."

"I think if I'd been raped, I wouldn't be falsely accusing anybody."

Moving on, Canty questioned her truthfulness when she claimed she hadn't been doing drugs in 1999 when she was arrested for prostitution in Sonoma and offered to make undercover buys for the arresting officer.

"Not true," she said. "Not true."

"Odd," Canty said. "So, if an officer wrote that in his report, he was lying?"

"Obviously, because I wasn't doing drugs then."

Canty circled back to the alleged rape incident, then started in on her again.

"What I'm asking is, you made up a story about being raped?"

"I didn't make it up. I would never make up a story like that. Never."

"Well, the reason you made up the story, am I correct, is that you believed that they had stolen your money?"

"Are you trying to make it seem like I'm a liar?" she asked. "I'm not. I would never make up a story like that because I believed somebody stole my money. That's ridiculous."

Clearly upset by the confrontational questions, Rachel turned to the judge and asked if they could take a break. He said yes.

But the break did nothing to interrupt Canty's line of questioning. He pointed out that the nurse who examined her found no evidence of assault after the second rape. In fact, he asked, "When that was all over, the police arrested you for filing a false report, correct?"

"I don't remember," Rachel said.

Canty continued with the litany of her arrests, asking her to confirm that she'd been arrested for pandering and lying to an officer in Salt Lake City.

When Rachel said she didn't remember, Canty asked if she remembered being arrested.

Rachel confirmed that she'd spent a few months in jail for pimping and pandering, but said the charge of "misleading a police officer" didn't ring a bell.

* * *

On redirect, Mazurek tried to clean up the damage the defense had done to his witness's credibility.

Asked what activities were to be covered by the $100 fee to which she and Wayne had agreed, she said, "Sexual intercourse."

Mazurek then asked her a series of questions about whether she consented to any of the violent acts that Wayne had committed against her, including binding, strangling and beating her, and punching and burning her in the vaginal area.

"No," she answered repeatedly.

"Did he ask you whether or not he could tie you up?"

"No, and if he had, I would have said no."

Mazurek asked if she felt sorry for Wayne today in the courtroom.

"No."

Asked to explain what she stole when she was arrested for burglary, Rachel said she took some clothes, which she planned to sell for money. Prostitution did not provide a very stable income, she said.

"In light of you told us everything that you've done in the past, including your convictions, your arrests, and the types of things you've been engaged in, if you had lied about the incident that Mr. Canty was talking about, would you tell us you lied?"

"Yes, I would."

"Okay. Were you lying about that?"

"No."

Mazurek closed by asking whether she'd been truthful in her testimony about being tied up, and engaging in vaginal and anal sex with the defendant, while being strangled, all without her consent.

"Yes," she replied.

* * *

Even after Rachel left the stand, Canty continued to tangle with Mazurek over her truthfulness. This debate continued for weeks as Canty kept trying to impeach her testimony, arguing with Mazurek and the judge, and calling several witnesses to dispute her statements about her 1999 rape report.

In short, Rachel had told police that she'd been grabbed and dragged into a motel room, slapped, and threatened with a knife while a half-dozen underage males poured alcohol down her throat until she passed out. When she woke up, she said, she was missing $400 and her pager, and "felt different down there."

Police subsequently found photos the young men had taken of her, posing naked and smiling. The men admitted to robbing her, and she, in turn, admitted to buying them beer. No rape charges were filed and it wasn't clear from the testimony whether any sexual assault had actually occurred.

Canty was upset. He didn't learn until after she'd flown back to San Francisco that Smith had granted Mazurek's request to issue a bench warrant in case she tried to avoid testifying. To Canty, this suggested that she was coerced into testifying and he had missed his chance to question her directly about it.

Canty dragged out the witness credibility debate until Smith and Mazurek expressed concern that they were spending more time on this side issue than the murder case itself.

"It takes us down the path of an issue that is completely collateral to what we're dealing with here," Smith said on April 24, just before the defense began presenting its case. "We're going to confuse the jury with these issues, and I don't see for what."

When all was said and done, Canty had succeeded in casting doubt on Rachel's credibility. But ultimately, it was not enough to outweigh the horrors of what she'd described to authorities and again in court about her night with Wayne Ford.

In 2008, Rachel recalled that testifying had been very difficult for her. She not only had to face her attacker again, but she was also torn apart by Canty, who kept asking what she thought were irrelevant questions.

She said it was the hardest thing she'd had to go through since being raped by Wayne a decade earlier, but she'd had no choice. Mazurek had forced her to come and testify.

Before the trial, she said, she'd been successful in putting the experience out of her mind. But while she was testifying, she said, "[Wayne] stared at me the whole time. It brought back all the bad memories."

The prosecution finished its case on April 12, 2006, sooner than anticipated, so Judge Smith called a recess until Monday, April 24, when the defense had scheduled its first witnesses. Given their prearranged flights, the defense team said it was not able to bring them in any sooner.

CHAPTER 23

DEFENSE: CONFUSED AND MENTALLY ILL

The defense began its case with Andy Lowery, who was called to elaborate on Wayne's state of mind during the period the crimes were occurring.

Lowery testified that Wayne had visited him monthly for about two years until just before he turned himself in. Mostly, he said, they discussed whether he had a conscience.

Mazurek objected, prompting Smith to question the relevance of Wayne's statements to Lowery.

"If he is conflicted over things that are going on at that time and is depressed and is looking for spiritual guidance, that's certainly an indicator from which one can argue an inference that he was not intentionally killing people," Canty said.

"Perhaps another inference is that he was conflicted

over the fact that he was intentionally killing people,"
Smith replied.

Canty argued that the defense had a right to counter
the prosecution's allegation that Wayne was evasive
during his statements to the detectives, a time when "he
was in fact sincerely involved in trying to resolve a moral
conflict in his life."

So the testimony—brief as it was—proceeded.

Canty then called Pastor James C. Ray, a Pentecostal
pastor who started visiting Wayne in jail after ministering
to the prisoner in the cell next door. The pastor said he
talked to Wayne through a slot in the door to his single
cell, singing hymns and Southern gospel songs and discussing the spiritual aspects of conviction, remorse, and
forgiveness.

"He asked if I thought God could forgive him," Ray
testified. "And the only thing that I can do is tell him
what the Scripture . . . says: all men who are in sin shall
be forgiven."

On cross-examination, Mazurek asked, "It's really not
all that unusual for people who don't care about spiritual things when they're not incarcerated to—when they
become incarcerated—want to talk about spiritual
things?"

"Sometimes," Ray replied.

On redirect, Canty asked, "Did Mr. Ford impress you
as someone who just suddenly wanted to talk about spiritual things?"

"No, I believe it was there all along. But he was wanting further counsel, spiritually, concerning things that
were already going on in his heart and mind, I believe."

* * *

Just before Canty was ready to call Wayne's friend Scott Hayes, Mazurek's objection to a photo of Wayne and Max in the pumpkin patch triggered a debate about the relevancy of testimony by Wayne's family and friends, whom Canty had intended to call to illustrate how events during his upbringing contributed to his current behavior.

"I don't think I need to litigate his entire childhood," Mazurek said, arguing that matters about Wayne's character, his family dynamics, and his social history were not relevant in the guilt phase of the trial, but more appropriate for the penalty phase, if they should get to that point.

Canty countered that much of this testimony was necessary to back up the opinions of their psychological expert, Reid Meloy, who believed that Wayne's various mental illnesses were attributable, at least in part, to interactions with his parents.

Smith, however, noted that such matters, even if they had contributed to Meloy's opinions, were not necessarily independently admissible.

Smith said he would allow Scott Hayes to testify since he was already on his way to the courtroom, but he would not allow the pumpkin patch photograph.

When the judge indicated other witnesses from Wayne's family and friends weren't going to be relevant, either, Canty asked for more time to research his argument before the judge made his final ruling.

The debate continued in the coming weeks, usually out of the jury's presence.

Canty said the defense had planned to call Gene Ford to testify about his ex-wife's behavior—including her sexual promiscuity, depression, mood swings, and suicide attempts—that may have influenced Wayne socially, but also could indicate that she passed on to him a genetic susceptibility for mental illness.

Canty said Gene was also going to talk about how Wayne's personality changed first at twelve, when his mother "said she no longer wanted him in the house and sent him to live with his father," and then later, after his head injury, when he became even more withdrawn and depressed.

"The only way for the jury to believe that these things were true and to understand that these facts do exist is for us to prove them," Canty said. "I think that we are not only entitled to prove them, that we have an obligation to prove them, in order to make the expert's opinion viable . . . with the jury."

Mazurek disagreed, saying the murder trial would turn into a family law dispute over Wayne's childhood history, and would take months to litigate. "We've got Dad saying Mom's a horrible parent. We've got Mom saying Dad's a horrible parent. We have disputes about things that happened twenty and thirty years ago."

"All of this stuff is not relevant to the . . . issue of whether he murdered these girls, and his intent at the time."

Judge Smith agreed, saying they didn't need "a credibility contest" between relatives as long as the defense expert had considered those discrepancies before rendering his opinion.

At Smith's request, Canty listed off the witnesses he'd intended to call—Wayne's aunts Ginger and Vickie and uncle Jimmy; Wayne's first stepfather, Steve Shurtluff; and Gene's friend Keith Hale—and detailed the gist of their anticipated testimony.

Canty said the defense had also planned to present depositions of Wayne's maternal grandmother, a videotape of Forbush's interview with Wayne's mother and a transcript of excerpts, along with some other witness interviews.

After Mazurek reiterated his objections, Smith ruled that any testimony by relatives or other witnesses about Wayne's emotional and mental history should be limited to the period just before he turned himself in.

"Whether or not he has remorse and understands the need for punishment afterward is a penalty phase issue, not a guilt phase issue, in the determination of what offense was actually committed," Smith said.

This ruling dramatically altered the scope and duration of the case the defense had intended to present.

"A lot of the time we were planning to spend has now been removed from the case," Canty told the judge.

So, in the end, Rodney was the only family member the defense was able to call, and briefly at that.

On Tuesday, April 25, one of the male jurors was excused after being hospitalized for a medical problem and his doctor suggested that he shouldn't continue with the trial. Smith seated one of the alternate jurors—a woman—in his place.

Next up, Canty called a neurologist and a radiologist, who had conducted tests on Wayne's brain and found some abnormalities.

Dr. Arthur Grant, the neurologist, had performed a twenty-four-hour video EEG study on Wayne at a hospital in the city of Orange in October 2002. The test was to measure his brain waves and videotape any seizures or spells that might occur, but none did.

In layman's terms, Grant found that Wayne's brain was like an eight-cylinder car running on six or seven cylinders, i.e., not functioning at its normal speed. One test result showed activity that was consistent with chronic alcoholics, even if they'd been sober for a while. Other possible causes could've been Wayne's head injury, but the doctor couldn't say for sure. He determined that these abnormalities had been present for quite some time, but he couldn't say how long.

On cross-examination, Mazurek asked if people with these mild abnormalities could still function in daily life.

"Most likely," Grant replied.

"There aren't any definitive studies in your field that say, 'People with these findings act this way'?" Mazurek asked.

"No, there are not."

"There's nothing that says people with these findings go out and murder people?" Mazurek asked.

"No, of course not."

Dr. Michael Green, the radiologist, testified that he conducted an MRI to look at the structure of Wayne's brain in September 2000.

The MRI, he said, showed mild to moderate atrophy in the cerebellum, the part of the brain that is used for sensory perception and coordination of muscles and movement. He said the atrophy could have been caused by alcoholism, certain medications, or congenital defects.

Once again, Mazurek cut to the chase on cross: "This type of cerebellar activity doesn't cause people to go out and commit crimes, right?"

"Not that I'm aware of."

"Doesn't cause people to go out and murder other people?"

"Not that I'm aware of."

* * *

On May 4, Canty decided to present to the jury the brief transcript excerpt from Forbush's interview with Brigitte that the judge had decided to allow, but not the videotape. Instead, Canty played the video taken while Wayne was being booked to illustrate his mental condition at the time.

After keeping the jury all morning without presenting any witnesses, Canty was concerned the panel would think the defense had done something wrong.

"I hope the court won't make it look like our fault," he said.

The judge said he would repeat his earlier explanation, that they had expected to have some testimony, but additional legal issues arose, and after discussing them, "much or some of that testimony was not available."

"You might even include that the defense had their witnesses here," Canty said.

"If you want me to," Smith said.

After the jury had been excused for the day, the judge revisited Mazurek's request to conduct a psychological exam of Wayne to use as rebuttal testimony to defense expert Reid Meloy's. Canty objected, arguing that psychologist Paul Berg had already done an interview with Wayne days after he surrendered.

Mazurek said he was planning to have Dr. Park Dietz do the exam, which prompted an unusual eruption from Wayne at the defense table.

"The guy is a liar, though. I won't talk to him," Wayne said.

Smith told Wayne that was something he could discuss with his attorney.

* * *

On the morning of Monday, May 8, Judge Smith announced that he would grant Mazurek's request for Dietz to do the exam, with Wayne's attorneys and Meloy present as observers. The exam would take place on May 15 at the courthouse, after Meloy had finished testifying.

Canty launched another objection to using Dietz, which explained the basis for Wayne's outburst.

"The ground for that involves our impression that Dr. Dietz has, in fact, participated in testifying to falsehoods in other cases, including a famous case in Texas, which resulted in a reversal of a conviction there, the [Andrea] Yates case, as a result of the falsehoods to which he testified and which were relied upon by the prosecution in that case," he said.

Smith overruled Canty's objection, saying those issues could be raised during cross-examination.

Next, the attorneys and judge debated what Meloy could and could not say in his presentation to the jury.

The prosecution's main concern was that Meloy shouldn't be allowed to give an opinion about whether Wayne had the capacity, intent, or premeditation to kill these women, and the judge agreed. Smith ruled that Meloy could discuss his research and different types of killers, but should leave it to the jury to decide which type Wayne was.

Before calling Meloy to the stand, Canty asked the judge to verify for the jury that the black and blue marks on his face were not the result of a fight. Apparently, both defense attorneys had dental work done the previous Friday.

"So that's the reason for any bruises or swelling, not that they were out doing anything else," Smith told the jury.

* * *

Meloy, a forensic psychologist and expert in sexual homicide, was the witness Canty hoped would pull together the complex aspects of the case for the jury. It also didn't hurt that he was a handsome witness.

As Canty led Meloy through his qualifications, Meloy said he had a Ph.D. and two master's degrees, one in psychiatric social work and one in theology. He ran his own nonprofit research company called Forensis, focusing on violent criminality. He'd published eight books, three of them on sexual homicide. And he'd been retained by the federal government on the Timothy McVeigh and Terry Nichols cases, the two men responsible for the Oklahoma City bombing massacre.

Meloy would be on the stand for three days, split almost evenly between direct and cross-examination— longer than any other witness during the trial. His testimony was crucial because it would help explain Wayne's complicated mental state and, the defense hoped, persuade the jury that he did not commit premeditated first-degree murder, let alone deserve the death penalty.

Meloy spent quite a bit of time explaining his methodology, which included interviewing Wayne for fifteen and a half hours, reviewing transcripts of interviews with family members, friends, and other witnesses, looking at crime scene photos, and reading various case reports. He also explained the series of tests he administered to Wayne before reaching his conclusions.

Severe mental disorders, he said, have both psychological and biological components, and although they may skip a generation, they are often passed down directly from parent to child. Traumatic events would typically make such disorders worse, causing people with "insult to the brain" to develop psychological problems.

Meloy explained that there are two types of homicides. The first is "predatory," which are planned killings and are committed without feeling, such as a contract murder, and the second is "affective," which are based in impulse or emotions such as anger or fear of a perceived threat. Following the judge's restrictions, Meloy carefully indicated that Wayne fit the second category.

One of the tests he gave Wayne was called the Psychopathy Checklist, on which he scored 24 out of 40 (the higher the score, the more psychopathic traits a person has).

"He's slightly more psychopathic than the average inmate who's in prison in the United States," Meloy said. "About 57 percent of inmates would be less psychopathic than him and 43 percent would be more psychopathic."

Mazurek would do his best on cross-examination to poke holes in Meloy's opinion that Wayne was not a severe psychopath.

Meloy then proceeded to lay out his complex diagnosis of Wayne, including his personality disorders and paraphilias, the formal term for a sexually deviant pattern of behaviors or perversions.

The four more common paraphilias were exhibitionism, sexual masochism, sexual sadism, and voyeurism. The rarer ones were picquerism, which is attaining sexual arousal through the insertion of needles, usually into a woman's breasts or buttocks; erotic asphyxia; partialism, an intense focus on one body part for sexual arousal, which in this case was the breast; and pseudonecrophilia, or isolated incidents of sex with a corpse that occur without preexisting fantasies or desires.

Meloy said Wayne had a recurrent major depressive disorder with psychotic features, noting that Wayne's military records showed that he was first diagnosed with depression when he was twenty-two, in April 1983, which indicated that the condition was chronic and started long before the killings.

"Psychotic is a general term that means a person at times will lose contact with the reality around him and will create in his mind an idiosyncratic, oftentimes bizarre reality," Meloy explained, adding that Wayne would still be in such a state if he weren't taking Paxil.

Mcloy said that Wayne was an alcoholic, dependent on liquor since at least 1983. He said alcohol, and Bacardi 151 rum in particular, helped lower his inhibitions and increase his impulsivity and depression during the year of the killings.

Next, he said, Wayne had three out of ten possible personality disorders, the first being a severe case of Antisocial Personality Disorder, for which he lacked only one criterion.

"This individual shows guilt and remorse," Meloy explained, adding that he not only observed Wayne "wracked with emotional pain and remorse for these acts he committed," but Wayne also discussed those feelings in detail with him.

Meloy later said that he believed these killings were out of character and perceived even by Wayne himself to be unacceptable behavior, which was "exceedingly troublesome and disturbing and guilt-inducing to Mr. Ford." Furthermore, he said, Wayne was not glib, superficially charming, or grandiose, as psychopaths often are.

He said Wayne also had a Borderline Personality Disorder, which was borne out in his history of attaching quickly and intensely to certain women. Initially, he would idealize them, but later, after the relationships grew rocky, he would devalue them, then turn angry and aggressive.

It is typical, Meloy said, for people with this condition to be sensitive to abandonment, reacting with rage and fury. Because their self-esteem is very unstable, they often act impulsively, exhibiting self-destructive behavior, such as suicide attempts, substance abuse, and risky sex.

"When alone, these individuals also feel very empty and . . . try to seek other people to take care of this feeling of emptiness inside. . . . [Wayne] shows the most instability in his relationships" with women, he said.

Wayne's last personality disorder, he said, was of the NOS, or "not otherwise specified," category, meaning he had features of several other disorders, but he fell short of having those full-blown conditions.

"Mr. Ford is very dependent on other people. Mr. Ford is quite narcissistic, and also is very self-defeating," Meloy said, adding that the latter feature, a term formerly known as masochism, surprised him. "I have not seen that in a case of this kind."

In his view, the dependent feature went back to Wayne's relationship with his mother, who admitted to Forbush that she never bonded with Wayne because she didn't want the pregnancy.

"She reports that she was raped to produce Mr. Ford. He was a product of rape. And she also told him this," Meloy said. "That kind of information being provided to a child is going to deeply affect self-esteem, and also the absence of an emotional connection with a mother . . . [is] going to leave its mark over the course of a person's life."

Wayne, he went on, also had a strong sense of entitlement and had exploited women, showing an absence of empathy while gratifying his own desires.

"This is one of many contradictions in this man's personality," he said.

Sometimes, he said, Wayne showed "striking empathy in his understanding of human relationships," and yet at other times, he demonstrated a striking lack of empathy by acting "extraordinarily cruel and aggressive."

Meloy said Wayne was not only sadistic but sadomasochistic, seeking out women who would inflict pain on him while having sex and vice versa.

Meloy cast blame on both of Wayne's parents for contributing to this behavior.

"Dad was an intimidating individual who could be suddenly and unpredictably aggressive in the family toward his wife, and oftentimes that aggression was sexualized," he said. "So Mr. Ford is raised and learned that this is what you do with women. You aggress against them suddenly and you aggress against them sexually."

Meloy said Wayne told him that when Wayne was seven years old, the family was sitting around the dinner table and his father suddenly "pulled out his mother's breast from under her blouse and showed it to the boys." Meloy acknowledged that he could not confirm this allegation.

Meloy said a mother's sexual promiscuity can factor into behaviors like Wayne's.

"Oftentimes that can teach the son, particularly if he's overstimulated, it can bring up feelings in him as a boy that he doesn't know how to deal with, such as fear, anger, or even excitement on the part of what his mother is doing. The indifference by the mother and the belittling by the father, I think, had an impact on both Mr. Ford's attitude toward women and distrusting and devaluing of them. And secondly, had a large impact on how he viewed himself, because of the verbal humiliation and intimidation by Dad. So he didn't think much of himself and, also, he did not trust women."

Meloy noted that the number of women and prostitutes Wayne said he'd been with varied, depending on whom he was talking to and when. At different times, he told Meloy he had been with four to ten prostitutes per week between the first and second victim, that he had been with a total of fifty to sixty prostitutes, and that he'd had no sexual partners between his third and fourth victim. He told detectives that he'd been with fifteen to twenty prostitutes, and he also told them that he'd used erotic asphyxiation on fifty women.

Overall, Meloy said, what those various figures "tell me is that he engaged in these paraphilic behaviors with a number of different women during this year's period, most of whom he paid for this kind of sexual activity, that were not killed and did not die."

Acknowledging that Wayne's transition from grief over losing his son to killing these women may seem bizarre on the surface, Meloy explained, however, that Wayne was not just grieving for his own son, "he's also grieving for what he never got [as a boy]. . . . In my opinion, the grief was genuine, real, and quite intense."

Meloy cited Wayne's admission that he was suicidal after his wife left with their son.

On its own, he said, the loss of a son would not cause a person to commit serial homicide. But here it was merely one ingredient that proved deadly when added to the personality disorders, the depression, the paranoia, the dislike toward women, the dangerous paraphilias, the impulsivity, and "the degree to which he sees women as being provocative."

"The combination of all these factors, in my opinion, was causative of the serial homicides," Meloy said. "The mix here was deadly. The recipe is very, very rare for this to occur."

Asked to explain the dismemberment of Wayne's first victim, Meloy said he felt Wayne was trying to hide evidence and was also sexually aroused through his paraphilias, using the breasts to masturbate, then cooking and freezing them so he would be in control of them.

Interestingly enough, he said, Wayne was reluctant

to admit some of these acts, telling Meloy, "I find that horrible and disgusting."

Unlike the first psychologist who worked on Wayne's case, Meloy said he didn't believe that Wayne had amnesia about the killings, acknowledging that the earlier finding would have been more favorable to the defense.

"He has clear memories of those events," he said. "There could be, literally, dozens and dozens of reasons to not admit [to that]."

Regardless, Meloy said, Wayne had a desire to stop killing, and that's why he turned himself in.

"This is an extraordinary behavior that I have never seen in a serial homicide case," Meloy said, adding that he'd also never read about such a case "where a person has walked into a police station with physical evidence, and over time confessed to the details of the crime, specifically to have himself stopped because he could not stop himself."

Because Canty was not allowed to ask, and Meloy was not allowed to give an opinion about Wayne's state of mind at the time of the killings, Canty closed his direct examination with this carefully worded question: "Your experience with what we might term the predatory or pure psychopathic killer is not one which there is a desire to stop?"

"Correct," Meloy said. "And that's because there's no conscience, there's no conflict, there's no guilt, there's no remorse. And there's an . . . increasing pleasure, oftentimes, in the actual killing itself."

Mazurek began his cross-examination of Meloy after lunch on May 9. From the very start, Mazurek pounded on the point that Wayne—not his mother, father, brother, or ex-wives—was to blame for these killings. To win a verdict of first-degree murder, Mazurek had to prove beyond a reasonable doubt that Wayne didn't act impulsively, but rather made a definite and premeditated choice to seek out these women to rape, torture, and strangle to death.

Meloy admitted that Wayne's wives, girlfriends, and prostitutes did not like or consent to such behavior, but Wayne proceeded to engage them in it as his behaviors escalated into violence.

One by one, Mazurek attempted to undermine Meloy's opinions about the contributing personality ingredients for this fatal "recipe" he had described, including the punishing behaviors by Wayne's parents. Meloy consistently responded that Mazurek was oversimplifying a very complicated psychological diagnosis.

"Lots of kids got spanked with a belt?" Mazurek asked.

"Oh, I'm sure they did," Meloy answered.

"And everybody that's spanked with a belt doesn't grow up to murder people?"

"Fortunately, not," Meloy replied. "Again, it's the confluence of all these different factors that we are talking about."

Trying to dissect Meloy's methodology, Mazurek noted that the expert took into account Wayne's statement about his father pulling out his mother's breast at the dinner table, even though it couldn't be corroborated anywhere in the record. Meloy explained that he'd specifically asked Forbush to pose that question to Wayne's mother, but that did not happen.

The prosecutor blasted Meloy for admitting that Wayne had exaggerated some of his personality test answers, and yet relying on those test results to form his opinions. On this, Meloy stuck to his guns, speaking in psychological jargon that rationalized his methods.

As Mazurek went through the various tests that Meloy

had administered, the prosecutor raised what he saw as inconsistencies between Meloy's testimony, the test results, and his published statements.

Meloy stood firm, although agitation crept into his voice as he answered Mazurek's questions. "I would never score a person just on the basis of the finding from one test, as I said probably half a dozen times," he said, referring to the Psychopathy Checklist.

Mazurek also confronted Meloy for contending that Wayne lied in certain instances, exaggerated or distorted facts in others, while still claiming that Wayne was truthful.

"My clinical interviews with him were not such that I found him to be a chronic liar," Meloy retorted.

During the questioning, some new information about the death of Jane Doe was revealed. Wayne told Meloy that he placed her body in a sleeping bag, took her back to his trailer, and went to bed. He woke up in the middle of the night, put her in the bathtub, cut her throat, and bled her out. The next day, he left her in the tub and went to work. When he came back, he cut off her breasts, head, arms, and legs, then sliced out her vagina.

"He didn't call anybody, he didn't call the paramedics, didn't notify anybody he just had this horrible accident and this girl died?" Mazurek asked.

"Correct."

This was all good fodder for Mazurek to dispute Meloy's finding that Wayne had shown guilt and remorse. The prosecutor presented a long list of Wayne's actions surrounding this incident, attempting to force Meloy to say they did not indicate remorse or guilt.

"Neither is putting her breasts in the oven and trying to melt them?" Mazurek asked.

After repeatedly saying Wayne did feel guilt and remorse, Meloy finally had to agree with Mazurek on this example, but he pointed out that the prosecutor had overlooked some details.

"You left out the fact that—that he also told me that he was dry heaving and vomiting during the dismemberment," Meloy said.

"Okay. That could be for a number of reasons?"

"It could be. One of them being disgust and horror at what he was doing."

"Of course, not so disgusted and horrified that he had to stop," Mazurek said.

"Correct."

The next morning, Mazurek used a similar line of questioning about Wayne's conduct after killing Tina Gibbs, again revealing some new details.

Wayne told Meloy that after strangling Tina with a tie, he went drinking and won $1,000 while gambling. Meloy said this was consistent with Wayne's history of numbing his emotions with alcohol.

"So, keeping her in the cab for three to five days after she's dead, is that consistent with remorse?" Mazurek asked.

Meloy gave a long answer, saying that behavior was consistent with his other findings about Wayne's paraphilias— but he said, "One could not confirm whether or not he was experiencing conflict at that moment."

"And keeping Ms. Gibbs's body and using it for necrophilia, for sexual intercourse, that's certainly not conduct consistent with remorse?"

"It could be," Meloy said, prompting the jury to snicker. He explained that Wayne's attempt to achieve sexual relief by gratifying his paraphilias could have been a way to manage the intolerable emotions resulting from what he had done.

Mazurek asked if Wayne knew these girls could die when he engaged in these behaviors.

"I think he was too disorganized and psychiatrically disturbed and agitated and personality-disordered to comprehend that," Meloy said. "It is my opinion that he was not aware that he was causing the death of anybody."

Asked to elaborate, Meloy read aloud from his interview notes, starting with Wayne's comments about Jane Doe:

"Bothersome feelings in her. She didn't want to be done. I felt awkward, not horny. The best I can think, she said something that set me off. Maybe I strangled her or punched her. I remember really enjoying sex with her firm, big breasts. In my car. Vaginal, oral sex on me. No anal. When I looked up at her, she wasn't breathing. I was face down on her. CPR trained. I'm scared she's hurt. Overdosed. Sex facilitated it. Drive to a hospital. Last time I was honest with police I got cruelty to animals. Shocked. Confused. I took her back to the trailer."

Similarly, Meloy said, Wayne denied knowing that he'd caused Tina Gibbs's death, claiming he'd initially thought he was drunk and "squished the piss out of her."

After discussing at length the many instances that seemed inconsistent with Wayne showing remorse, Mazurek tried one more time to get Meloy to admit he was wrong: "Even with all of that, we don't even get a maybe that there's a lack of remorse or guilt?"

"Correct," Meloy said.

"No matter what I ask you, basically, you're not going to change your score to that?" Mazurek said, referring to the Psychopathy Checklist.

"Correct."

Reading aloud one of Meloy's published statements, Mazurek asked if he would agree with it: "The use of tests to determine state of mind at the time of the crime is, at best, wholly inferential, and, at worst, grossly misleading?"

"I would agree with that, generally, given what I just said," Meloy said.

As Mazurek finished up his cross-examination, he tried one last time to get Meloy to say that Wayne engaged in his lethal paraphilias "with reckless disregard" for his victims. But Meloy still wouldn't go there.

The erotic asphyxiation didn't start as a means to kill these women, he said, "I think it started as a paraphilia, but I think then, when you talk about . . . the disregulated fury, the impulsivity we've just discussed, the person is at great risk of being killed."

On redirect, Canty went back over Meloy's most significant findings.

"Can people do horrible things repeatedly and still have a conscience and still have remorse?"

"Yes."

Countering Mazurek's rhetorical drumbeat that Wayne made a premeditated choice to kill these women, Canty asked if an Antisocial Personality Disorder is thought to have a genetic component.

"Yes . . . People do not choose to have an Antisocial Personality Disorder, nor did they choose to have psychopathic traits."

The following week, on Wednesday, May 17, Canty called psychologist Paul Berg, who had interviewed Wayne in the Eureka jail.

Although he'd initially been hired by the Humboldt County District Attorney's Office, Berg's testimony proved helpful to the defense.

"Did you get any sense, in evaluating Mr. Ford, that his presentation involved malingering?" Canty asked.

"No, there were a number of reasons I didn't."

Berg said Wayne did not do what defendants generally do when they're trying to "con the doctor." They either "act like a prisoner of war" and refuse to discuss anything, or they try to befriend and butter up the doctor.

"He did neither of those," he said. "He was kind of straight."

On cross-examination, Mazurek asked if they could write off Wayne's depression as a natural, common reaction to being in jail.

Berg said no, because Wayne was not just depressed, he was "profoundly depressed."

"What I believe Mr. Ford was depressed about was what had happened and what he did. And the reason I say that is, he was not arrested. He didn't get stopped on the highway, picked up at his home. . . . It was by [his own] volition that he turned himself in. It wouldn't make sense that he's been depressed about being in, because . . . [it] was his own choice."

Despite objections by the defense, Wayne's two ex-wives testified as prosecution rebuttal witnesses after lunch—and out of order; the defense had yet to rest its case.

While Elizabeth was on the stand, Mazurek peppered her with questions about the time and attention Wayne paid to his son, Max.

During their marriage, Elizabeth said, Wayne would occasionally hold Max, but only until he cried; then Wayne would hand him back to her. He didn't feed Max, try to change his diaper, or bathe him.

When Wayne came to see Elizabeth and Max after the separation, Mazurek asked, "Did he visit with Max?"

"No."

"Did he hold Max?"

"No."

"Feed Max?"

"No."

Elizabeth said Wayne spent more time talking to her than paying attention to his son. Throughout 1997, Wayne did not call and ask to talk to Max, send him greeting cards, or call to check on his welfare. Even during the October 1997 visit, she said, Wayne spent only ninety minutes with his son and the other four and a half hours talking to her and his friends.

"Did you take Max and hide him from the defendant so he would never have any contact with his son?" Mazurek asked.

"No."

"And, in fact, you encouraged him to have some contact with his son?"

"Yes."

On cross-examination, Canty brought up situations that characterized Wayne as just the opposite—emotionally attached to and interested in the welfare of his son.

While Elizabeth was pregnant and went in for her ultrasound, Canty asked, "He viewed the picture of the child?"

"Yes."

"And he was emotional about it?"

"Yes."

"Cry?"

"Yes."

"And was he there for the birth of the child?"

"Yes."

Elizabeth acknowledged that Wayne also took out a $10,000 loan to help support the family when the couple was having financial problems in Las Vegas, and after the separation, he sold parts of his Jeep to help pay for an emergency room visit for Max.

She also acknowledged that Wayne was depressed throughout the relationship, and he had spent four days with his friends Scott and Linda Hayes, contemplating suicide, after the breakup.

After the brief testimony of Ron Forbush and DA investigator Christine Murillo, the defense officially rested.

CHAPTER 24

REBUTTAL: MALINGERING?

Dr. Park Dietz, a forensic psychiatrist and the prosecution's next rebuttal witness, met with Wayne on May 15 and 19 to conduct the psychological evaluation in preparation for Dietz's testimony.

Although he was initially retained on the case in November 1999 by prosecutor David Whitney, a former FBI agent who was one of Dietz's associates had worked on it alone until recently. Together they had racked up more than $58,000 in fees, subsidized by taxpayers, so that Dietz could rebut Dr. Meloy's findings and conclusions.

When Dietz took the stand on Wednesday, May 31, Mazurek led the psychiatrist through his qualifications, which included running two consulting firms: Park Dietz & Associates, and Threat Assessment Group, Inc. Dietz said he'd also coauthored a book and published articles on sexual masochism and sexual sadism, and had helped craft the language for sections on paraphilias and impulse control disorder in the *Diagnostic and Statistical Manual of Mental Disorders (DSM)*, which sets standards for the mental-health field. He also consulted for the TV show *Law & Order*.

As part of the high-profile cases with which he'd been involved, he evaluated John Hinckley Jr., the attempted assassin of President Reagan, serial killer Jeffrey Dahmer, DC snipers John Malvo and John Muhammad, and a half-dozen other serial killers that Mazurek cited.

Rather than wait for the defense to attack the witness on his point of weakness, Mazurek had Dietz explain how he'd run into trouble with the case of Andrea Yates, the Texas mother with postpartum depression who drowned her five children in the bathtub. He said he'd accidentally misspoken during his testimony and later tried to correct the record. However, the prosecutor had used his statement in his closing argument, and it later fueled an appeal that led to her conviction being overturned.

As Mazurek had Dietz dissect and rebut Meloy's findings, the psychiatrist testified that he disagreed with many of them because of insufficient evidence or proof to support them.

In some cases, he simply differed with the methodology or definition Meloy had used, including his finding that Wayne showed "affective" versus "predatory" aggression. He said those terms applied to an event, not a person, and were not appropriate to describe criminal behavior, because crimes could involve elements of both.

"One would have to know what actually happened to make that judgment," he said. But in this case, one of the two witnesses to each of Wayne's crimes was dead; the other witness—Wayne—claimed amnesia.

Dietz also disputed Meloy's opinion that Wayne was depressed the year of the killings, saying, "I don't think that the evidence is quite as convincing."

For one, he said, if someone is drinking alcohol, it's impossible to tell he is depressed, because the alcohol can heighten those symptoms, so "we don't know if it's drinking or depression."

Suggesting that Wayne may have sought mental-health treatment because he was seeking an excuse for his crimes, he completely dismissed Meloy's opinion that Wayne had psychotic features along with his depression because he had no history of hallucinations, delusions, or thought disorders.

The use of the term "catatonic" in Wayne's military records about the Okinawa incident, he said, was not applied properly because Wayne was still able to talk; he simply chose not to. Dietz said Wayne may have faked certain symptoms, prompting a diagnosis of psychosis, which went hand in hand with the Antisocial Personality Disorder. Wayne's records reflected that the military doctors gave him Haldol because he was violent and aggressive, not psychotic, Dietz said.

Dietz concluded that the evidence concerning the head injury from 1980 could not be "associated with the onset of emotional collectivity, impulsivity, temper, or aggression" because such symptoms do not grow over time; they tend to come on immediately. This, he said, conflicted with the testimony by Wayne's wife, Kelly, who said he was nicer after the head injury, and also with Wayne's history of starting fights with men and showing aggression to women before and after his head injury.

Although Dietz said he agreed with Meloy's diagnoses of Antisocial and Borderline Personality Disorders, he disagreed with the labels of "impulsive" and "explosive."

With impulsive aggression, he said, "there is no gain,

no apparent motive." But in this case, Wayne did have a motive—to gain sexual arousal. He was able to function well in the marines for a time and also to hold a series of jobs and control his aggression when his wives or girl-friends asked him to.

Also, Wayne told Dietz that "he taught himself how to look like he had an explosive temper to avoid being pushed around," modeling on his father's behavior.

Asked to discuss how paraphilias are developed, Dietz launched into a lengthy explanation, saying the cause was unknown, but the specifics seemed to be learned, primarily by males, between the ages of eight and twelve.

Paraphilias are thought to develop by chance associa-tion, he said. He gave the jury an example of a man he'd treated who couldn't sustain a healthy relationship with women. Dietz was able to trace the man's problem years back to when he masturbated while looking at his father's detective magazines, which often featured a sexy woman with a knife to her throat or tied to the radiator.

Similarly, he said, Wayne had access during puberty to the porno magazine *Screw,* which Dietz said "had some unusual pictures in it, and that he found exciting, used for this purpose, and still remembers to this day." (Wayne had also told Meloy that he'd looked at bondage and sadomasochism magazines when he was about nine years old. Gene said they weren't his and he had no idea where Wayne would've gotten ahold of such publications.)

Dietz did concur with Meloy's opinions about the par-tialism and sexual masochism, revealing that Wayne had not only performed erotic asphyxiation on women, but also on himself, using a necktie to enhance his own or-gasms and asking women to strangle him during sex. He told Dietz that he'd bound, burned, and pierced his own genitals for pleasure.

"Could that be a way of him trying to explain why he

does certain things to women in these cases, because he says he does it to himself?" Mazurek asked.

Mapes objected to the question. "Calls for speculation," he said.

"Sustained," Smith replied.

Dietz acknowledged that Wayne was a sexual sadist, but he explained that even sadists can satisfy their needs without hurting anybody—by using fantasy, masturbating to pornographic images, or simulating acts with consenting partners. Violent crime, he added, was "the gratification of last resort" and, thankfully, the rarest.

Asked if paraphilias could cause a man to act a certain way and remove his self-control, Dietz said, "No. All the paraphilia does is dictate what causes erection, not what one does with the erection or what one does in the rest of one's sex life. . . . A person can't help what turns them on. They do control what they do about it, if anything. . . . Overall, only a tiny, tiny fraction are going to commit any crime."

Countering Meloy's statement that Wayne's case was unique because he turned himself in, Dietz said he knew of at least eight other cases of sexually motivated serial killers who did the same thing, two at the urging of siblings.

Furthermore, he said, "Remorse at a subsequent point does not inform us of the mental state at the time of the crime."

Canty began his cross-examination on June 1, using some of the same impeachment techniques against Dietz that Mazurek had used on Meloy, sparring with Dietz over semantics and arcane psychological jargon.

For example, Canty brought up a comment Dietz made on *60 Minutes II* as he tried to cast the psychiatrist and his philosophy in an unsympathetic light: "Treating private psychiatric patients means listening endlessly to people with fairly normal lives whine about why their lives aren't as great as they wished."

In particular, Canty battled with Dietz over his definition of depression, attempting to prove to the jury that Wayne was psychotic and that his extreme fear of abandonment caused him to make decisions from an abnormal perspective.

Canty pointed out that Wayne's military medical records show a diagnosis of "acute psychosis" in September 1984. Dietz shrugged that off, saying no symptoms fitting that diagnosis were recorded, even after Canty showed him a second notation by a nurse.

"So your assessment is that he was probably malingering in order to get out of the Marine Corps?" Canty asked.

"No. I'm saying that's a possibility," Dietz replied.

Noting that Wayne disliked the side effects of Haldol, Canty suggested that Wayne wouldn't keep throwing angry outbursts in the hospital if he knew he'd be forced to take the drug.

Canty also noted that Rodney had said Wayne was babbling and talking incoherently the day he turned himself in.

"Would that be consistent with what you refer to as a thought disorder?" Canty asked, referring to one of the necessary components of psychosis that Dietz had listed.

"It might be," Dietz said, but he still wouldn't commit, saying he would need to interview Rodney to know for sure.

Ultimately Dietz acknowledged the possibility that Wayne was psychotic in 1984, but said that didn't necessarily mean Wayne was still psychotic in 1997.

"Psychosis is . . . a mental state that's time limited," Dietz said, adding that some people could go for years without symptoms.

After Dietz finished testifying on Wednesday, June 7, both sides rested.

CHAPTER 25

HAUNTING WHISPERS

Mazurek delivered his closing argument on June 14, three months after the trial began, taking two hours and fifteen minutes to sum up his case for the jury.

He started by harking back to his childhood, when he loved watching horror movies that featured monsters, even though they made him terrified to get out of bed in case he ran into one on his way to the bathroom. When he became an adult, he said, he decided there were no such things as monsters.

But he was wrong.

"There are monsters in the world and they don't look like monsters in the movies," he said. "They look like human beings and sometimes they look exactly like Mr. Ford. 'Cause Mr. Ford is, in fact, a monster. He devoured young women to satisfy his sadistic—"

Mazurek had barely gotten started and Canty was already objecting. Canty said he didn't like his use of the word "monster," because it suggested that the defendant

was somehow less than human and therefore entitled
to less consideration than other defendants.

Smith told Mazurek to tone down his rhetoric, but
overruled Canty's objection.

"As I was saying," Mazurek continued, "the defendant
devoured these vulnerable young women to satisfy his
sexually sadistic appetite, leaving their dead, decomposing, and sometimes dismembered bodies scattered like
trash throughout the state of California. And when you
look at those pictures, you know in your heart . . . this was
nothing other than cold-blooded murder."

Mazurek quickly ran through the highlights of the evidence for each of the victims' deaths, wading through
the legal terminology to help the jury understand its instructions.

He also explained the three elements of first-degree
murder the jury needed to reach a guilty verdict and to
confirm the special circumstance allegation: 1) the defendant caused the death of another person; 2) he had a
state of mind called malice aforethought, or intent to kill;
and 3) he didn't have a lawful excuse or justification.

Even though the pathologists testified that they
couldn't definitively determine the cause of death for
two of the victims, Mazurek said, other evidence showed
that all four deaths shared a common cause and motive:
strangulation to achieve sexual gratification through
sadism and to express anger over Wayne's wife leaving
and taking their son.

"Causing somebody's death is absolutely the ultimate
act of sadism," Mazurek said, adding that strangulation
was one of the most "personal ways" to do it.

"You're squeezing the life out of them. Think about how
long it takes to do that. Not how long it takes to render
somebody unconscious . . . but how long it takes to kill

them. . . . What do you think is going through your mind for those three to seven minutes?"

Even if these victims were more physically vulnerable to death because they were prostitutes, had heart conditions from drug abuse, or had been drinking, that's no defense for murder, he said. Besides, he added, the defendant admitted that he was responsible for causing at least two of the deaths.

He said the jury could draw inferences about Wayne's intent and mental state during the killings from the testimony of "Sonoma County Doe."

"There is a basic pattern, a basic plan. It's common to all the girls. . . . You can also use it to negate the claim . . . that the defendant was doing something accidentally. . . . It's not something that just suddenly occurs to him."

After reminding the jury that Wayne cut up Jane Doe in his bathtub, kept her body parts, and used them to masturbate, Mazurek asked rhetorically, "Does that sound like an accident?"

He used the same rationale with the other victims, noting that Wayne dumped their naked bodies miles away from where they lived, so they couldn't be identified.

"If this were truly an accident, would you go through that much effort to dispose of the evidence?"

Trying to repair whatever damage the defense had caused to the credibility of "Sonoma County Doe," Mazurek acknowledged that she was "a little rough around the edges," but he said she had no agenda or motive to lie in court about what Wayne had done to her.

"I wish I could bring in twelve nuns and a priest [as witnesses], but twelve nuns and a priest aren't what the defendant associates with," he said.

Mazurek said Wayne was lying about not remembering how these women died, leaving the jury "no option but to conclude that he intended to kill them.

"At the time he acted, he knew his act was dangerous to human life and he deliberately acted with . . . reckless disregard for the health and safety of another person," which constitutes murder, he said.

"He selected his victims based on their young age, size, and vulnerability—choosing ones he knew he could control—using goal-directed behaviors to satisfy his sadism," he said.

"Strangling somebody, we all know, is dangerous to human life. They die. You don't have to be a rocket scientist to figure that out. . . . If he didn't know this was dangerous . . . or could potentially cause them death, he wouldn't be doing it."

After the lunch break, Canty objected once again to the monster reference and also to the prosecutor's implication that Wayne's failure to testify was somehow questionable. The judge said that statement caught his attention as well and offered to give additional jury instructions to explain that that decision could not be held against Wayne.

Canty argued the point again after Mazurek's closing and moved for a mistrial. The judge denied the motion, offering again to talk to the jury, but Canty declined, saying it would only "highlight the issue."

Next, Mazurek disputed Wayne's claim that he squeezed these women's necks to intensify their orgasms, underscoring Meloy's testimony that Wayne distrusted, devalued, and hated women.

"Do you really think that makes sense, based upon what we know about the defendant, or is that a lie to make what he's done . . . not sound so insidious or sinister, but to sound more like an accident? . . . How many guys pay prostitutes so they can pleasure the prostitutes?"

The evidence presented in court, he said, and the diagnosis of sadism proved that Wayne was not "concerned about other people's pleasure. He's concerned about their pain," because it excites and arouses him.

Summing up, Mazurek asked the jury once again to provide the justice that these four young women deserved: 4 first-degree murder convictions and confirmation of the special circumstance allegation.

Mapes and Canty split up their closing argument so that Mapes gave his forty-minute portion that afternoon, laying the foundation for Canty's statement the next day.

After delivering a broad-brush explanation of the law and jury instructions, Mapes asked jurors to try to put themselves in Wayne's shoes—and in his mind—so they could determine his mental state.

"You took an oath to follow law, no matter what it is. No matter how it comes out, even if you don't like it," he said. "If you find that it's not his fault—even then, you have to find him not guilty, whether you like it or not."

That meant the jury should consider the four deaths separately, he said, not lump them together as Mazurek did in his closing.

"He wanted to supply facts from one to the other, and the law doesn't allow you to do that," Mapes said.

Nor, he said, were the jurors allowed to speculate, as Mazurek suggested. "He's trying to make up for his burden of reasonable doubt. . . . Don't assume. . . . Look at the facts first and decide. . . . Apply the law as you see fit, not as the DA sees fit."

To determine whether Wayne premeditated and carefully planned his crimes, Mapes said, jurors needed to consider his recent divorce, his depression, the loss of his son, his Borderline Personality Disorder and his alcoholism. Only then could they decide if Wayne had carefully weighed the pros and cons and realized the consequences of what he was doing.

Mapes suggested that the jury try to imagine drinking ten shots of alcohol in a contest, doing wild things at a party, then waking up the next morning and thinking, "'Oh, my gosh, did I say that? I hope I didn't say that.'"

"And as the fog lifts off, you realize you did say or do something. That's the closest thing I might be able to think of for us who don't have mental disorders [to understand] the lack of deliberation that a person who has mental disorders might experience."

Even "Sonoma County Doe" testified that Wayne was frantic and didn't know what he was doing at times, he said.

Mapes defended his questions about victims experiencing arrhythmias due to their past drug abuse, reminding the jury about the pathologists' testimony that this factor could have contributed to the deaths.

"The reason I asked my question is when it comes to intent to kill, it makes a difference. . . . My argument would be, 'Well, no, a person may have experienced an arrhythmia after a much shorter period of time, and that doesn't show an intent to kill.'"

As Canty began his portion of the closing the next morning, he warned the jury that he was going to speak for quite a while. By the time he finished during the afternoon session, the defense's entire closing had lasted three hours.

His primary goal was to rebut Mazurek's argument that Wayne made a choice to kill those women, and persuade the jury that Wayne was a victim of a mental condition over which he had no control. He argued that Wayne's acts were the result of genetic, physical, and environmental factors from which he used alcohol to escape, and that his was a world in which he felt like the "unwanted product of a rape . . . [who] cannot understand women or relate to them."

"I'm hoping that you're going on this journey with me to try to put yourself in the place of a person who is, in fact, afflicted with these disorders: an impaired ability to think, concentrate, and make decisions. . . . Memory difficulties. A person who cannot make relationships work, unable to perform self-care and personal hygiene."

Canty told the jury that Wayne turned himself in because his conscience and "goodness prevailed."

"As you recall, in a conversation with Detective Freeman, Mr. Ford told him that he felt like God was involved and Detective Freeman indicated, 'Yes, God sent you to me.'"

Canty took a swipe at Dietz and his bias, highlighting the doctor's lack of a California medical license and the fact that he hadn't treated a patient in twenty-five years.

"You might expect that a physician would be kind of interested in the welfare of the patients and ridding the world of disease and things of that sort. But that's just too boring for Dr. Dietz," Canty said, alleging that he was "unable to understand empathy and . . . understand the feelings of other people."

"His business is testifying," he said.

Canty listed a series of questions for jurors to consider as they deliberated how mental illness affected Wayne's decision-making process, contending that the answer to one final question would answer all the others.

"How can you reason from one point to another if you have the mental illnesses described, and everybody agrees are present, in this case? And the answer is, you can't. . . . You are stuck in a different world. You make choices based on what you see: hopelessness, loneliness, abandonment, self-destruction, misinterpretation of events. And you are frantic. And you're very ill. And you can't get help. This produces unregulated emotion. Departure of reason. Inability to plan. Panic. And you are controlled by your impulses."

Canty said common sense dictates that someone who dismembers another is severely disturbed because it is a horrifying concept.

"Someone who turns himself in and wishes to stop killing must have suffered the same horror himself. He must have had difficulty in imagining that he could do these things. Isn't that the reasonable and simple explanation? And then I guess my question is—why, then, are we looking for another?"

Canty pointed out that even Mazurek felt it necessary to defend "Sonoma County Doe" as a credible witness. Given the evidence that she had falsely accused others, and had engaged in criminal behaviors herself, Canty asked, "What specific facts that she testified to you about can we say are actually true?"

He also noted that the jury heard evidence that Wayne had sex with women with whom he did not engage in paraphilic behaviors, underscoring that "most did not die."

"So I guess the question is, why are we going to transfer 'Sonoma Doe' over to the four homicides?"

Canty reminded the jury of Wayne's head injury from 1980 and the three medical tests that showed he had brain abnormalities. Canty also revealed that Wayne had suffered a previously undisclosed boxing injury while in the marines.

"We're mentioning them because sometimes head injuries can change a person's personality," he said.

Add in some stressors and the triggering event— Wayne's visit with Max at the pumpkin patch—just before the first killing, Canty said, "and we suggest to you that that creates a considerable amount of reasonable doubt as to the various mental states that you're presented to consider in this case."

The fact that Wayne visited bookstore owner Andy Lowery month after month to try to understand what was going on in his life, Canty said, "is not consistent with the man who is out stalking and psychopathically killing women. You can't do both."

Alluding to the storyline of the ex-convict hero seeking redemption in *Les Misérables* by Victor Hugo, Canty quoted from the book to illustrate Wayne's dilemma: "If I speak, I am condemned. If I stay silent, I am damned."

But, he said, Wayne, like Hugo's protagonist Jean Valjean, turned himself in, carrying evidence in his pocket that would forever connect him to his crimes.

In conclusion, Canty prepared the jury to watch Wayne's booking video with a few last questions in mind.

"Is he one of these people who turns himself in, in order to make a plea bargain to get something out of it? He didn't ask for anything. In fact, he said he thought they were going to kill him. . . . Is this one of these persons who was just tired of running? Well, he isn't running from anything."

As in any trial, Mazurek, as the prosecutor, got to have the last word before the jury began its deliberations. His opening gambit was to ask the jury to consider what was real and what wasn't.

"What is real in this case, and what we know for certain, is that four young girls lost their lives at the hands of this defendant while they were engaged in sexual acts with him. Their deaths are very real."

Jumping onto Canty's allusion to *Les Misérables*, Mazurek came up with his own cautionary tale—"The Emperor's New Clothes"—to impeach the defense's psychological expert witness.

"I would suggest to you the little tale about the emperor has no clothes relates directly to the testimony of Dr. Meloy," he said, referring to the expert's claim that Wayne's driving around and having sex with Tina Gibbs's body could be consistent with remorse.

"Now, I know I was not the only one in this courtroom that raised my eyebrow and went, 'What? What are you talking about? What are you trying to sell us?'"

By the same measure, Mazurek asked the jury to question whether any of Meloy's testimony was credible. Comparing Meloy to a snake oil salesman, Mazurek urged the jury to weigh the qualifications of Meloy versus Dietz, noting that Meloy relied on the *DSM* as a standard, while Dietz actually wrote parts of the book. He also attacked Meloy for relying on selective details that fit his theory, even in the face of conflicting information.

"Dr. Meloy chose to believe that Dad raped Mom, even though Dad said, 'No, I didn't,' and Dr. Meloy chooses to accept the fact that the defendant was abandoned by his mother as a child, even though Mother says, 'We were divorced, son wanted to go live with Dad.'"

Mazurek said Meloy relied on unreliable information for his findings, some from Wayne himself, even after admitting the defendant was a liar.

Why, Mazurek asked rhetorically, would Wayne say he had been in a coma for three or nine days back in 1980?

"It's part of his malingering, part of trying to make things in his past sound worse, so that it benefits him now. 'Cause if you believe he had this coma, then you believe he has this head trauma, then you believe he can't control his actions. There is no independent evidence of a coma . . . so we know that it's not real."

Neither, he said, was the alleged trauma of losing his son, Max. Mazurek reminded the jury of Elizabeth's testimony that Wayne's relationship with Max was virtually nonexistent.

"He didn't care. He wasn't actively involved. He was more interested in trying to get back with Elizabeth than he was with his son, Max."

Claiming there was no evidence that Wayne was severely depressed, Mazurek contended that Wayne was cunning, manipulative, and faking his symptoms during his interviews with the detectives so they would sympathize with him, just as he cried to "Sonoma County Doe" so she wouldn't report the rape to police.

Mazurek defended Dietz's résumé, noting that it described his practice as forensic psychiatry in consulting, *not* treatment and diagnosis.

"What the defense wants you to believe is that just because he hasn't got a medical license, when he crosses the border from somewhere else into California, he becomes a moron, that his opinion isn't valid. . . . If he weren't qualified, do you think the FBI would" ask him to be a criminal-profiling consultant?

Mazurek also reminded the jury about Dietz's testimony that Wayne was not psychotic.

"Paraphilic behavior is not an illness. . . . He is sick and twisted . . . but he is not mentally ill, and he is not mentally impaired."

Mazurek contended that Wayne didn't surrender out of remorse, but rather to catch a break from authorities.

"Rodney Ford is the true hero in this particular case," he said. "He is the person that saves lives and solves crimes, and he is the one that did the right thing."

Wayne may have seemed depressed in the booking video the jury just watched, he said, "but what is he depressed about? Is he depressed about the killings? Or is he now depressed and in a panic . . . that now the police are looking for him because he's killed four people, and when you're caught, they're going to give you the death penalty. That would make you incoherent and inconsolable."

Finally, Mazurek said that the defendant has a constitutional right to a jury trial and "for all twelve of you members and voices of this community to tell him that he is guilty of first-degree murder. Go back and tell him."

After delivering instructions to the jury of seven women and five men, Judge Smith told them to take the weekend off and begin deliberating Monday morning, June 19.

On the third day of their deliberations, the jury broke around 1:00 P.M., leaving two questions for the judge, who answered them in the jury room the following day.

First, the jurors wanted the date of the "Orange County Doe" rape, which occurred on June 16, 1998.

Second, they asked: "Was there a photo of the evidence from the campsite when it was all laid out at the crime lab? We saw it during Judy Taylor's testimony, March 15, '06." Smith directed them to the photographic exhibits that illustrated those items.

That Friday, the jury had four more queries.

One, the jurors wanted portions read to them from the testimony of pathologist Robert Lawrence.

Two, they wanted to make sure they had the stipulation concerning DNA evidence from April 3.

Third, they asked: "Do we get to look at the autopsy reports themselves?" The answer was no.

And finally, they asked for a legal definition of "mayhem."

After discussing these questions with the attorneys, Smith explained to the jury that it should disregard the mention of "mayhem" on the transcript of the Freeman interview because Wayne had never been charged with that crime.

* * *

The jury deliberated for all or part of seven days. Because the material was so intense, some days the panel could only manage to debate for two or three hours; others, they went a full five hours.

The jurors agreed not to take a straw vote until they had sorted through all the evidence in the case, which took a couple of days.

On the first vote, for the murder of Jane Doe in Humboldt, the group was split between first-degree and second-degree murder. Initially, some members had difficulty going for first-degree because of the slim autopsy evidence, but that got hammered out within a day or so after they went over the forensics again. The final vote was unanimous.

After that, the deliberations progressed fairly quickly. The jury had no trouble agreeing on first-degree for the other three murders and the special circumstance allegation.

Finally, on Tuesday, June 27, 2006, at 11:52 A.M., the foreperson told the bailiff that the jury had reached a verdict.

Smith set a time of 2:00 P.M. so the media and other interested parties had a chance to get to the courthouse for the announcement.

Once court was in session, Smith asked his clerk, Evi Roberson, to do the honors.

Wayne showed no emotion as Roberson read each of the four verdicts.

"Superior Court of California, County of San Bernardino. The People of the State of California, plaintiff, versus Wayne Adam Ford, defendant. Case number

FSB 027247. Verdict 1: We, the jury in the above entitled action, find the defendant, Wayne Adam Ford, guilty of the crime of murder in the first degree as charged in count one."

Roberson continued to read the three others, which were all the same: guilty, guilty, and guilty.

Then came the decision on the pro forma multiple murder allegation: "We, the jury in the above entitled action, find the offenses charged in counts 1, 2, 3 and 4, are a special allegation within the meaning of Penal Code section 190.2 (a) (3), to wit, more than one offense of murder, to be true."

Canty requested to have the jurors polled individually, and each of them confirmed the verdicts.

"All right," Smith said. "Ladies and gentlemen of the jury, by virtue of the verdicts that you rendered and the special circumstance allegation, we are now then going to proceed with the second phase of the trial, the penalty phase. People, ready to call your first witness?"

"No," Mazurek said as laughter rippled throughout the courtroom, breaking the tension. Even Wayne laughed.

Smith explained that he was being facetious. Obviously, the attorneys had no way of knowing the verdict or when it would come down, so no arrangements for witnesses had been made.

Smith told the jury that he and the attorneys expected to start the penalty trial on July 12 and finish presenting the evidence by late July or early August, when the jury would begin deliberations for a second verdict.

Like her fellow jurors, Darlena Murray would have to wait another month before she could talk about the case to anyone, including her live-in boyfriend, who had been following the proceedings in the newspaper.

Complying with the judge's order not to discuss the case with anyone, which meant holding in her emotions, had been difficult for Murray. Ever since she'd heard Wayne's soft, low-talking voice on the taped interviews with detectives, she'd been waking up in the middle of the night and thinking she heard his voice in her bedroom. Not being allowed to tell anyone about these creepy early-morning awakenings made them even harder to cope with. Two years later, she would still get the chills thinking about Wayne's whispery voice.

CHAPTER 26

LIFE OR DEATH

By the time the second phase of the trial started in July, a new chapter in Wayne's complicated history with women was revealed.

Her name was Victoria Redstall and she came from quite a different educational and socioeconomic background than Wayne's—not to mention the prostitutes with whom he'd been consorting before his arrest.

The attractive British-born blonde, who had an athletic frame of five feet nine inches and 130 pounds, was described by England's *Daily Mail* as the "privately educated daughter of a chartered surveyor from Esher, Surrey, a wellspoken 'firmly upper-middleclass' young woman whose uncle is a knight and whose cousin married into the Sangster racing dynasty."

But what American media found more relevant was that she was an actress and former spokesmodel for Grobust, an herbal supplement, ironically, for breast enhancement, which had worked for her.

Victoria said she started visiting Wayne at the West Valley Detention Center in April after deciding she wanted to make a documentary about a serial killer. She persuaded a correctional deputy to take her to Wayne's unit in protective custody, then started meeting with him every other day.

As soon as Wayne's attorneys found out about the visits, they immediately put a stop to them. Victoria was banned from the jail and the deputy was told he'd be fired if he let her in again.

"It was very unethical for that deputy to do that, and it just shows how cunning she is and how she uses herself to do what she does," Forbush said.

Through these initial meetings, and later, daily collect calls from jail, Victoria said, she and Wayne connected on a deep level, forging a "strong emotional bond" as she gathered material for her documentary.

"This is a professional relationship," she told the *Daily Mail* in August 2006 after the visits had been blocked. "We have never touched. Our letters do not contain anything romantic. . . . The story has taken over my life and I admit to being obsessed by him, but not in a sexual way."

Over time, however, this alliance would grow increasingly intimate.

The gregarious Victoria sat with the reporters covering the trial and boasted about her experiences with Wayne—allegedly singing country-western songs together through the bulletproof glass in the jailhouse visiting room. She also told them how upset the defense was about her visits with Wayne.

Victoria, who lived in Studio City in Los Angeles County, said she initially gave a different name to Wayne, because he was, after all, a serial killer. She also used a different name when she submitted forms to Judge Smith, requesting permission to take video footage and photos of Wayne in the courtroom.

Court officials don't look fondly on people who don't put their legal names on media request forms, especially when they aren't employed by a media organization.

Concerned about the photos and video Victoria was taking of Wayne in the courtroom, the defense asked the judge to issue some restrictions, which Victoria proceeded to ignore. She continued to take video footage, then claimed she hadn't done anything wrong because her camera wasn't taking "photos" but video.

The bailiff confiscated her camera and escorted her out of the courtroom. When she was allowed back in, her eyes were red and teary.

In a May 2006 posting on localnewsgroup.co.uk, which she wrote to respond to a news story in her home country, she denied being reprimanded by court officials. She also made at least one other claim that was misleading at best.

"Last year, I was reading the weather on the morning News on the number one Los Angeles Station KTLA 5," she wrote.

KTLA officials said Victoria participated in a promotional audition, but she was never hired.

In addition, she wrote that she "trained to be a Los Angeles County Sheriff and was accepted by a station here." Sheriff's officials said they could not confirm or deny her statement because of confidentiality and privacy laws, but people involved in the case were skeptical.

Victoria posted one other comment, however, that proved quite telling: "I have NEVER been obsessed with

Serial Killers. I have, however, been fascinated with the mind of a Serial Killer since I was a teenager."

The penalty trial, which began as scheduled on July 12, was attended by several newspaper reporters, the author of this book, and Victoria.

The $64,000 question was this: Would the fact that Wayne turned himself in and cooperated with authorities help persuade the jury that he should be spared the death penalty?

After the trial, Judge Smith said he believed that Wayne showed remorse and that his tears were genuine. Nonetheless, he said, "I thought there was a high likelihood they [the jury] would return with the death penalty just because of the nature of the crimes and how many there were."

But that morning, Smith gave no sign of his personal feelings as he welcomed the jurors back to his courtroom.

As Mazurek delivered his ten-minute opening statement, he described the trial's penalty phase as "the rest of the story," after which the jury would choose between recommending the death penalty and the lesser punishment of life without the possibility of parole.

"In these cases, you compare sometimes to people throwing a rock into a pond and it ripples out and creates a bigger effect on the people that surround the victims. It's not just their deaths, but the impact the death had on their mothers, fathers, brothers and sisters, and families."

He closed by asking the jury to return "the greater punishment."

"When I first got up and gave my opening, I told you the defendant knows what he did and knows what he is. Well, he also knows, if you remember back to the interviews, what he deserves. And at the end of this, based upon all the circumstances that we're going to talk about, we all know what he's going to deserve."

The defense reserved its opening until the start of its case, so Mazurek went right into his first witnesses, all of whom were correctional officers from Humboldt and San Bernardino Counties.

Three of them testified that they'd found makeshift weapons during searches of Wayne's single cells. These included a blade that had been removed from a disposable razor and was stuck to the bottom of a table with glazing compound from the window, thirteen days after he surrendered; a five-inch piece of chain-link bent into an L-shape, sharpened at one end and lodged underneath the cell's door frame; and two 1-inch screws, sharpened at one end, and stored on the bolts holding the table against the wall.

The other three officers testified about Wayne's bad behavior in jail. In one instance, Wayne got angry and threatened to injure an officer who picked up a piece of Wayne's candy off the floor and wouldn't give it back.

In a second incident, Wayne refused to give back his metal food tray until he could speak to a sergeant about a broken pay phone. When he didn't comply with the deputy's orders to give back the tray, and threatened to "go to town" on him, the deputy called in four others and a sergeant for a "cell extraction." They shot pepper spray three times through the food tray slot in Wayne's cell door before he agreed to put his wrists to the slot and be handcuffed.

* * *

Mazurek conducted pretrial interviews with the identified victims' parents, exploring their experiences with grief so that he could have them relate the most poignant moments for the jury.

At the end of the day on July 12, Mazurek called Ron Sharp, Tina Gibbs's stepfather, and then Mary Sharp, Tina's mother. Debra White, Lanett's mother, and Rudolfo Tamez, Patricia's father, testified the following morning.

Even now, Mary Sharp said, she was troubled when she saw a missing or murdered child on television. Her heart went out to those poor families, with whom she felt a strong bond. She knew that most other people didn't understand what they were going through.

But she did.

Her daughter Tina's birthday and Mother's Day were always the worst; Mary so missed seeing her daughter's smile and hearing her laugh. She even missed the way Tina used to roll her eyes when she didn't get her way.

Ron felt those pangs, too, but what hurt him most were the years of watching Mary suffer over losing Tina. Mary was still dealing with chronic depression, for which she saw a psychiatrist several times a month.

"It's destroyed me," Ron told the jury. "I don't know what to do. I know I got to go on. I've got too much to take care of. We've been married twenty-six years. I plan on making it forever. She's tough. But I got to take care of her right now."

Once Mary found out how Tina died, she started having a recurrent nightmare with scenes of a big rig coming down the highway, clothes being thrown out a window, and flashes of Tina's face. She was also haunted by the thoughts of what terrible things Tina must have endured in her final hour. It was all too unbearable to imagine.

The only solace Mary had found was a small garden she'd planted in Tina's memory, with purple, yellow, and white flowers—her daughter's favorite colors—and an angel in the middle.

Mary still couldn't help but hope that she would answer the door one day and see her daughter standing on the doorstep.

She would give anything to hear Tina say, "Mommy, I love you," just once more.

Debra White felt she would never get over the shock of losing Lanett. It was heartbreaking to watch her grandchildren grow up without a mother and apart from one another.

Amanda, Carlos, and David each went to live with their respective fathers. Michael, who stayed with Debra and Bill, was only a toddler when Lanett died, so he didn't understand.

"Nana, I know how we can see my mom," he said to Debra one day. "We can get some balloons and put them up in the air and hold on to them, and they will take us up to see my mom."

Michael kept Debra from going off the deep end. It helped her to know that she was raising her baby's baby.

Every day, Debra saw something that reminded her of Lanett, and that she was never coming back.

The holidays were difficult, because Lanett had liked all of them. She always took the kids to see fireworks on the Fourth of July and dressed them up for Easter.

"On Easter, there's no more Easter baskets, no more pretty clothes for the kids," Debra told the jury. "It's just like a big, old empty space that's left in me that's never going to get filled again."

Amanda's birthday, Christmas, Mother's Day, and Lanett's birthday were even tougher.

"When I brought her into this world, it was hard for me to bring her in, and for someone to take her from me, I just don't understand why," Debra said. "Why would they want to take my baby away from me?"

Like Mary, Debra often wondered about Lanett's final moments. All she could hope was that her daughter died quickly and didn't suffer.

"I wonder how she even managed to be where she was at. How she got there. 'Cause, knowing my daughter, she would never just go and get in a vehicle or something with just anybody. I just don't know how she could ever end up that way. . . . I just wonder what it was [like], her last, last breath."

Debra said the doctors wanted to medicate her and put her in therapy, but she refused. None of that would bring her baby back.

"She didn't deserve this . . . and it's the most horrible-est thing any mother, father, sister, or brother could ever have to deal with in their life."

In the time it took to get this case to trial, Rudolfo Tamez said he felt like he'd aged thirty years.

A parent wasn't supposed to lose a child this way. His life would never be the same.

"A million times I wish it had been me that was murdered that day. A million times. The pain is just—you can't put into words. . . . It just—just was incredible."

He still had a few happy days, but they were always tinged by the sadness about his daughter Patricia's passing. Even when he laughed, part of him still could not be joyful. Other people didn't understand this, because they hadn't lived through it.

Some days he thought he wouldn't cry, but then the smallest thing would set him off. He just couldn't stop crying.

Rudolfo had always hoped that he could help Patricia beat her addiction. Make a better life. Overcome her demons. But now he had lost that chance and he would always regret it.

He couldn't bring himself to attend the rest of the trial, not because he didn't love his daughter, but because he didn't want the publicity. He also didn't want his granddaughter to find out what had happened to her mother. One day, he would tell the little girl, but for now, he wanted to protect her from the horror.

He understood that sometimes you could lose a child to illness, but Rudolfo couldn't understand how a man like Wayne could be wired to take Patricia's life just to experience pleasure.

Rudolfo saw Wayne as a coward who thought the whole process was a joke and wanted to be the center of attention. Before the trial started, Rudolfo told Mazurek that he hoped Wayne would get the death penalty. He felt it would help him heal and bring justice for his daughter.

On the stand in the penalty phase, Rudolfo described the thoughts that clung to his mind. "My words can never come close to the image of the way she died, being taken to the edge of death and brought back—"

"That's not true," Wayne blurted out from the defense table, interrupting Rudolfo midsentence. "That never happened."

Judge Smith directed Wayne to be quiet. "Mr. Ford, it's probably best that you not say anything to Mr. Tamez."

Rudolfo tried to speak again, but this time it was Canty who spoke over him.

"Well, I'm sorry," Canty said to the court.

When Rudolfo tried once more, Canty interrupted him again with an objection. He didn't think Rudolfo's statement was an appropriate answer to Mazurek's question, and the judge agreed. So Mazurek rephrased the question, to which Rudolfo replied that he often thought about what had happened during Patricia's last minutes.

"Is that hard for you to do?" the prosecutor asked.

"Yeah, very, very difficult for me to think about it."

Mazurek asked if there was an image of Patricia, alive, that he'd like jurors to take with them.

"The way she used to laugh," Rudolfo said. "You know, she had this laughter that was contagious and made you feel like . . . here's somebody that loves life and is . . . right at the essence of what life is. . . . That, and her tremendous, tremendous heart. That's what I'd like you to remember."

On Thursday, July 20, Mapes gave an opening statement that was even shorter than Mazurek's, taking the jury into Wayne's mind while he was in the woods, pondering what he'd done and what to do next.

"There is a lot of prayer involved. But I know that's all I can do. There's nothing I can do to make things right, other than that. So, I take that long journey down that road to that motel, and every step that I take, I can sense my freedom slipping away. But I know that I've resolved that I have to do the right thing. After having done so much wrong. So I call my brother . . . the one I trust could still help me turn myself in, 'cause that's what I have to do."

Mapes told the jury the defense was going to recall Rodney in a few minutes, then some deputies from Humboldt County, one of whom would talk about how tough it was for Wayne in jail on Max's birthday that first year.

"We have to do that, because the DA said that he didn't love his son. And he did."

Mapes asked the jury to give Wayne a life sentence. "This case is about a man who did the right thing after doing so many wrong and awful things. . . . And so what that means is that we're going to ask you, as jurors, to do the right thing for a man who had a conscience and turned himself in."

When Rodney had taken the stand the first time on May 11, Canty led him through the events leading up to Wayne's arrest in the sheriff's lobby.

This time, on July 20, Mapes showed Rodney a photo of Rodney and Wayne as boys, and asked why Wayne's hands were in Rodney's lap.

"We were always close," Rodney said. "We've been close our whole lives."

Rodney, who sat calmly with his hands in front of him, said Wayne changed after his head injury in 1980.

"He was just not my brother," he said.

As for the doctors who testified otherwise, he said, "He's not their brother. I've known him his whole life."

Asked if he thought Wayne loved Max, Rodney said, "Definitely. Everything he did after Max was born, he did for Max. I mean, he was excited to have a son. You know, he left a perfectly good job to follow his then-wife to Vegas. . . . He took a lesser-paying job just so he could be close to his son and help take care of him."

"If he loved Max so much, why did he eventually leave Las Vegas?"

Rodney said he told Wayne to do so. "He really wasn't getting anywhere in life, and he was just focusing too much on what he couldn't have any more. His marriage was over. And I told him he needed to move on and focus on his life."

Mapes asked if Rodney thought Wayne was mentally or emotionally unbalanced.

"Yeah, I think he's got problems."

"But you love him in spite of those problems?"

"Yes. He's my brother."

"Whose idea was it for him to turn himself in?"

"His. He called me. I mean, I didn't go looking for him. . . . He realized what he had done was wrong. He turned himself in. You know, he told me a number of times that he didn't want to hurt people anymore and that he needed to be put away."

Mapes asked what effect it would have on Rodney if Wayne got the death penalty.

"Devastating effect."

"Why is that?"

"I love him. I don't want to see him die."

The following Tuesday, July 25, the defense called criminalist John Thornton, who had worked for Wayne's first attorney, Kevin Robinson. Canty and Mapes had originally intended to call Thornton and Robinson during the guilt phase to illustrate that Wayne had a conscience and felt remorse about his crimes because he helped authorities search for Jane Doe's body parts in the Mad River. They held off, however, in light of a tricky ruling by the judge concerning a limited waiver of attorney-client privilege.

"We would have drowned if we had gotten in the water at all, and even then, we wouldn't have been able to find a concrete block," Thornton testified about their first trip to the river in December 1998.

On cross-examination, Thornton acknowledged that he was unaware Wayne had already been out to the area with Freeman and "that they had looked for [the head] and basically determined it had been washed away."

"So you didn't document that he sent you to look for something he knew was gone?"

"Objection," Canty said. "Argumentative."

"Sustained," Smith said.

On redirect, Mapes raised the possibility that the river could have deposited silt and rocks that buried the cement block and head even deeper, making them impossible to find.

"I certainly wouldn't set that possibility aside," Thornton said.

Next, the defense called two Humboldt correctional officers who testified about two incidents in which Wayne was so depressed that they were concerned he was going to harm himself.

The first was on Max's birthday in December 1998, when he called on the intercom for a mental-health worker, or he might hurt himself. The second time was after a visit with his father in August 1999.

The defense also called a correctional officer and a sheriff's sergeant to discuss assault statistics from San Bernardino County jails to establish that Wayne had a reason to collect and fashion makeshift weapons—the jails were a dangerous place, even for inmates like Wayne in protective custody.

"You did have a person who was in protective custody

who was murdered this year?" Mapes asked sheriff's
Sergeant Jay Blankenship.

"Yes."

"So it's impossible to protect everybody, correct?"

"Yes."

"And that person was murdered by another inmate?"

"That's correct."

Both sides rested on July 27.

The judge gave the jury its new instructions, explaining that after listening to the attorneys' closing arguments, the panel should consider evidence presented in both phases of the trial, weigh a specified list of eleven aggravating and mitigating circumstances against each other, and then decide what punishment to recommend for the defendant.

As Mazurek flashed photos of the women's dead and dismembered bodies on a projection screen, he and his ninety-minute closing were interrupted by Canty's half-dozen objections to inappropriate arguments about the death penalty and other matters.

Alluding to the "Drugs Destroy Dreams" ribbon that Patricia Tamez had given to her father, Mazurek conveyed a similar theme he wanted the jury to take into deliberations: "The defendant destroys dreams and hopes and lives, and not just the lives of the four dead victims in this case, but of their families as well."

Choosing a punishment of life without the possibility of parole might be the easy way to go, he said, but it would not result in justice.

"The real objective is to fit—fashion a punishment that

fits the crime and the criminal. And protecting society has nothing to do with what this defendant deserves."

Quoting from philosopher Immanuel Kant, Mazurek explained why society imposes the death penalty: "If we favor executing murderers, it's not because we want to, rather because, however much we do not want to, we consider ourselves obliged to. . . . It is our moral duty to provide justice."

As Mazurek gave his analysis of the aggravating and mitigating factors the jury would be asked to consider, he negated all the mitigating factors, which included whether the victims participated or consented to the defendant's homicidal conduct, whether Wayne acted under "extreme duress" or "substantial domination" of another person, whether he had an accomplice, and whether he was under the influence of "extreme mental disturbance" or was too impaired by mental disease, defect, or intoxication to understand the criminality of his conduct.

"None of these apply to his conduct . . . and had the defendant not been able to conform his conduct to the law or . . . was impaired, there would be some other verdict than first-degree murder," Mazurek said, prompting Canty to voice an objection that the judge sustained.

Rather than putting themselves in Wayne's shoes, as the defense suggested, Mazurek urged the jurors to put themselves in the victims' shoes as Wayne raped and strangled the life out of them.

"The last face they ever see on this earth [is] not any other family members, it's this defendant. Imagine that for a while. . . . Justice is the death penalty for these four girls. Justice demands that death be imposed."

In Canty's forty-five-minute closing, he told the jury that no one was trying to excuse Wayne's behavior, devalue the victims' lives, or diminish their relatives' feelings of loss.

Canty noted that Wayne may have made threats to assault correctional officers since he'd been behind bars, but he'd never actually carried them out.

"Mr. Ford is going to spend the rest of his life in prison, whatever verdict you decide upon. So this is not about excusing behavior. He is going to be punished. The issue is what is the appropriate penalty."

Canty painted a picture of what Wayne's life in prison would be for the next forty years if he was spared the death penalty.

"He will look back over a life in a single cell, in protective custody, living in a place of constant violence, where your day is scheduled, and a place where inmates hold trays hostage to be able to talk to a sergeant, a place where you do not decide when the lights go on, when the lights go off, or when to eat your meals, or even what to eat—a place where your single solitary concern is survival."

Canty reminded the jury that it did not speak for the victims or their families, but rather the community at large. And like the blindfolded statue of Lady Justice, who holds a scale in one hand and a sword in the other, he said, the jury held "the power to use that sword for execution or for life."

He also encouraged the jury to consider sympathy, compassion, and mercy in their deliberations, because Wayne had surrendered to authorities.

This time quoting William Shakespeare, Canty cited a statement by the attorney character Portia: "The quality of mercy is not strained. It droppeth like gentle rain from Heaven upon the place beneath. It is twice blessed. It blesses him that gives and him that takes."

Wayne Ford was in court today, Canty said, because he'd repented.

"[He] now is in your hands. And you have the power to decide whether to condemn him or allow him to live out his life in prison. The decision you make will speak to society about the consequences of turning yourself in. You have the power, because Mr. Ford presented himself to you to make this decision voluntarily, by walking into that jail in 1998. Please do not condemn this man."

Canty and Mapes raised some concerns about Victoria Redstall's videotaping future proceedings along with the "legitimate media," so Smith called a hearing for the next morning so that Victoria could present, under penalty of perjury, her press credentials and some documentation about her project.

At the hearing, Victoria presented an e-mail, reportedly from the owner of a production company with whom she said she was working. She also presented an unsigned contract, admitted she had been paid nothing so far, and said she'd been financing the documentary with her credit cards.

Under questioning by Mapes, she admitted to giving the name "Victoria Clare" when visiting Wayne.

"I went into the jail with my true ID," she said. "I don't have fake ID. I trained to be a deputy sheriff, so I know the rules. I know the law."

"Are you aware that at some time there was a bulletin with your photograph at the jail saying, Do not let this person in?" Mapes asked.

"Never," she said.

"Previously you were ordered by a bailiff in this courtroom . . . not to take pictures pursuant to a judge's order, correct?"

"No, she actually said to me when I was sitting down that—she threw me out of the courtroom for using my camera, when I had been specifically given written permission by the judge. She threw me out and she defiled me."

Victoria, who had already said that she'd applied for press credentials from the sheriff's department, switched course and said she wasn't actually media.

"I'm doing a documentary," she said.

"And you agreed you gave a false name to the jail when you went there?"

"No, I gave my real name, Victoria Clare."

"You didn't give 'Redstall'?"

"I didn't give my last name because I was obviously wanting to protect my identity."

"From the jail?"

"From the jail."

In the end, Judge Smith did not take away Victoria's privileges and allowed her to film alongside the news reporters and photographers, who have their own innate sense of who is one of them.

On August 2, Judge Brian McCarville was filling in for the vacationing Judge Smith, when two questions arose from the jury.

The jurors wanted to know if they could see Forbush's interview with Wayne's mother, and also the transcript read in court from the investigator's interview with Melva Lenore Ward, the dispatcher in Redding who had taken Wayne in as a teenager.

McCarville told the jury that although the psychological experts made reference to Brigitte's interview during their testimony, the interview itself would not be available. The judge promised to deliver the Ward interview transcript, however, which had been inadvertently withheld.

A week later, on August 9, one of the jurors asked for extra clarification on jury instructions concerning whether "'mental illness' should be a serious consideration."

After conferring with the attorneys, McCarville read parts of the instructions to the panel once more, including three of the relevant mitigating factors.

"You do not all need to agree whether such factors exist," McCarville said. "If any juror individually concluded that a factor exists, that juror may give the factor whatever weight he or she believes is appropriate."

With Victoria's help, word of her antics soon spread around the globe.

A story in the *Los Angeles Times* that ran on August 1 quoted her saying she'd driven her red convertible next to Wayne's bus as it headed back to jail so that he could watch "her blond hair blowing and her jewelry glimmering in the sunlight."

Victoria also told the *Times* that she'd been sued by her former homeowners association because she used to stand on her condominium balcony in her nightdress so that news helicopters would fly over and shine their spotlights down on her. She didn't explain how the helicopters knew she was there.

Newspapers in Victoria's native England followed up with their own stories, which were loaded with the irony of a former breast-enhancement spokesmodel, who wore tight clothes that accentuated her breasts, befriending a serial killer with a breast fetish.

Around the same time, Court TV's Crime Library Web site ran a story with the headline VICTORIA REDSTALL'S FIXATION, calling her a serial killer groupie. The story quoted her as saying that Wayne wasn't the same man as he was when he killed those women.

"We all have evil in us," Victoria told Court TV.

"Even as she shed tears over his apparent show of conscience, she thought it was 'hysterical' that this offender with a breast fetish had become so attuned to a model for breast enhancement," the story stated.

Complaining that the media was printing horrible things about her, Victoria went on the former MSNBC program *Scarborough Country* to defend herself the day after the *Times* story ran.

Host Joe Scarborough, a former U.S. Representative from Florida, asked Victoria what positive things she hoped to achieve for society by visiting "this cold-blooded killer" in jail when Wayne's own attorneys wanted her to stay away.

"Because a serial killer is made, they're not born," Victoria said in her usual rapid-fire speech. "And it's a component, a lethal cocktail, of obviously bad childhoods, abusive relationships, a bang on the head, which he had in 1980. He had an accident which caused him to go into a coma. A lot of this hasn't come up in the trial . . . and I know he wants to get that out."

Asked why she trusted him so much, Victoria said, "Because he wouldn't be a danger to anyone coming in contact with him, because he's on the medication that has made him normal now, completely normal and completely leveled him out."

Referring to Wayne's breast fixation, Scarborough asked, "What's that all about?"

"When I met Mr. Wayne Adam Ford, I didn't know that was the extent of—he had a breast fetish," she said. "I knew that he dismembered some of his victims. So what it is, is, again, slandering the truth and making me look like, 'Oh, I've got to go after him because he's into breasts.' Absolutely not. I dress very professionally in the jail and in the courtroom, and it's just a coincidence that people are going to make a story about it."

Later that month, Victoria didn't do herself any favors by telling the San Bernardino *Sun* that she and her documentary film crew were heading up to Humboldt County to search for Jane Doe's missing head.

"'I'm going head-hunting,' Redstall said with a laugh," the story stated.

Mazurek said he was disturbed by Victoria's comments.

"She's either crazy, or it's very appalling by trying to get publicity with the facts in this case and these poor victims that were dismembered," he told the *Sun*.

CHAPTER 27

No Mercy

This time, the jury deliberated for nine days.

For the past five months, these jurors had been listening to testimony and looking at the gruesome photos and notes they'd taped to the jury room wall to remind them about the serious nature of this case. They'd also taped up the factors they were supposed to weigh and went through every one of them.

"It was hard to come up with what was mitigating," Darlena Murray said later.

But now they were faced with the hardest part of all, the momentous job of deciding whether this man on trial deserved to keep his life.

"Nobody wanted to make the wrong decision," Murray said.

At long last, seven months after these twelve citizens were selected to serve their civic duty, they reached their second verdict, on the afternoon of Thursday, August 10, 2006.

* * *

Judge Smith was still on vacation, so Judge McCarville gave the interested parties an hour and twenty-five minutes to gather for the reading at 4:35 P.M.

Once the parties were assembled, McCarville asked the clerk to read the verdict.

"The People of the State of California, plaintiff, versus Wayne Adam Ford, defendant. Case number FSB027247," Evi Roberson said. "Verdict one: We, the jury in the above entitled action, find that the appropriate penalty shall be death."

The jury confirmed for the judge that this indeed was its collective decision, then was polled individually at the defense's request. Yes. Yes. And yes.

Mazurek felt a sense of accomplishment that he had been able to wade through the massive amount of information and won a conviction against Wayne Adam Ford.

"I felt I brought some closure for the families and that Wayne got what he deserved in the end," he said.

Afterward, several of the jurors discussed their experiences and thoughts with the attorneys and media.

Three of the jurors told reporters that the victims' photos gave many of them nightmares, and most were planning to get therapy.

"It was the most horrendous thing I've ever seen in my life," Murray said.

The jurors said that most, if not all, of their colleagues had been leaning toward the death penalty, but they weren't able to reach a unanimous verdict until one man could decide how much weight to give Wayne's mental problems. Murray later said it also took some soul-searching by a couple of jurors with deep religious beliefs to get their minds around such a punishment.

Given that Mazurek had tried to keep teachers off the jury, Murray had to ask him, "Why me?"

"Because you seemed so honest," Mazurek replied.

Murray thought Wayne clearly knew what he'd been doing and knew right from wrong. As for motive, "self-gratification is all we can come up with," she told the reporters, echoing the prosecution's argument.

Although she didn't feel sympathy for Wayne, Murray said, she did feel empathy for him. "He almost seemed like he was two different people."

Elecia Morris, a twenty-five-year-old public health worker, said she saw no signs of remorse in Wayne, given that he was able to eat a burrito and make deliveries after killing his victims.

Most of the jurors suspected that Wayne had lied about his "amnesia" during the killings. But they knew for sure that he had been lying when he shouted out during Rudolfo Tamez's testimony.

"If he knew that, then he knew what he did with the others," Murray said. "So there was no amnesia."

Murray later said that all but a couple of jurors believed that Rodney, who kept his brother at the sheriff's station when he wanted to leave, was the only reason that Wayne was on trial. They also felt bad for what Rodney must have gone through, turning his brother in for murder.

Murray said she was among the jurors who left the courthouse believing there were more than four young women who had died at Wayne's hands.

After the trial, Murray stayed in touch with a couple of other jurors and found it hard to let go of the case.

For weeks afterward, she searched the Internet for more information on the trial and issues that had come up, wanting to learn even more than what the attorneys had provided.

But Murray said she would remain haunted by one question most of all: Who was the Jane Doe from Humboldt County?

CHAPTER 28

WAYNE: ACCIDENTS AND MISCONCEPTIONS

Probation officer Marixa Mathews interviewed Wayne on October 17, 2006, for a presentence report, which stated that Wayne was "very sorry about all that has happened." However, he still believed he was "not guilty of four counts of first-degree murder. If anything, he is guilty of four counts of 'accidental death.'"

Wayne insisted that none of the victims was tortured. "There was no struggling and no pain inflicted upon the victims," Wayne told Mathews. "All acts and activities were consensual. Anything that might have appeared to be painful or torturous was done postmortem.

"Most serial killers are proud of their work—not me," he said.

Mathews wrote that Wayne was upset that the victims' family members, citing Rudolfo Tamez in particular, "have been left to dwell on these misconceptions."

Wayne said his attorneys had "plenty of opportunity to

tell the jurors how the victims' deaths were related to the defendant's psychological problems. For whatever reason, they chose not to," the officer wrote.

Wayne declined to comment on the jury's death recommendation, but said he didn't understand why people were so fascinated by the fact that he'd surrendered to authorities.

"If someone breaks the law or does something wrong, they are supposed to turn themselves in—which is exactly what I did. Why would anyone question why I would do that? Then they don't believe me when I tell them certain things about an incident. Why would I turn myself in just to lie?"

Three women who accused Wayne of raping and torturing them were interviewed for the report, but their names and statements were not disclosed to the public. Wayne denied the allegations, saying, "They were all prostitutes and they all got paid for their services. They all agreed to participate in anything and everything that went on during those encounters."

Mathews said the Probation Department recommended that Wayne be required to pay $20,000 in restitution fines. It also agreed with the jury's recommendation that he receive the death penalty.

In February 2007, Victoria sent an electronic voice file to John F. Berry, a reporter at the Riverside *Press-Enterprise,* in which Wayne spoke directly to the reporter.

Berry wrote a story on February 17, quoting Wayne as saying that the truth never came out during his trial.

"The fact I'm being executed doesn't bother me one bit," Wayne said. "But the fact the truth wasn't told, and the people were hurt beyond what they should have been hurt, that bothers me."

Trying to explain his actions, Wayne said, "It does not mean I was sitting there, enjoying myself, reviving them and torturing them. That never happened."

Victoria told Berry that Wayne believed he had blacked out during the killings, a result of his old head injury.

"I got into the mind of a serial killer," Victoria told Berry. "I should be respected for that."

Based on another audio clip of Wayne's voice that was posted on the Web site for Victoria's documentary project—RoomZerotheMovie.com—it's unclear what Victoria's motives were in contacting Berry.

In the clip, Wayne said: "Is your recorder on? You have exclusive, you, Victoria Redstall, have exclusive on everything to do with me. I'm not talking to any other media source unless they go through you. Period. That's all there is to it. I don't care if it's the president of the United States. I don't have to talk to anybody and will not, unless they go through you first. And you tell me that you want me to talk to them. You have that on tape now? Don't lose it."

Victoria announced to the media that her documentary was set to go out for bid on March 16, 2007, the day of Wayne's sentencing hearing. However, when that day came, she said she was still several months away from finishing. She said the same thing in an interview in August.

Seven months after the death penalty portion of his trial had concluded, the day of Wayne's sentencing finally arrived, delayed in part because Mazurek had been appointed to the bench and another prosecutor had to take his place.

None of Wayne's relatives came to the hearing, and of the victims' families, only Lanett White's attended.

A small group of photographers was finally allowed to film during the proceedings.

Wayne repeatedly stared at Victoria as she took video alongside the media, the click of camera shutters filling the courtroom.

Wayne sat calmly and emotionless for most of the hearing, his face blank until just before he received the sentence, when he clenched his eyes tightly, bracing for the impact of the judge's final words, or perhaps fighting to hold back tears.

As Judge Smith read off the long list of mitigating factors, Lanett's father, Bill White Sr., got up and left the courtroom, apparently worried that the judge was going to let Wayne off. Bill Sr. returned in time to utter an exclamation as the judge made his decision known.

Smith confirmed the jury's finding for the death penalty and denied the defense's motion for a new trial.

Reporters crowded around Bill White Sr. in the hallway after the hearing.

Bill nodded when a TV reporter asked if he felt a sense of justice.

"He's a dog," Bill said.

Asked if he would go to San Quentin to watch the execution, he said, "Sure would love to be there if at all possible. I'd like to see him hang."

As for Lanett, Bill said, "I remember her the way she was—happy. Didn't have no fear. No such thing. She's looking at him [now] get what he deserved."

Canty told the *Inland Valley Daily Bulletin* that he was pleased the judge seemed to take Wayne's remorse into account. But, he said, "He couldn't redecide the case for the jury. He could only decide whether there was enough evidence to support the verdicts."

Deputy District Attorney Michael McDowell, who took

over for Mazurek at the sentencing, predicted that Wayne would die of natural causes before he would be executed.

Forbush later said the defense team had felt that the jury might vote for a life sentence because Wayne had turned himself in, "but I don't think we were lulled into a sense that we were going to prevail."

Nonetheless, he said, he thought there were some very promising appellate issues to pursue.

Wayne Adam Ford was transferred to San Quentin soon after the hearing.

In a letter he sent to Rodney in June 2007, addressed, "Dear Big Brother, From My Bayside Villa," Wayne wrote that he'd stopped taking Paxil, which had rendered him "not mentally gifted for the couch potato life with zero initiative as I have been for the last 8–9 years."

However, he said, he would like to go back on the drug because it had helped by "leveling my unregulatable [sic] emotional system and I'm once again being beat up by my own disfunctional [sic] electro-chemical brain chemistry."

That said, he told Rodney that he felt he would be able to mask his dysfunction "until my eventual slaughter at the hand of the state. I can't wait."

Wayne said he would appreciate a visit from his brother once or twice a year, but he would understand if Rodney wasn't comfortable doing that.

He said Victoria, whom he'd nicknamed "Speedy," cared about him and "does all she can to help me be happy," including buying him a TV and promising to get him a Sony Discman. In addition to the documentary, he said, she was going to help him publish a book he wanted to write.

"If this works out, maybe in a couple of years I can support myself. At least I hope."

He enclosed a letter that he said Victoria had sent to him.

"I will kiss your eyes, drink your tears (if you have any) kiss every part of you that I can (without getting into trouble) hold your hand, kiss your hand, your arm, your fingers, your lips . . ." the letter said. "I love you like a drug that I cannot get enough of, and will prove that as soon as we can touch."

So much for the "emotional" relationship.

In the letter, Victoria called Wayne "my baby, my perfect baby," and said she would give him the shirt off her back. "I was going to say I would give you my right arm to make you happy, but that would have sounded like a bad joke!!!"

Wayne also sent Rodney some photos of Victoria in which she and another woman were posing, washing cars. Victoria was wearing a skimpy pink halter top, pink heels, and short shorts, bending over to show cleavage for the camera.

Wayne scribbled a note to Rodney on the same page on which she'd printed the photo from her computer, explaining that she'd taken these pictures at his request to pose in "Daisy Dukes," which are extremely short, formfitting, denim cutoff shorts, named after the southern character Daisy Duke from the TV series *The Dukes of Hazzard*.

Wayne wrote Rodney that she was "not sophisticated enough to be evil. She's been careful to be respectful while making the documentary that may never get off the ground."

Forbush, however, said he was concerned that the hours of conversations she had tape-recorded with Wayne could harm his chances of winning his appeals.

"The effect may be undermining everything that we tried to do throughout the whole trial," he said. "It's been borne out that she's not helping Wayne, that she's going to end up hurting Wayne."

But, Forbush said, Wayne has pointed out to him that he might do the same thing if he were in his place, befriended by an attractive woman like Victoria, saying, "I mean, what do you want me to do?"

After his trial, Wayne told Rodney that he hoped his appeals would be successful, so he could go free.

But even if he lost his appeals, Wayne was still many years away from being executed—at least for the time being.

When he first arrived on Death Row at San Quentin, none of his fellow prisoners had been executed for more than a year, and only thirteen since the death penalty had been reinstated nationally in 1976.

In February 2006, the execution of Michael Morales was called off after a last-minute volley of appeals, because prison officials couldn't find a medical professional to monitor the process. Doctors said to do so would have violated the Hippocratic oath, in which they vow to save lives, not take them.

Previously, doctors had only confirmed that a prisoner was dead, but a federal district judge, Jeremy Fogel, ordered the new requirement when he ruled that the state's death-by-lethal-injection protocol had to be changed.

Fogel also ordered that the prison stick to barbiturates rather than the three-drug cocktail used previously. The first drug that was injected—through a tube that went through a wall and into another room so that the "executioners" could remain anonymous and hidden from view of the media and other witnesses watching on the other side—was the analgesic sodium pentothal. The second was pancuronium bromide, which paralyzes all muscles in the body, including the diaphragm, and stops a person from breathing. The third was potassium chloride, which stops the heart from beating and, without sufficient anesthetic, apparently causes a person to feel as though his veins are on fire.

Fogel's actions had essentially instituted a temporary moratorium on executions in California, one of thirty-six states that had capital punishment on its books at the time. New Jersey had just eliminated it, and Colorado and Maryland were looking at abolishing it.

By 2007, the issue moved to a larger stage when the U.S. Supreme Court agreed to consider the appeal of two Kentucky inmates and the question of whether lethal injections violated the Constitution's ban on cruel and unusual punishment by being too painful.

By 2008, the California Commission on the Fair Administration of Justice was also reviewing the state's death penalty system, considering in particular whether to narrow the definition of what constituted a capital crime. At the time, the law allowed for thirty-three "special circumstance" crimes that went along with first-degree murder, such as using poison, raping the victim, and committing multiple murders.

Meanwhile, as a way to close the state's gaping budget gap, California Governor Arnold Schwarzenegger proposed the release of 22,000 nonviolent prisoners at the same time the state was moving ahead with a $337 million project to build a new execution chamber and add hundreds of cells to Death Row.

California had the largest backlog of cases and Death Row population in the nation. Its death penalty system had been operating at such a slow pace that about fifty Death Row inmates had already died of natural causes before they could be executed, and more than thirty had seen their appeals go for longer than a quarter century.

That meant taxpayers had been paying to house these inmates for life terms, anyway—after already paying the higher cost of prosecuting them as death cases and subsidizing the appeals that went along with that. (The annual cost to house a regular prisoner is $34,000, and presumably more for an inmate on Death Row, which is made up of single cells.)

"That is the most expensive possible system imaginable," said Richard Dieter, executive director of the Death Penalty Information Center, an organization that says it is critical of the death penalty, but not on moral grounds. "It's the worst of both worlds."

EPILOGUE

In October 2007, years after Gene and his second wife had adopted a dozen disabled children, he and Rodney agreed to meet for an interview for this book in Sacramento. This was the first time since Wayne had turned himself in that Gene or Rodney had agreed to talk to someone other than the family and defense team about the case (outside of court, that is).

In light of Victoria's documentary and conflicting statements by Wayne's mother and other people, Gene said he felt it was important to state his version of events.

"I'm really proud of Rodney. I'm not so proud of Wayne anymore, but at one time, I was very proud of him," Gene said.

When he first heard what Wayne had done, Gene said, "I felt betrayed, felt he betrayed the family, got the family involved in his sordid lifestyle. It really bothered me. I tried to clean up the mess," he said, explaining that he retrieved the family's vehicles, including the trailer, to make sure no one could buy them to make money off Wayne's notoriety.

So far, neither Gene nor Rodney had gone to visit Wayne at San Quentin, saying they were angry he was trying to manipulate them from behind bars through letters and phone calls, asking them for money, and urging them to talk to Victoria for her documentary.

"I said I want nothing to do with her," Gene said, adding that he'd told Wayne that twice, before and after he'd been transferred to San Quentin.

"I love him, but I don't like what he's done," Gene said. "I'm disappointed in him, but he's still my son."

Gene said he thought Wayne was in the best place he could be, where he couldn't escape. "I don't want him on the street again. . . . He's made his bed, he'll sleep in it, and I'll start visiting him when I'm in the right frame of mind."

Looking back, Gene said he didn't think he could have done anything different in raising his boys. "You raise them the best you can, with the experience you have. When you have children, they don't come with a manual."

Rodney said he didn't have a clue why Wayne committed these crimes, but he speculated that he "dislikes women so much that something inside of him snapped. He has a very low approval of women that, I think, are prostitutes, wanton women, who are sluts or whatever."

Rodney and Gene said they believe Wayne may have killed the first victim accidentally and didn't know what to do with her body, so he cut her up because he was scared and wanted to get rid of the evidence.

"After that, if he was displeased, you can't burn twice for murder, so it didn't make it probably such an obstacle to kill one, two, or three," Gene said.

Gene and Rodney shared the belief that Wayne turned himself in because he couldn't live with the guilt or the pain of what he'd done.

"As a human being, he was done. That's why he called me," Rodney said. "All our lives, I always helped him. We used to fight like cats and dogs, but we still loved each other, and when the chips were down, we were there for each other."

Rodney acknowledged that Wayne no longer believes he murdered those women.

Asked why Wayne might feel that way, Rodney said, "I don't know. He's demented. . . . He still thinks he's going to get out. He's going to win some of these appeals and he's going to get the death penalty off the table. He's got something up his sleeve. . . . I think it's a pipe dream, but in this day and age with the kind of attorneys you have out there, it might not be."

But even if that happened, Rodney said, he would never trust Wayne with anybody but him. "I would not trust my brother to be alone with my children or my wife."

Rodney said he's had death threats because of this case. Some of his company's clients have requested that he not participate in certain jobs. And he is still scared that someone who is angry at Wayne will try to hurt Rodney's family.

Several years before the trial, Rodney and Gene each talked to Wayne about giving up his parental rights to Max, so that the boy could have a normal life.

"If you love your son, you need to give up your parental rights," Rodney told him. "The best thing for your son is to let him go. You need to let your son disappear. . . . You need to do the right thing."

"He's my son. Why should I give up my rights?" Wayne asked, saying he wanted Max to have his tools and be aware that Wayne was his father.

But eventually, Wayne relented and signed the papers so that Elizabeth's new husband, whom she married in April 1999, could adopt the boy, then three and a half years old.

Rodney said he hoped Wayne would never get out of prison; he'd already come to terms with the fact that Wayne was going to be executed. He just didn't know whether he would be able to watch, even if Wayne asked him to be there.

"He's going on a journey," Rodney said. "We all have to answer to a higher power at the end of our world."

AUTHOR'S NOTE AND ACKNOWLEDGMENTS

Much of the information in this book came out of materials I was allowed to review after the trial, including court exhibits and documents that were submitted during discovery but never made their way into the jury's hands. As such, I was able to read every word from the taped interviews Wayne gave to authorities in the days after he turned himself in. The materials also included a sizeable excerpt of the eight-hour interview with Wayne's mother that Ron Forbush conducted in India, his interviews with other Ford family members, and Wayne's military medical files.

Detectives Juan Freeman, Frank Gonzales, Mike Jones, Joe Herrera, and Gary Rhoades graciously supplied me with information and let me question them repeatedly about their investigations and interviews.

I interviewed Wayne's father, Gene, and his brother, Rodney, for an entire day in a hotel room in Sacramento, most of which was focused on Gene. The next day, I talked with Rodney alone. Although Gene was reticent to speak with me at first, he and Rodney proved to be extremely cooperative. Gene told me that he'd even turned down an interview with the producer for Dan Rather, among many others, when the story first broke.

Ron Forbush was also reticent at first, but he later proved to be tremendously helpful. Joe Canty, who had been his best friend for decades, had initially agreed to be interviewed for this book, but, unfortunately, he died of a heart attack in June 2007 before I was able to speak with him. A month earlier, he'd been recognized by the county Board of Supervisors with the Award for Excellence for the "passion and creativity" he showed in defending Wayne, as well as for his long career as a hardworking government attorney. Ron's help with the case history was also important because Governor Schwarzenegger appointed Steven Mapes to the bench the same month that Canty died. As a judge, Mapes apparently didn't feel it was appropriate to talk to me for this book, Ron said.

When I initially contacted Wayne's mother in India via e-mail, she said she would be willing to answer questions about his family history. However, after I sent her a four-page list of questions that included Gene's perspective, she apologized but said she had to renege. She didn't want to be part of any book in which Gene and Rodney were involved, given that their versions of events were so far apart from hers.

I wrote a letter to Wayne, asking if he would cooperate with me for this project, but he did not respond. Based on the audio clip posted on Victoria Redstall's documentary Web site, Wayne sees her as his media liaison and believes everyone needs to go through her. When I told her I wanted to talk to him, she said she didn't think Wayne would answer my letter.

I interviewed Lanett White's daughter at the courthouse, where Lanett's parents agreed to be interviewed later. However, through a series of e-mails, Bill Jr., Lanett's brother, subsequently told me his parents wouldn't talk or let me publish Lanett's photo without payment. After I told him I was planning to read through her criminal record to try to understand what made her get into Wayne's truck, he cut off communication altogether. I tried reaching the other victims' families through the Victims Services Office, but no luck. So, instead, I based the victims' chapters on court and police records, testimony, and summaries of Dave Mazurek's pretrial interviews with the parents. Mazurek was extremely helpful and cooperative, answering questions about the case for hours.

The chapters about Wayne's relationships with his ex-wives and girlfriend Wadad were based on interviews that Detective Freeman conducted. Wayne's most recent ex-wife, Elizabeth, who has long since remarried, politely declined my interview request, understandably choosing to put this behind her.

Whenever possible, I drew from official sources, such as interview transcripts or court records, to write the dialogue. Scenes that include dialogue that was reconstructed and approximated by people I interviewed were cross-checked with other people involved in those conversations when I could reach them. Dialogue drawn from the voluminous transcripts of the trial or interviews with Wayne and witnesses had to be edited for storytelling purposes, but most of that was done by deletion. Nothing was added or created or exaggerated. Wayne often spoke in sentence fragments that didn't make sense and the detectives jumped around during their interviews, but I was careful to maintain the flow of the conversation and not take anything out of context.

Any errors that may have occurred along the way are purely accidental and unintentional.

On a purely personal note, I found the researching and writing of this book to be fascinating yet grueling as my past came back to haunt me. I learned only after marrying my late husband that he was an alcoholic, had a Borderline Personality Disorder, and, as the first of two adopted sons, felt emotionally abandoned by his adoptive mother and disconnected from his father.

I sensed when I met him that he had dark secrets, but I didn't know the extent of them until it was too late. Although he'd told me about some of his past exploits, I was shocked after his death to find two locked brief-cases containing documents he wanted to keep secret from me, as well as a stack of old photos of mostly unat-tractive women in what looked like hotel rooms.

He was very bright and could be sweet, generous, and loving when he was sober. But he, too, suffered from de-pression, often cried, and told me many lies. When he drank, he was a completely different person—verbally abusive, threatening, and, once, even violent. Toward the end, it was very difficult to watch him disintegrate and, ultimately, he committed suicide. I bring this up only because I feel it gave me some personal insight into Wayne Adam Ford's psyche.

I want to thank all the people I've mentioned above for their help, time, and trust, and for sharing their files with me as I gathered the information, photos, and per-missions I needed to tell this important story.

I'd also like to express my appreciation to the follow-ing folks for their assistance:

John McCutchen for his photographic contributions.

For the research and/or photo help, Blondie Freeman and Vonda Kay Jones; Melva Paris, Brenda Godsey, and Gary Philp, of the Humboldt County Sheriff's Depart-ment; Ramon Denby and the Las Vegas Metropolitan Police Department; Ron Fleshman, of the Ocean Grove Lodge; Rachel Holt; Judge Michael Smith, Jerry McBur-ney, Stacie Franco, Kim Rezendes, Cyndi Gomez, Robert McDaniel, Evi Roberson, and Theresa Wolfe, from the San

Bernardino County court system; David Whitney, Diana Soren, and Michael McDowell, from the prosecution team; Bob Pottberg, Nancy Reichard, Lynne Sarty, from Humboldt; Jennie McCue, of Saddleback College; Mark Folghum, of the Tacoma Police Department; John F. Berry, from the Riverside *Press-Enterprise;* Michael Miller, from the state water department; juror Darlena Murray; Denise Cattern, from Chino; and Richard Dieter and Krista McKim, from the Death Penalty Information Center.

Mike Shohl and Michaela Hamilton, from Kensington, for their continued support and enthusiasm for my work.

My agent, Gary Heidt, for his efforts to keep me sane and fed.

My readers, Alexa Capeloto and Mark Sauer.

And Carole Scott, Samuel Autman, Bob Koven, Jon Sidener, and Writing Women for your support, encouragement, and help getting me through the dark places to which this book took me.

Don't miss Caitlin Rother's
masterful true-crime thriller

LOST GIRLS

Available from Pinnacle

Here's a compelling excerpt . . .

CHAPTER 1

John Gardner's mother was worried. The bipolar mood swings, erratic behavior and suicidal impulses that had periodically plagued her thirty-year-old son since he was a child were not only back but worse than she'd ever seen them.

When Cathy Osborn left her condo for her psychiatric nursing job the morning of February 25, 2010, John was asleep on the futon in her home office, where he stayed when he visited. Cathy called his cell phone and texted him numerous times throughout the day to see how he was doing, but she got no response. When he didn't answer his phone, something was usually up.

That evening after work, John was still missing in action, so she decided to combine her usual run with a search for her wayward son, an unemployed electrician and unmarried father of twin sons. Having completed fifteen full marathons, as well as fifteen half marathons, Cathy routinely jogged five to seven miles around Lake Hodges in nearby Rancho Bernardo Community Park. But she was so worried about John and his well-being that she didn't really feel like doing the full route.

She jogged about a mile through the neighborhood, turned at the white railing off Duenda Road, and started down the narrow path that widened as it left the residential area and fed into the vast, beautiful open space of the San Dieguito River Valley. Depending on the time of day, sometimes she couldn't see another soul for miles in any direction. It was so peaceful out there, far away from the stresses of the city. So isolated. So still. And so deadly quiet.

But her nerves were on edge that evening as she ran along the sandy trail at dusk. She jerked to an abrupt halt, startled to see a snake off to the right. Once she realized it had no head and posed no danger, she continued heading toward the slate blue of the lake up ahead, hoping to find John in one of his usual haunts. He'd told her that he liked to sit on the benchlike boulders that were positioned along the trails, posted with informational placards about the Kumeyaay Indians and the natural wildlife habitat. Knowing his two favorites overlooked a waterfall and the lake, she kept her eyes peeled for discarded beer cans and cigarette butts. But she saw no sign of him.

This is the wrong spot, or he's been here and he's just not drinking beer or smoking cigarettes, she thought.

Cathy had spent nearly three decades managing her son's medical and psychological treatment, ferrying him to countless doctors and therapists who had prescribed more than a dozen medications. Starting at age four, John had begun with Ritalin for his attention-deficit/hyperactivity disorder (ADHD). As he grew older, his behavioral problems became more complicated. As a teenager, he was diagnosed with bipolar disorder, but he had experienced so many side effects to the drugs that he'd stopped taking them in high school. He had been on and off them ever since. Mostly off.

John also had a history of psychiatric hospitalizations, and by now, Cathy was very familiar with the danger signs that he was reaching a crisis point. In the last couple of months, he had totaled two cars, running one into a pole and the other into a cement barrier. So on

February 8, she had driven him to the walk-in psychiatric clinic at the county hospital in Riverside, where both of them hoped he would be admitted as an inpatient. But even after John told the psychiatrist he might qualify as a "5150"—someone who is in danger of hurting himself or others—the doctor said he didn't think such treatment was necessary. He simply gave John some more pills and sent him on his way. Five days later, John went on a suicidal binge of methamphetamine and other illicit drugs, which landed him in the emergency room.

All of this made for a complicatedly close relationship between John and his mother. Things had escalated recently after he'd started using methamphetamine and increasing his drinking. The crazier he acted, the crazier Cathy's own emotional roller coaster became. If she didn't watch over him, she feared he would go right back to the same druggie friends he partied with during his nearly fatal binge, a pattern she'd seen over the past eighteen months. Or worse yet, he'd be successful and actually kill himself.

John had been "living" at his grandmother Linda Osborn's house in Riverside County since January, going back and forth to his mom's condo in Rancho Bernardo, a San Diego suburb, an hour south. But because Linda had also been admitted to the same hospital as John, Cathy decided on February 19 to take him home with her for a few days. Clearly, he was in no state of mind to be left to his own devices at his grandmother's, or in the care of his aunt Cynthia, who had her own emotional problems.

"It's time for you to get some more intense treatment," Cathy told him.

John agreed, saying he'd been trying to get help, but not succeeding. "I need you to help me because I can't seem to get it done on my own," he said.